Ethics and Public Policy

Ethics and Public Policy: A Philosophical Inquiry is the first book to subject important and controversial areas of public policy to philosophical scrutiny. Jonathan Wolff, a renowned philosopher and veteran of many public committees, such as the Gambling Review Body, introduces and assesses core problems and controversies in public policy from a philosophical standpoint. Each chapter is centred on an important area of public policy where there is considerable moral and political disagreement. Topics discussed include:

- Can we defend inflicting suffering on animals in scientific experiments for human benefit?
- What limits to gambling can be achieved through legislation?
- What assumptions underlie drug policy? Can we justify punishing those who engage in actions that harm only themselves?
- What is so bad about crime? What is the point of punishment?

Other chapters discuss health care, disability, safety and the free market. Throughout the book, fundamental questions for both philosopher and policy maker recur: what are the best methods for connecting philosophy and public policy? Should thinking about public policy be guided by 'an ideal world' or the world we live in now? If there are 'knock down' arguments in philosophy why are there none in public policy?

Each chapter concludes with 'Lessons for Philosophy' making this book not only an ideal introduction for those coming to philosophy, ethics or public policy for the first time, but also a vital resource for anyone grappling with the moral complexity underlying policy debates.

Jonathan Wolff is Professor of Philosophy at University College London, where he is also Director of the UCL Centre for Philosophy, Justice and Health. He is a member of the Nuffield Council on Bioethics and was a member of its Working Party on the ethics of research involving animals, as well as the Academy of Medical Sciences's Working Party on drug futures. He is a member of the Advisory Council of Demos and was a trustee for the Responsibility in Gambling Trust (2003–9). He is editor, with Tim Crane, of the *Routledge Philosophy Guidebooks* series. He writes a monthly column on higher education for the *Guardian* newspaper.

PRAISE FOR *ETHICS AND PUBLIC POLICY*

'A first-class examination of where philosophy meets public policy by one of the leading political philosophers today. I have no doubt that this book will set a new benchmark for all future work, as well as offer a substantial contribution to policy analysis. I cannot recommend it highly enough.'

– Thom Brooks, Newcastle University, UK

'Not only does Jonathan Wolff provide the invaluable service of helping us explore the ethical dimension of decision making through a historical and concrete understanding of specific policy dilemmas but he does so in a way which is authoritative, clear and engaging. This book is strongly recommended for putative decision makers who want to think and act wisely and for the philosophically-inclined wishing to test their ideas against the hard realities of policy making.'

– Matthew Taylor, Chief Executive, RSA

'This book sets the bar for how moral philosophy can inform, and be informed by, public policy debates. It will be of great value to students interested in ethics, philosophy, political science, economics, and public policy as well as those with interests in the important social issues Wolff addresses.'

– Debra Satz, Stanford University, USA

'Many books promise to introduce the reader to philosophy and ethics; very few do it with such wit, elegance, and intellectual honesty.'

– Richard Ashcroft, Queen Mary University, UK

'This is the book we have been waiting for: a treatise on the ethics of public policy by a major political philosopher. An ideal text for a course on practical ethics, or on contemporary social problems: understandable but not at all dumbed-down.'

– Daniel Wikler, Harvard University, USA

'A model contribution of political philosophy to the development of public policy – and, as importantly, of the practice of public policy to theory. Policy makers and philosophers will learn an enormous amount from reading it.'

– Leslie Pickering Francis, University of Utah, USA

'A beautifully crafted, clear and concisely formulated survey of many controversial and pressing issues in public policy. Wolff's writing conceals an apparently effort-less command of a wealth of philosophical argument, and helps painlessly to steer the reader through complex material.'

– David Archard, Lancaster University, UK

Jonathan Wolff

Ethics and Public Policy

A Philosophical Inquiry

Routledge
Taylor & Francis Group

LONDON AND NEW YORK

First published 2011
by Routledge
2 Park Square, Milton Park, Abingdon, Oxon OX14 4RN

Simultaneously published in the USA and Canada
by Routledge
711 Third Avenue, New York, NY 10017

*Routledge is an imprint of the Taylor & Francis Group,
an informa business*

British Library Cataloguing in Publication Data
A catalogue record for this book is available from the British
Library

Library of Congress Cataloging in Publication Data
Wolff, Jonathan.
   Ethics and public policy : a philosophical inquiry / by
Jonathan Wolff.
      p. cm.
   Includes bibliographical references and index.
   1. Public administration–Moral and ethical aspects.
2. Policy sciences–Moral and ethical aspects. I. Title.
   JF1525.E8W65 2011
   172–dc22   2010052482

ISBN: 978-0-415-66852-1 (hbk)
ISBN: 978-0-415-66853-8 (pbk)
ISBN: 978-0-203-81638-7 (ebk)

Typeset in Joanna and DIDOT
by Taylor & Francis Books

For my mother and in memory of my father

Contents

Acknowledgements

This book has come into being slowly, over the course of ten years or more. Every chapter has been presented, in various forms, to numerous audiences: in my teaching, to philosophy societies, at conferences, as public lectures and to professional groups. I have learnt a huge amount from the hundreds of comments and questions I have had. Unfortunately, one of my bad habits is that I rarely take written notes (or if I do, I can never find them again), normally relying on my memory. And another of my flaws is that my memory is never as reliable as I expect it to be. So in many cases I must have incorporated ideas that I have heard from others. If you recognize any of your own ideas in what follows, then I'm immensely grateful for your help. If you don't, thank you for reading anyway. But the events are fresh enough for me to be able to thank Mark Hannam and Carina Fourie for their very valuable comments on a near complete draft, and to four readers for the publisher for their acute reports on the penultimate version. I hope that my response to all these readers has improved the book. I am also very grateful to Tony Bruce of Routledge for his support and encouragement.

Shortly before I submitted the final version for publication, Kim Angell, Beate Elvebakk and Robert Huseby, on behalf of the Nordic Network on Political Ethics, organized a two-day symposium on the manuscript at the University of Oslo. I'm immensely grateful to them for doing this, and to the other participants, including Thom Brooks, Martin O'Neill, Eli Feiring, Hilde Nagell, Hallvard Fossheim, Jakob Elster and Lene Bomann-Larsen, for their excellent papers and other contributions which have helped me improve the focus and formulation of a number of my positions and arguments. I'm also very grateful to Li Sa Ng who helped produce the index and also made some valuable suggestions for improvement.

The process of turning this manuscript from a collection of writings produced for other purposes into a book took place largely on the balcony of a house called Felsted in Anne Port, Jersey, in the Channel Islands, where, in my distracted moments I could study the sea, and distant shores of France. This happened over a succession of summers and I'm extraordinarily grateful to my hosts, Jane, Michael, Alice and Grace Bravery. Indeed had it not been for the hugely generous hospitality of the Braverys, as well as Lisa, Simon, Todd, Lulu, Joss and Martha MacDonald and Jane, Martin, Maeve and Stella Greene in Jersey, this book would have been finished a lot sooner.

Introduction

A telephone message: could I please call the Home Office, the implausible sounding Liquor, Gambling and Data Protection Unit. I did, and to my astonishment they didn't want to talk about data protection. So began my first practical exploration of an issue in public policy where it was thought that the perspective of a philosopher could be of use – in this case a review of the law of gambling. Since then I have been involved in projects concerning railway safety, crime, the law of homicide, the regulation of drugs, animal experiments, the distribution of health resources, disability support, sustainability, and personalized health care. In each case I agreed to join in largely because it sounded interesting and worthwhile. I also thought, rather pompously, that political philosophers have a responsibility to take matters of public policy seriously, and it is a duty for those of us paid out of the public purse to make a contribution where we can. It also seemed that philosophers should have something to contribute to all of these policy areas. But what I had not expected, at least not at first, was that each of these encounters would teach me something about philosophy.

To give an example, let me describe my first extended encounter with the question of the morality of human treatment of animals, while I was a member of the Nuffield Council on Bioethics Working Party on the ethics of research involving animals (our final report is NCB 2005). The great majority of members of the working party had a scientific background, and for some of them experimenting on animals had been a routine part of their scientific practice for decades. Many of the scientists were experts in some area where animals were used, either for basic research, or to test either the efficacy or the safety of new pharmaceuticals. Each of us was asked, initially, to provide a brief report of the state of knowledge in our area. Drafted in as a moral philosopher, even though I had never worked on ethical questions about animals, my first task was to provide a report explaining the current 'state of knowledge' in ethical thinking.

Accordingly I undertook a review of some of the major contributions to the philosophical literature, as well as some surveys. (For example, Singer 1989, 1995, Carruthers 1992 and DeGrazia 2002.) One thing that was obvious from a first glance was that there was no such thing as the current state of knowledge. The debate was divided. At one extreme were those who argued that current practices of eating and experimenting on at least some more complex and developed animals was in principle no different to doing the same thing to human beings, and therefore not just wrong but morally horrific. At the other end of the scale were those who had views that would apparently have been consistent with finding nothing morally objectionable to cockfighting, bear-baiting and torturing animals for fun, although no one seemed quite ready to draw those conclusions.

Now, I was perfectly happy to report disagreement, just as the scientists reported disagreement about such things as the feasibility of replacing some current experiments with computer modelling, or the degree to which fish feel pain. However I was far less comfortable reporting the views giving rise to these disagreements. For on the whole, philosophers seemed to defend views that were so far from current practice as to seem, to the non-philosopher, quite outrageous. The idea that society could adopt any of the views put forward seemed almost laughable. To put it mildly, from the point of view of public policy the views were unreasonable and unacceptable.

This was a shock. Moral and political philosophy, I had assumed, is made for the analysis of public policy, exploring foundational values, and consolidating them into theories and prototype policies that could, with reasonable adjustment, fit practical needs to improve the moral quality of our public lives. But this common view, it seems, overlooks one crucial point. Moral and political philosophy are, after all, branches of philosophy. And, it seems, in contrast to some other disciplines, the way in which philosophy has developed makes it fit rather badly with public policy needs. In science and in social science a researcher makes his or her name by presenting a view that others find attractive or useful and build upon. By and large the situation in philosophy is the reverse. A philosopher becomes famous by arguing for a view that is highly surprising, even to the point of being irritating, but is also resistant to easy refutation. The more paradoxical, or further from common sense, the better. Philosophy thrives on disagreement, and there is no pressure to come to an agreement. Indeed agreement is unhelpful as it cuts discussion short. At a conference or seminar series no one takes minutes of the meeting in order to provide a common statement representing the views of the group. A seminar group can have as many different views as it has members – indeed, to recycle an old joke – it will often have more views than members. In public policy, however, a report must be written, or a recommendation made, or a law or policy drafted, just as in science and social science a practical outcome is sought. A need to agree on a practical outcome creates pressure towards convergence. Philosophy, under no such pressure, thrives on what Freud in another context called the 'narcissism of minor difference' (Freud 1963 [1930]).

There may be no better illustration of the difficulties philosophers face in coming to agreement, even when they are trying very hard, than in a book published in 1912, called *The New Realism: Cooperative Studies in Philosophy*, by six eminent American philosophers who wished to found a new, realist school of philosophy (Holt 1912). The book, as its subtitle documents, is written in a rare spirit of cooperation, and part of the project is to set out, in the appendix, what is called the 'Program and First Platform', or in other words a kind of manifesto. Yet the authors don't seem to have been able to bring themselves to sign up to words drafted by others, and so the book concludes with not one program and first platform, but six, subtly different, one by each author. (This failed episode in philosophical cooperation was drawn to my attention by the late Burton Dreben.)

Philosophers find it hard to compromise. This may be a problem when it comes to committee work. But it is also a great strength. The foundation of all intellectual enquiry is the pursuit of ideas and reasoning for their own sake. Without pure philosophical reflection, and the dogged pursuit of what may seem to others crazy ideas, intellectual discussion would be flat and static. The issue, in the present context, is not at all to dismiss philosophical reasoning but to explore how to connect it to public policy. It is tempting to think that the way to approach a moral problem that arises in the context of public policy is to formulate the correct moral theory, show how it would resolve the policy issue under consideration, and then to argue for it, hoping to convince policy makers of the correctness of one's moral theory and its resolution of the policy difficulty. Of course such contributions are an indispensable part of the formulation of public policy. Yet typically they will not take the debate very far. It is unrealistic to think that moral argument can have such power, unless there is already a very broad consensus. By contrast, on many issues there is trenchant advocacy of a number of different views, some, but not all, based on moral considerations – which may conflict with other moral considerations – and some linked to powerful interests, including the interests of government to obtain re-election. Accordingly governments can feel limited in their ability to make decisions that they fear will be unpopular with the press or the electorate. Whatever the power of one's arguments in intellectual terms, it has to be accepted that public policy is not a sphere of pure reason. And even if it were, the challenge of convincing others would remain.

In the public policy arena, debate differs from abstract moral argument in at least three ways. First, there is little space for 'agreeing to disagree': some policy or other is needed. Second, there is an inevitable bias towards the status quo. At any time, some public policy will be in place, and in most circumstances the burden of argument for change is higher than for reflective or un-reflective continuation of current policy. Third, whether a moral view is correct, or right, or persuasive, takes second place to whether it is widely shared, or at least widely accepted in the sense of enough people being prepared to live with it. This is not to endorse any form of subjectivism or relativism, but rather to accept the practical implications of what Rawls called 'the burdens of judge-ment': that given the free use of reason, conscientious, reasonable moral thinkers may come to differing and conflicting judgements (Rawls 1989). If this is so, then there is little prospect of demon-strating that any view is true or correct. Even broad acceptance could be out of reach, but it is a reasonable hope, and, in most circumstances, the best we can reasonably hope for.

I've suggested that in public life, first of all we must have some policy. Second, we start from where we are. Third, the best chance for moving forward is to draw more people into a consensus view, so that policy can be more widely endorsed, even if different peo-ple's reasons for the policy differ. In this respect it is worth drawing an analogy with another Rawlsian idea: that of an overlapping consensus (Rawls 1989). It could be that a particular public policy is defensible even on conflicting moral assumptions. To take a very simple example, despite their deep disagreements, Kantians, who believe in absolute moral requirements, and utilitarians, who want to maximize the balance of pleasure over pain, agree that it is wrong to murder innocents when no good could come of it. There are many other examples, of course, to illustrate the point that not all philosophical disagreement makes a difference at policy level.

Murder is the easy case. It is not true that there is always convergence. If there was then the moral dilemmas that generate the concerns of this book would not arise in the first place. In the face of such disagreement we noted that some writers on topics in applied ethics or the ethics of public policy begin by setting out the ethical framework or principles which they will use to settle the questions that they discuss. Doing this makes their work appear highly rigorous and principled, as if this is the way professional ethicists should behave. My view, as will become clearer throughout the book, is that this is a noble idea, but it is ultimately unsuccessful. There are many sources of our values, coming from numerous philosophical, cultural and religious traditions. Some need to be rejected, and others refined, but it would be some sort of miracle if they could all be put into a tidy order, like the rules of a game or the axioms of geometry. Ethics is, in my view, more like the science of medicine than physics. Theoretical and technical knowledge is important, but there is no reason in advance to think that it can all be stated in terms of clear, simple principles, or made to fit into a single, complete coherent framework, or that every problem can be solved with a complex algorithm.

In this respect the general methodology I shall follow bears comparison with some comments by Joel Feinberg. In the introduction to his book, *Harm to Others*, which is the first of four volumes on the moral limits of the criminal law, Feinberg writes: 'I appeal at various places, quite unselfconsciously, to all kinds of reasons normally produced in practical discourse, from efficiency and utility to fairness, coherence and human rights. But I make no effort to derive some of these reasons from others, or to rank them in terms of their degree of basicness. ... Progress on the penultimate questions need not wait for solutions to the ultimate ones' (Feinberg 1987, 18). Feinberg does not express scepticism about the possibility of an overall, systematic, comprehensive framework. Rather, he simply points out that such a framework is not necessary to make progress on the issues he discusses. I am sorely tempted to go further than Feinberg's agnosticism, but like Feinberg, have for present purposes no need to do so.

It is also worth bringing out a further aspect of the methodology adopted here. Before criticizing I seek to understand, where I can.

That is, it seems to me worthwhile to try to understand why it is we have the policies we do have before advocating change. In some cases there may be a reasonable pattern of moral argument that can be constructed to explain why we have a particular set of policies. There is, after, all, something to the idea of the wisdom of ages. On the other hand, as John Stuart Mill and others have pointed out, there is also the prejudice of ages, and some policies may simply be a reflection or hangover of value systems that are outmoded or should never have been accepted in the first place. But history can matter. Existing policies may be cobbled together to respond to previous historical circumstances, including policy failure, and being aware of the history of a policy area can help us become sensitive to possible pitfalls with new recommendations. Of course, explaining how we got where we are will never, in itself, provide a sufficient justification for standing still. But it can make us aware both of the reasons others have thought current policies are the best that can be achieved, and, sometimes, the restricted possibilities for doing much better.

We will see the points made above, as well as many others, illustrated in the chapters to come. Much of this book draws on work written for other reasons, and several chapters are based on work that has been published elsewhere. I did not set out to write a book on public policy; rather I found out that I was half way to having done so, without realizing it. Hence the topics I discuss here are ones I have thought about for some time, rather than those that might be most salient in the public mind at the moment. As a result there is nothing here, for example, about war, terrorism, immigration or climate change. This book, however, has a particular rationale. Of course part of the purpose is to apply philosophical reasoning to a series of highly important policy areas, although in some cases, such as safety and the value of life, it may not be apparent to the non-specialist that any such debates exist. But equally I want to draw out messages for philosophy from the discussion. Each chapter will allow us to make a different methodological point – sometimes more than one – that will help us approach other policy areas in future. The point, therefore, of this book is not only to introduce discussion under the themes discussed, but also to equip the reader to consider other policy areas in a more philosophically informed, but non-dogmatic, fashion. Hence at the end of each chapter the methodological conclusions will be emphasized, and these are drawn together in the final chapter, which also makes some more general points about the prospects for philosophical thinking to inform public policy.

The chapters in this book reflect my attempts to think through the issues presented to me. In many cases they were my input into forms of joint deliberation with other people from different backgrounds, and the resulting joint report will often be rather different from the accounts set out here. I should also be clear that this book is not intended to be a full treatment of how philosophers can engage in public policy. There is nothing here about writing letters to the newspapers, appearing in the media, setting up pressure groups, helping fund campaigns, or getting elected to public office. All of these are valuable and would reward discussion. My focus here is on the ways in which philosophers can intervene by way of argument into policy debates. In my own case this has often taken the form of committee work, but it could equally take other forms. But I do not want to be thought to be suggesting that all philosophers can do is make arguments (and distinctions, and detect ambiguity or confusion, and reflect on the logical relations between ideas, and so on), although arguably this is all they can do as philosophers. Neither do I want to suggest that only philosophers can do these things. Academics in other spheres, civil servants and those who work in law, accountancy, business, journalism and elsewhere, can be just as capable as philosophers at spotting confusion and mistakes in arguments. Our advantage, as philosophers, is that we do this informed by our training and scholarship. Generations of philosophers have agonized about similar questions and much of our working life is spent studying and reflecting on how they have done so, and how it could be done better. Of course, part of the argument of this book is that such a background doesn't give us any sort of short cut to the right answers. But it does provides extra resources for considering the ethical dilemmas of public policy, and helps bring a variety of perspectives to debates. We will return to this in the final chapter.

I should also make clear that although I reject a particular way of connecting philosophy and public policy, I do not claim to be the first to have seen things the way I do. Far from it. This book is part of an emerging tradition of thought in moral and political philosophy, which is characterized by a rejection of what we might think of as a 'first choose your theory' approach to practical political and moral problems. It is becoming increasingly common to distinguish 'top-down' (or theory-driven) from 'bottom-up' (problem-driven) approaches to applied ethics. This book, naturally enough, aims to be a contribution to bottom-up theorizing, where the first task is to try to understand enough about the policy area to be able to comprehend why it generates moral difficulties, and then to connect those difficulties or dilemmas with patterns of philosophical reasoning and reflection. I think I first heard the approach explained by Janet Radcliffe Richards, in relation to her practice in teaching ethics to medical students. There is now a growing body of work, to be found in journals such as the *Journal of Applied Philosophy*, that follows similar lines. A good, relatively early, statement of the general idea, this time applied to political philosophy, comes from John Dunn:

> The purpose of political theory is to diagnose practical predicaments and to show us how best to confront them. To do this it needs to train us in three relatively distinct skills: firstly in ascertaining how the social, political, and economic setting of our lives now is and in understanding why it is as it is; secondly in working through for ourselves how we could coherently and justifiably wish that world to be or become; and thirdly in judging how far, and through what actions, and at what risk,

we can realistically hope to move this world as it now stands towards
the way we might excusably wish it to be.

(Dunn 1990, 193)

Colin Farrelly has followed Dunn in a recent book that is critical of
'ideal theory' in political philosophy (Farrelly 2007), and Amartya
Sen has come close to setting out an agenda for this approach in his
recent book *The Idea of Justice* (2009), although arguably the approach
is even better exemplified in his earlier work, such as *Development as
Freedom* (1999). I will mention other work that has influenced my
approach in subsequent chapters.

As this book is intended for a diverse audience, including those
with a philosophical background who wish to extend their thinking
into public policy, and those in policy who would like to look at
some of the philosophical issues that arise in their policy area,
there is a question of how much, and what sort of, background
knowledge I can presuppose. What I have decided to do is to
explain all the issues as they arise, so that they can be understood
in context, rather than to have separate sections or chapters in which
philosophical or policy issues are explained. No doubt some discussion will go too slowly for some readers and too quickly for others. I
apologize in advance, but I see no way round that problem. Which
means, I suppose, I don't really apologize at all.

1

Scientific experiments on animals

INTRODUCTION

How should human beings treat non-human animals? This question is often debated under the heading of 'animal rights' or, rather differently, 'animal liberation' (you might want to liberate animals even if, strictly thinking, you don't think animals can have rights). This may well be, from the perspective of the future, the defining question of our age. Will future human beings look back at contemporary practices of eating meat and using animals for scientific experiments with the horror we have for earlier practices of slavery? Indeed on some views what we do to animals is far worse than what was at least routinely done to slaves.

It is unlikely that we can come to an accurate view about what future generations will think of us. But we can try to come to a view about the correct approach to the ethical question of the treatment of animals. My main task here, however, is not to argue for any particular answer to that question, although I will towards the end of this paper set out some tentative conclusions. Rather I will attempt to argue that one standard way of approaching the moral question of our treatment of non-human animals is unhelpful, and an alternative framework is much more promising both philosophically and for policy debates. My discussion will focus on the use of animals in scientific research, and I will say very little about other practices such as eating animals or hunting them for sport.

THE USE OF ANIMALS IN SCIENTIFIC EXPERIMENTS

Before getting started on philosophical discussion, it is worth looking at some of the details about the use of animals in scientific research. My discussion will focus on animal experimentation in the UK, where, it is sometimes said, the regulations are the most restrictive in the world. Nevertheless, similar considerations also apply elsewhere. In the UK the main legislation is the Animals (Scientific Procedures) Act 1986. Each year the Home Office provides a set of statistics concerning the licences granted for the year. It is not always necessary to obtain a licence, but as the Home Office explains, 'Under this Act any scientific procedure carried out on any living vertebrate animal, or one species of octopus (*Octopus vulgaris*), which is likely to cause that animal pain, suffering, distress or lasting harm is a regulated procedure requiring licence authority' (Home Office 2009, 3). No licence has been granted in the UK for experiments on the great apes (chimpanzees, gorillas and orang-utans) since the current Act of Parliament has been in force.

A licence will only be granted if, in the opinion of the authority, the benefits of the research outweigh the harms, and experimenting on animals is the only feasible way of obtaining the information sought. This is not intended to rule out 'basic' scientific research with no obvious, immediate application, but it must at least be plausible that the experiment will contribute to the scientific enterprise, with possible eventual benefits to human or to animal welfare. Experiments, or other licensed procedures, are divided into four classifications, mild, moderate, severe and unclassified. Unclassified are those where the animal suffers no pain, as, for example, in experiments where it remains unconscious throughout the procedure and never regains consciousness (we will look at such cases in more detail later). Mild, moderate and severe refer to the degree of pain or suffering involved, although how a particular procedure is classified is generally a matter of judgement and experience, as coming up with an operational definition of the boundaries is probably an impossible task. Relatively few licences are granted for severe procedures, but the majority of licences are for moderate ones.

The sheer numbers of animals involved, however, may come as a surprise. In 2008 licences were granted for 3.7 million procedures, up from about 3.2 million the previous year, but a long way down from the peak of above 5 million in the 1970s. The very great majority of animals used are mice, rats and fish, although together dogs, cats and non-human primates numbered over 11,000. Pigs, turkeys and other farm animals were also used in experiments relating to veterinary medicine. Although many types of experiments are carried out, animals are used particularly for drug discovery and testing. At an early stage animals are used to attempt to establish the effects of particular substances, normally a chemical compound. These compounds are likely either to have been manufactured in the lab or derived from a natural source, often the rain forest, or even the sea bed. Perhaps it is no surprise, given evolution, that nature seems to be a wonderful source of compounds with health-protective properties. Once a desirable effect is detected, and firmly established, the next stage is to test the compound to see if it is safe, or whether it has adverse side effects, prior to testing the substance on human beings.

The scientific use of animals has a long history, especially in dissection. Indeed in the seventeenth century the philosopher Descartes reveals himself in his writings to be an enthusiastic devotee of animal dissection, in order to further his understanding of human anatomy (Descartes 1985 [1637]). It may well have been that Descartes even performed vivisection: experiments on living animals. Vivisection became more common in the eighteenth and nineteenth centuries, and began to spark considerable protest and disquiet. Experimentation on the mass scale we now see began only in the twentieth century with the use of animals anaesthetized with ether and chloroform. The use of animals in research has always been accompanied by protest, although it has been stronger and more vocal, and, indeed, even violently active at certain times (NCB 2005). And the extent to which animal experimentation takes place is not always made explicit. For example, when you put money in the collecting tin for heart or cancer research there is a high chance that the money you give will pay for experiments on animals. Indeed those who support antivivisection charities may well, unwittingly, in their support of other charities, be funding exactly the work they want to ban. In collecting evidence for the Nuffield Council we found that among the strongest supporters of animal experiments were societies and charities desperately seeking a cure for a severe medical conditions.

MORAL PHILOSOPHY AND POLICY DEBATES: ANIMAL EXPERIMENTATION

In the Introduction to this book I mentioned some of the difficulties in trying to influence public policy on the topic of animal experimentation by means of philosophical argument. Given that philosophers have such radical disagreements among themselves, and their views often have implications that are very far from current practices, philosophical discussions, on their own, are likely to be treated as fairly marginal to practical debates in policy. But I do not for a second want to diminish the effect that philosophers can have on changing the intellectual climate. Peter Singer's arguments for 'animal liberation', for example, have had a huge influence on how these questions are considered and discussed, and as a result of the efforts of Singer and others very significant changes have been made. Many of the types of experiments once taken for granted in the 1960s and 70s, which inflicted great harm and suffering merely to satisfy the curiosity of the researchers, are now outlawed. But one can hardly argue that animals are now liberated, or that the world is on its way there, even if some of the worst abuses have been eliminated. This sets the question of how philosophers can have greater influence, or even any influence at all, in practical areas of policy.

There is also a second background issue that needs to be brought out before going further. In public debates about the ethics of animal research, two distinct but intermingled questions need to be separated. The first is the scientific question of whether experimenting on animals is a useful way of finding out about human beings: do the animal models 'work'? Some critics say they fail: if chocolate had been safety-tested on beagles it would never have reached the market, so it is said. Apparently a beagle could die if it ate a whole box of dark chocolates. Others take a more nuanced view. One researcher said to me, 'I know an awful lot about pain in rats. I don't know how much I know about pain in human beings'. Hence there is a scientific debate to be had about the efficacy of the science of animal experiments.

It is possible, however, to believe that a well-defined animal experiment can teach us a great deal, yet still be morally wrong. After all, we can imagine numerous experiments on humans that would yield very useful information – the Nazi scientists on trial at Nuremberg did some of them – yet most of us have a strong view that it would be wrong to do this type of experiment on unwilling subjects, however much that would increase our knowledge. Indeed some people think it is wrong to use the information gained in the Nazi experiments, even if significant benefit would come of it (Moe 1984). But the main point is that even if animal experiments work, this doesn't settle the moral question of whether they should be permitted. Conversely, however, if it is shown that the experiments do not work then, for all but the most extreme view, that would be enough to show that the experiments are not only scientifically flawed, but also morally wrong. Hence arguments about the efficacy of experiments can, on their own, only show that experimenting is wrong; they cannot show it is right. Different types of empirical evidence – for example, about the capacity to feel pain – may have greater bearing, of course.

THE STANDARD APPROACH: DEFINING THE MORAL COMMUNITY

One popular way of trying to advance the debate on the morally proper treatment of animals is to try to define what it is about humans being that makes us 'members of the moral community' and to explore whether this — whatever it is — is also true of at least some animals. Now, there is one obvious proposal that would settle the matter immediately: the critical morally relevant property is 'being a human being' and this would explain why it is that all and only human beings are members of the moral community. Such a view resonates with the often-heard expression that it is 'obvious that human beings are more important than animals'. However the form of this claim is suspiciously like the claims once heard that it is 'obvious that men are more important than women' or that 'whites are more important than blacks'. Rather than statements of the moral obvious they are now, of course, taken to be statements of sexism and racism, and the term 'speciesism' has been coined to make a similar point in the current context (Ryder 1975; Singer 1995). In effect, the challenge is to find why being a human being is so important. Is there a morally significant property that human beings have, and at least some animals do not, which would then justify drawing the bounds of the moral community in such a way that it leaves out those animals we eat, hunt or experiment upon, or in other words treat in ways we would never treat human beings? On this view, the property 'human being' is not sufficient: membership in a species has no moral weight in itself.

We need then, to look for some underlying property to explain why human beings are morally special. To jump ahead, some possible candidates offered by moral philosophers are sentience, autonomy, possession of a conception of the good, capability to flourish, sociability and possession of a life. These are all properties typically held by human beings, and to varying degrees, by animals. Our question, then, is whether any of them provides a criterion for membership of the moral community. An immediate difficulty was pointed out by John Rawls. On the face of it many of these properties come in degrees, but it seems that, as far as the moral community is concerned, you are either a member of it, or not. Hence, Rawls argued, we need what he called a 'range property': one such that either you have it or you do not. Rawls' example was whether or not a point on a plane was 'inside the circle'. Of course one point could be closer to the centre of a circle than another, but this is not the same as being 'more inside' the circle. Either the point is inside the circle or it is outside (ignoring those points that hit the line). Similarly, it seems, in the current context of trying to draw the boundaries of the moral community we need a property that is either had, or is not had (Rawls 1971, 508).

The first suggestion on the list was 'sentience', to be understood as the capacity to suffer or feel pleasure and pain. Possibly this could be a range property. Of course some creatures may have a capacity to feel differing ranges or intensities of pain and pleasure, but it is not unreasonable to suppose that an entity either has a capacity or fails to do so. As Jeremy Bentham put it, 'the question is not whether they can talk or reason but whether they can suffer' (Bentham 1996 [1781], 283). Yet it is well known that there are problems with this approach in that it gives a rather uncomfortable answer to the question of the boundaries of the moral community. On this view more or less any creature with a nervous system is a member of the moral community. Indeed, there is an interesting echo of this thought in the UK regulations mentioned above. As we saw, a licence is needed to experiment on all vertebrates and the common octopus. Presumably the justification for this is that we know that such creatures have a very clear capability to suffer. However, one obvious, and rather troubling, consequence of the position that a capacity to suffer puts a creature into the moral community is that it would seem to leave a small number of human beings out: those with a seriously malfunctioning nervous system or those in a permanent coma (although perhaps these individuals can be regarded as suffering in other ways).

Some will be very happy to accept sentience as the basis of entry into the moral community, but we should be aware of the very radical consequences of doing so: that there is no moral privilege to human status. This, of course, will be welcomed by many who object to our current treatment of animals. However, the further implications of such a view are not so clear. Often it is assumed that it entails that animals have rights, on the basis that if human beings have rights and there is no moral distinction between human beings and other sentient animals then such animals must have rights too. Yet Bentham, who, as we saw, is a defender of the view that sentience is what matters, equally famously denied that human beings had rights in any substantial sense (Bentham 1987 [1796]). For Bentham the consequence of drawing the bounds of the moral community in terms of sentience is that other animals have, not rights, but equal weight in the utilitarian calculus with human beings. For this reason, perhaps, Peter Singer, a contemporary utilitarian, named his book *Animal Liberation* rather than *Animal Rights*.

We will return later to the question of rights versus utilitarian aggregation. In the meantime, we should look at a second approach to drawing the bounds of the moral community, which draws more on the Kantian tradition in moral thought. It comes in a number of variants, but all take as the qualifying property for the moral community something like autonomy, will or freedom, which either is, or is based on, some sort of higher-level cognitive functioning, possibly involving the ability to reflect on the thinker's own thoughts. Accordingly it draws the bounds of the moral community much more tightly than the sentience approach, leaving out almost all, if not all, non-human animals. Perhaps a case can be made for great apes and dolphins, but not much more.

While many may be pleased to draw the line in a way that allows us to continue to eat and experiment on animals there are two well-known immediate consequences that should give us pause. First, those creatures that do not have higher-level cognitive functioning are therefore excluded from the moral community. It appears to follow from this that they are, therefore, owed no more concern than inanimate objects. Animals, then, could be treated just as we treat plants or mineral ores, and so on, which is to say without regard for their own welfare or interests in any respect. This is a notorious consequence of the Kantian view. Kant's own response was that we should treat animals well out of a concern for ourselves, so as not to demean our own moral status (Kant 1997, 212). But this seems to get things exactly the wrong way round. If it were not in some way wrong to treat animals badly it is hard to see why it would be demeaning of our own humanity to treat them so.

The other obvious problem is that, just as with the sentience approach, some human beings would also be left out of account. In this case, though, the problem is much more serious. Babies, adults with severe learning difficulties and those suffering dementia would also be excluded. Babies could, perhaps, be rescued on the basis of potential moral status, but the other categories are much more problematic.

Now other properties have been proposed as possible bases for membership of the moral community, such as sociability or possession of a life, but rather than go through them one by one, we can note it seems unlikely that any of them is capable of generating the 'common-sense' position that we owe moral concern to (many) non-human animals, but we need not treat (all of these) animals the way we treat human beings. Even if we are justified in killing animals for food, few would think that we need show no concern about how they are kept or treated. However, on the approach we are considering, if we think in terms of a 'range' property, then, to put it crudely, you are either in or out, and so the common-sense position that we owe something to animals but not the same as we owe to human beings is unsupportable. On the 'moral-community' approach we should either treat animals as we do human beings, or we have no moral duties to them at all. The fact that the philosophical debate is so polarized in this way is the crux of the matter of why philosophers' views match up so poorly with current policy and regulations, which appears more complex in structure than is typically offered by philosophers. This, of course, cannot be offered as an argument that public policy is right and philosophical theories wrong. But before we can make progress we should at least try to understand the moral assumptions behind the common-sense view.

AN ALTERNATIVE APPROACH: MORALLY RELEVANT PROPERTIES

The obvious alternative is to deny that we need a range property, but that membership of the moral community is a matter of more or less. Perhaps we need to find some sort of 'sliding-scale' property to explain why we should treat some creatures, such as human beings, in a different way to others, such as mice, which in turn should be treated in a different way to ants. There is, I think, something to this idea, but I think the way it is stated is misleading. First, the notion of 'moral community' is unhelpful and should be abandoned. It suggests a cut-off point: as we said, either you are in or you are out. But once a sliding scale or continuum is adopted there seems no reason for even thinking there is a boundary line that we need to police in some way.

Second, the assumption that we should explain the grounding of moral duties on a single 'sliding-scale' property is probably the wrong way of trying to generate a more complex account. We can see this by reviewing, once again, the properties that we have already mentioned: sentience, autonomy or higher cognitive functioning, possession of a conception of the good, capability to flourish, sociability and possession of a life. Now, some of these could be turned into sliding-scale properties, it is true. But to do so and pick one as the essential property would appear to imply that we should treat the others as being of no moral relevance at all. But this seems hard to justify. Let us consider sentience as an example. Once we know that a creature is capable of feeling pain, how could we not feel morally obliged to take that into account in working out how to treat it? I am not suggesting that this alone justifies an absolute prohibition on causing pain, but rather it would be inhumanely callous simply to ignore the fact that a creature can feel pain, even if we find reasons to justify experimenting on it.

Having agreed that we must take pain into account, it would seem very strange to conclude that this is all we must do; that we have found the relevant property and that is that. Some animals are capable of higher cognitive capacities, or will by instinct live in groups. Once more it would simply seem wrong to ignore such facts about creatures when deciding how to act towards them. And once more I am not supposing that we should argue from the premise that an animal has higher cognitive capabilities or that it lives in groups to the conclusion that we must treat it in the same way as we treat human beings. Rather the conclusion is much less precise: that we should take this fact about the animal into account when working out how to treat it. This could, of course, mean treating it with as much respect as we do human beings, or, more modestly, housing it in particular types of environment, or ensuring that it has particular forms of stimulation. The argument then, is that we can match concerns about particular types of treatment with particular properties of the creature. The fact that a creature can feel pain is relevant only to the forms of treatment that threaten to cause it pain. The fact that a creature is sociable by nature is relevant only to those issues that bring sociability into play, perhaps in how it is kept or how other creatures might suffer at its absence or distress.

In other words, rather than setting the terms of membership of the moral community and then supposing that membership brings with it full moral concern, we can approach things a different way. Rather we can say that a very wide range of objects in the world have morally relevant features. These objects include humans and animals, and might also include such things as plants, mountains and rivers, although that is not our direct concern here. But the point is that moral agents have a duty to take all morally relevant features into account in their treatment of those objects. A patchwork of morally relevant properties generates a patchwork of potentially problematic forms of treatment. Rather than suggesting that there is a single 'sliding-scale' property, we can observe that if creatures differ in their morally relevant features, something resembling a sliding scale will be generated. It will not be a smooth graduation, but may involve differences in principle between different types of animals. For example, great apes and dolphins may well be thought to have more substantial morally relevant properties than, say, dogs and rabbits, which would then correlate with how they are now treated as a matter of policy in the UK and a few other countries. But a creature could be 'higher' than another in one respect, but 'lower' in another. The point is not to generate a biological league table, but to ensure that in our treatment of animals we take all their morally relevant properties seriously.

Which features are morally relevant is a matter on which there can be some debate, although, with one very important exception to which I shall return, these are likely to involve rather small-scale controversies. How these features should be taken into account is, though, going to be much more a matter of disagreement. This, in fact, is where the action is, and where we can model and understand the real issues driving debates on the ethics of our treatment of animals.

UNDERSTANDING PHILOSOPHICAL DISAGREEMENT

The burden of the argument so far is really to suggest that the standard philosophical debate about animal ethics has, in a sense, painted itself into an impossible corner. By framing the question in terms of possession of what property provides a creature with a passport to the moral community, philosophers have saddled themselves with literally unbelievable consequences. If the condition is sentience then humans are absolute moral equals with all animals with a nervous system. If the condition is higher cognitive functioning, then there are no moral constraints on the permitted treatment of many animals, at least not for the sake of those animals (as distinct from the human-centred objection that we can demean ourselves in acting in such ways). My suggestion is that, rather, a whole range of properties are morally relevant and should all be taken into account. Yet this does not explain how they should be taken into account, and here, as I have said, we hit the heart of current debates, even though those who take part in the debates may not see things in these terms.

To see the force of the question of how properties can be taken account of in different ways, consider, for example, how some have taken inspiration from the work of Peter Singer, arguing that as animals can feel pain just as human beings can, they should be treated with the same moral concern. Singer's book, called *Animal Liberation*, is sometimes said to be 'the bible of the animal rights movement'. But as noted above, Singer's book is not called '*Animal Rights*'. To say that human beings and animals should be treated the same way is not yet to say what that treatment should be. One could read Singer and conclude that we should start eating other human beings or perform highly invasive experiments upon them. Those who think that Singer has provided a defence of animal rights appear to argue that if a creature is capable of feeling pain then there is an absolute moral requirement not to inflict pain, or allow the infliction of pain, on that creature, perhaps unless it is for its own good.

This is a very strong conclusion. Even if all animals are equal, it is not true that all pains are equal. We sometimes permit the infliction of avoidable pain, or at least discomfort, on human beings for the sake of the greater good. Forms of crowd control are often intensely uncomfortable and in some circumstances, say, standing in a con-fined space, can be painful. Yet we would sometimes forcibly require this of people if there is an emergency and the police need to clear a space by penning people into a small area. But that aside, the main point is that while Singer and animal rights activists can both agree that the capacity to feel pain is a morally important property, and how we treat a creature should take into account its possible pain, they do not agree about the moral consequences of the possession of this capacity. The animal rights theorist argues that possession of this property is a sufficient reason to justify an absolute prohibition on action that causes pain, while Singer, as a consequentialist must take a different view. Pain, of course, must be weighed in the consequentialist scales, but there is no reason why it should not regularly be outweighed by other factors.

What matters, then, is how each morally relevant feature is to be taken into account, and the main candidates are whether they generate absolute prohibitions on possible forms of treatment, or whether they are simply properties to be put in the balance to be measured against other factors, such as the prevention of greater pain. Clearly, treating a morally relevant property as generating an absolute (or even near-absolute) prohibition is very close to the idea that the possessor of that property has a right not to have it violated. Whether all theorists will want to draw this conclusion will depend on their theory of rights, but that need not detain us here. By contrast, treating a feature as something to be taken into account, rather than as generating an absolute prohibition, seems to be friendly to the idea that, though weighed in the balance, it can be overturned by other considerations. For example, other things being equal we should not cause mild anxiety in any creature, but when weighed against the possible benefits of a major medical breakthrough, it could be that the consequentialist calculation comes out in favour of permitting the anxiety. Of course, the calculation could also go the other way; much depends on the probabilities of harm and benefit, and the particular weights given to the different factors, which, when we get down to the real details, could differ between theorists even if they accept the same 'high-level' theory.

To illustrate the different ways in which moral factors can be taken into account it is worth exploring the moral underpinnings of the current UK regulations for experiments upon animals, but also broadening the discussion to include experiments on human subjects. As in many other countries, the regulatory regimes apparently rest on a combination of assumptions. The rule for experiments on human subjects is that no one should be subject to any sort of potentially harmful intervention without their consent. The respect given to the idea of 'informed consent' in medical practice, medical research and other research involving human beings, shows how important this idea is in common currency. It is now, for example, virtually impossible to obtain ethical approval for any experiment on human beings that involves deception, thus making highly problematic a whole range of studies in social psychology and elsewhere. For example, it would no longer be possible to conduct the famous Milgram 'obedience to authority' experiments in which the subjects were tricked into believing they were giving other human beings severe, even fatal, electric shocks (Milgram 1974). Many of the experiments on which the contemporary discipline of social psychology is now founded could not have been done under present regulations; hence informed consent has not always been given the weight it now has. Perhaps in the past deception was considered acceptable if the scientific objectives were deemed sufficiently important. Now, though, informed consent is at the heart of medical ethics and research involving human beings.

Should such regard be extended to creatures presumed to be of high cognitive power, but who do not have human language in which to express their wishes? As we saw, in the UK no licence will be granted to conduct invasive scientific experiments on great apes, for example, although not all countries have followed the UK's lead. But other primates, such as monkeys, and mice, rats, rabbits, dogs, fish and other animals are typically treated as if they do not have the capacity to give or withhold consent, although it certainly appears that dissent can be expressed by most animals, by running away if they get the chance. However, we can sum up the moral assumption in question as: those creatures who are capable of autonomous thought should be given the right to determine whether or not they are subjected to invasive treatment (where 'invasion' is understood widely, and mere deception would be treated as a form of invasive treatment). Those creatures of high cognitive capacity that do not explicitly consent are presumed to dissent.

The capacity to feel pain and suffering, however, is treated as a rather different matter. On the face of it current UK regulations do not allow severe, prolonged pain to any creature, either as part of a scientific experiment or as a by-product of raising or slaughtering animals for food or other purposes. Hence wherever possible, experiments are conducted with anaesthetized animals, and farm animals are stunned before slaughter. Where pain is impossible to avoid as part of the experiment, as in the obvious example of testing painkillers, scientists do whatever they can to reduce the duration and intensity of pain to the lowest degree possible. The UK regulations seem to make a distinction between severe and prolonged pain and suffering, on the one hand, and milder forms, perhaps of the sort that would normally be part of the daily or weekly experience of any sentient creature. Severe and prolonged pain creates something close to an absolute prohibition, or at least is given very high weight in the consequentialist balancing. Animals have a 'near right', we might say, not to suffer prolonged severe pain as a consequence of human treatment. We see this concern run right through laws and regulations regarding animals, such as the types of traps hunters are allowed to use to catch wild animals. Short-term mild pain, mild suffering or mild distress is treated as an undoubted harm, but one that can be outweighed by other factors. In between is a large grey area – prolonged mild pain, short severe pain, moderate pain of any duration – on which decisions will also need to be made.

Let us move next to the morally relevant feature of 'having a good'. Here the idea is that there are forms of treatment that are good or bad for an animal in the sense of furthering or impeding its flourishing, given the type of animal it is. The most obvious way in which such issues are taken into account as a matter of current practice is by means of the conditions in which animals are housed. Where possible some semblance of 'natural conditions' will be attempted. For example, foraging creatures will often be placed in environments to allow them to root around in wood shavings or similar material. Animals that live in social groups are often housed together. Once more we see an illustration of how morally relevant features of any animal can be used to determine how that animal should be treated, although the conditions of scientific research and farming mean that the constraint is interpreted in different ways. In the case of scientific research all aspects need to be controlled, and so simulated forms of expressing natural behaviour are likely to be offered, if anything is. This, of course, adds to the cost of scientific research, but in a rather minor way, compared to the immense cost of many experiments and procedures. Furthermore scientists often argue that contented, non-anxious animals make for better scientific subjects, and so in purely scientific terms the money is well spent. In the case of farming, marginal costs are more important as they must be passed on to customers in a highly competitive market, although product differentiation through 'humane' forms of farming is also common, as in the case of 'free-range' eggs. However there is less need to regulate all aspects of a farm animal's life, and so forms of behaviour that allow normal functioning are sometimes possible, although, of course, by no means the norm. But it is rather troubling that in the case of farming we often allow minor cost considerations to outweigh a creature's ability to live a life that is natural to the type of creature it is.

The final feature I shall discuss, which is not to presume that the list is complete, is 'possession of a life'. Here matters are somewhat more dramatic and potentially controversial. As things stand, while, as we have seen, pain and suffering is treated with great seriousness in the UK regulations, death of an animal, by contrast, is treated as a 'humane end point'. A research scientist, a farmer or slaughterhouse worker has to learn to accept the death of an animal as morally unproblematic, provided it happens the right way. The experiences that happen within a life, such as pain and suffering, are one thing; the life is quite another, and is treated as of little, if any, moment.

Take, for example, the experimental procedure known as 'anaesthesia without recovery', which is used to try to determine the immediate effects of an experimental substance (often referred to as a 'compound') on an animal, usually a rabbit, mouse or rat. In one version of this type of procedure, the animal is fitted with two catheters, one to deliver the anaesthetic, the other to deliver the compound under test. First, the animal is rendered unconscious by means of the anaesthetic. Next the animal is subjected to a series of radical surgical incisions to expose its internal organs. Its skin is peeled back and then it is pinned out on the laboratory bench to keep it immobile and its internal organs exposed. Various probes are then placed on its organs and blood vessels, in order to monitor their state during the experiment. The compound is then introduced and precise observations can be made concerning its effects on blood flow, metabolism or whatever else is under investigation. The anaesthetic is topped up as necessary to keep the animal unconscious and hence not in pain. When the experiment is concluded, after a matter perhaps of some hours, the dose of anaesthetic is increased until the animal dies: a 'humane end point', without pain.

Such experiments are not uncommon, although being labour-intensive they are comparatively expensive. But, of course, they are far from the only method by which animals are killed for human purposes, whether within science, agriculture or recreation. It appears that current regulations in all these areas assume that an animal's life in itself has no, or very little, value, again as distinct from the experiences which happen within a life, which can have both positive and negative value. (Note that it is assumed that the preservation of a species is of great value, but this is not to say that such value is somehow 'spread out' among all the members of that species.)

Now, if human beings and other animals all have lives, yet human life is treated with reverence while animal life is treated as of no value, then, prima facie, there is an unjustified partiality in favour of human beings, unless some relevant points of differentiation can be made to explain the difference. In response it should be noted that some philosophers argue that for human beings it is not true that life, itself, has value for the person whose life it is. Of course, family, friends, even admirers, can find value in the life of that other person – in their company, support or achievements, and so on. But none of this entails that the life itself has value for its possessor.

Still, it seems very odd to deny that life has value for human beings, especially in the face of the evidence that the overwhelming majority of human beings take steps to prolong their lives as long as they can. But perhaps this can be understood in terms of the hopes, desires and fears of the agent concerning his or her future. Perhaps, then, it is the continuation of these plans and projects that have value rather than the life itself. Someone with no plans, no sources of enjoyment, no family and no friends, and no prospect of any of these things, may see little or no value in the continuation of his or her life. And, indeed, although it may sound strange to say such a thing, the thesis that life has no value in itself is not an unfamiliar one. For example it is sometimes said that to believe the alternative – that life does have value – entails a duty to create as much life as possible, which seems an unappealing doctrine. Whether this really does follow appears to rest on some fairly strong assumptions concerning the relationship between value and duty. But be that as it may, we can draw some conclusions. First, current regulations concerning animal use assume that life, if it is of value at all, has weak value which is easily outweighed by other factors. Second, such an assumption does not necessarily show that there is an unjustified partiality in our practices in favour of human beings, for it is possible that the apparent extra value given to human life derives from other recognized sources of value, such as the value of the plans of the person or their desires or their place in a wider social networks, including mutual relationships of care, and so on.

THE PROBLEMATIC STATUS OF HUMAN TREATMENT OF ANIMALS

So far, though, I have done no more than describe how to understand disagreement about human use of animals, and to consider the moral assumptions most likely to underlie contemporary regulations. Roughly the position is this. First, creatures with high cognitive capacity have strong rights against interference. Second, sentient creatures have a 'near right' not to be subjected to pain that is both severe and prolonged, while more moderate pain and suffering are a matter of concern and are taken note of within a consequentialist calculation. Finally, sociability and the possession of a good are also taken account of to some lesser degree, but little or no weight is given to life itself. I have not, however, said whether I think that any such view is defensible. For my own part, I simply do not know whether to accept that life has no value, whether it is the life of a human being, a non-human animal or a plant. Other things being equal, it is a worse world if a living creature or plant perishes, but this could be explained by a wide range of factors. If there is value to life itself, then there is something to regret in the death of any animal in scientific research or in farming. Equally, and this sounds less plausible, there is something to regret in the death of every plant, including those grown as an annual crop, although it is easier to see the loss in the death or destruction of, say, a large tree or well-established bush.

But leaving aside the case of plants, if there is value in animal life, then the moral assumptions underlying current regulations are questionable. As we have seen, there seems no recognition of the (possible) value of life. But perhaps even more problematic is the one-sided consequentialism of the regulations. Costs are weighed against benefits, and a judgement is made as to whether the benefits sufficiently outweigh the costs. Even if it is right that there is need for a balance between various factors, and that it can be acceptable to allow small and moderate pains, or confinement and restrictions on natural behaviour, for the sake of great possible benefits, there is something deeply suspicious about the fact that the costs all fall on non-humans while the benefits rebound to human beings. Even when experiments are undertaken to devise pharmaceuticals for use on animals, the benefits are usually sought for human purposes, and the particular individual animals that suffer do not also benefit. Generally when suffering is systematically imposed on one group or individual for the benefit of another group or individual we consider it to be, at least, exploitative. It is hard, therefore, to escape the charge that human beings exploit animals in a way that is problematic.

A common response is to argue that the animals who suffer also benefit in a quite different way. After all, in the vast majority of cases the particular animals in question would not exist at all if it were not for human purposes. Most animals used by humans are bred specifically for such purposes and hence if life has a value this value is conferred on any animal brought into existence. In addition, or alternatively, the lives of many animals used by human beings may contain a significant balance of positive experience over negative to make that life worthwhile, and hence the charge of exploitation is somewhat mitigated (Scruton 2000).

While this defence may be appropriate in some cases, the fact that so few animals used by human beings are allowed to live to an age where they die a natural death should give us pause. Consider the way in which animals such as dogs and monkeys are used in safety tests. After a short exposure – a few weeks or months – to the compound under trial they will be 'euthanized' so that a post-mortem can take place to see whether their internal organs have been affected. These are animals otherwise in the prime of life (and this is why they have been chosen for the experiments). Consider also the example of anaesthesia without recovery described earlier. Think too, of food production. Sheep on the hills seem to have a rather utopian life. Yet the lamb we generally eat, as distinct from the adult sheep kept for their wool, or for breeding, are slaughtered when between a month and a year old: presumably when the combination of their size and tenderness brings greatest economic rewards. A simple awareness of the facts can make many people, including myself, very sympathetic to the moral case for ending animal experiments and for vegetarianism.

Yet the peculiarity is that, for me at least, I do not find that such arguments, however intellectually compelling, of very strong motivational force. I still use medicines and household products that have been tested on animals. I do not protest against the animal experiments that take place in my university. I continue to eat meat, albeit rather guiltily. The moral philosopher R.M. Hare would respond to this combination of professed belief and action by arguing that my claims are insincere (1952). Hare argued that sincere moral belief is always expressed in action, but as my actions don't follow my claimed beliefs, any moral argument I make against harmful treatment of animals is necessarily insincere. This seems to me, however, dogmatic and uncompelling. Phenomenologically, it seems to me that moral argument hits hardest at the level of *conscience*, and whether it spurs *action* is a further issue. Partly, I think, we must take into account the consequences of acting on one's moral beliefs. Where it is costly, or even awkward or inconvenient, to act as your conscience prompts, individuals may find themselves acting in ways which they, themselves, at some level disapprove of. Consider, by way of analogy, the existence of slavery in the American south in the nineteenth century. I find it very hard to believe that every slave owner sincerely believed that there was nothing wrong with the practice of one human purchasing another and holding arbitrary power over him or her. No doubt many did think that somehow it was in the natural order of things, but surely some had their doubts? These 'guilty masters' may well have accepted the moral argument that no one should be a slave of another, yet did not seriously consider liberating his or her slaves, believing that there was no other way of surviving at an acceptable standard of living. By analogy many of us are unwilling to give up the benefits of what, in reflective moments, we take to be morally unacceptable uses of animals, as doing so would make our lives more inconvenient and uncomfortable.

If the actions we choose to pursue are, we believe, morally unjustified, then we have a choice. We can live with the apparent hypocrisy, or change our way of life or adjust our moral beliefs. Politically or structurally, however, there is a further option: institutional or technical advance which allows us to pursue our ends without accepting behaviour we believe to be unjustified. Presumably slavery was easier to abolish when it became clear that it had become economically possible to remain in business without slaves. By analogy, if we can find ways of producing non-animal foods which are just as delicious and nutritious as meat, or ways of testing pharmaceuticals that do not involve animals, then we can continue to pursue the ends we seek without acting in ways that are morally troubling. In effect such an ambition is to solve the moral problem by avoiding it.

In the case of animal experimentation the leading suggestion in the direction of avoidance is the doctrine of the 'three Rs' proposed by Russell and Burch (1959). The three Rs are refinement, reduction and replacement. Refinement is the idea that experiments should be modified so that they are as little harmful as they could be to animals. Reduction, naturally enough, calls for a reduction in the number of animals used. Replacement is the idea that the knowledge sought by experimenting on animals might be achieved in some other way.

Refinement and reduction are generally welcomed by scientists. After all, if you could reduce the pain to animals, or the number of animals involved, without compromising the science, what could be the objection? Replacement is rather more complicated. In some cases it is a matter of conducting experiments on cells or tissues that have been cultivated in the lab – so-called *in vitro* experiments. These can yield useful knowledge but at the moment tend to be used only at an early stage of research. Another possibility is computer modelling, but this is in its infancy, and at the moment seems very limited, as computer models will always be a simplification of the real world. But there are other methods of replacement. Consider, for example, experiments conducted in the 1960s in which infant monkeys were removed from their mothers' care to see how they responded. The scientists conducting some of these experiments claimed that they were hoping to gain insight into human depression (Kaufman and Rosenblum 1967). But it seems that such experiments are scientifically very strange, even independently of the ethical questions. For surely psychological and sociological studies would be a much more effective way of obtaining this sort of information. More generally, sometimes a research question might better be addressed by social science or statistical analysis than by animal experiments. This is likely to make experimental scientists nervous: nervous of redundancy. Replacement is the goal of those who oppose animal experiments, but, of course, it is hardest of the three Rs to crack.

PROGRESS IN PUBLIC POLICY

In the present context we can split moral attitudes to the human use of animals in scientific experiments roughly into three groups. First, there are those who think that harms to animals are, on balance, outweighed by the scientific and medical benefits such experimentation allows. Second, there are those who see irrefutable arguments on both sides, and conclude that this is a genuine moral dilemma with no clear solution. Third, there are those who feel that the moral considerations show that we are wrong to use animals in scientific research. Of these groups the first find their views most clearly reflected in current regulations. But still, partially in deference to the second and third groups, changes are regularly being made. In essence the regulators have taken their question to be how we can modify our treatment of animals so that more and more people find it less and less objectionable. In other words, the regulators are attempting to bring together what, in the Introduction, we called, following Rawls, an overlapping consensus. Think of the changes made over recent decades: much more attention to animal welfare in farming and slaughtering, banning of animal testing for cosmetics and household products, banning of tests on great apes, and seeking out alternatives to animal experiments through test-tube and computer models. Although it would be wrong to say that such moves have fully satisfied those who argue against human use of animals, they must see them as steps in the right direction. At the same time those who have found their activities limited by such new regulations have not, in general, had to give up very much. In general they can adapt to the new situation. Hence there appears to be moral progress in public policy at relatively little cost, by a series of concessions around the edges. But equally clearly, in this case, there remains work to be done.

This is not to say that radical, discontinuous, change is impossible. Slavery was abolished. Neither must there always be a consensus behind change. Often change is highly contentious or unpopular. The banning of hunting with dogs is an example, although as we will explore later, changing law in absence of widespread agreement can create important problems of compliance. In the case of human treatment of animals in research and farming, for the moment the best we can hope for in the short to medium term is to make current practices less objectionable to more people.

CONCLUSION: LESSONS FOR PHILOSOPHY

This chapter has, I hope, illustrated in detail a point made briefly in the Introduction to this book. Approaching a problem in public policy by means of the methodology 'first choose your theory', as if you were signing up for some sort of crusade, could lead to interesting philosophical consequences but it is very unlikely to lead to a usable contribution to current policy debates. Of course as I hope I have also made clear, radical philosophical arguments are a vital part of the debate, and add to the stock of ideas that enrich discussion. But on their own they will settle nothing. The methodology implicitly recommended here suggests that when thinking about a practical issue, we should start at the other end: not at the philosophical theories but current disagreements in the public policy area. We need to ask: what do people think they disagree about? And is that the best way of understanding their disagreement? Is there a better way? And if so, does that open up new avenues for making progress? It is a commonplace to say that philosophers can help clarify the terms of public debate. Philosophers are not the only people who can do this, of course, but it is part of our training to make distinctions, to follow arguments out to their conclusions, and to reconstruct relatively loose arguments in a more rigorous form. But to do this one has first to become immersed in the debate in which one wishes to intervene.

It is implied in the methodology I am suggesting that participants in public debates do not always fully comprehend or perfectly articulate what they disagree about. A simple slogan or principle, while helpful for campaigning, can have a distorting effect on argument. In my view, contemporary public policy debates about human treatment of animals are not, centrally, debates about whether animals have rights, or whether all animals are equal. They are not even debates about which properties of creatures are morally relevant. Rather they are debates about how morally relevant properties of animals should be taken into account in human treatment of them.

I have also made a further point about moral argument and human motivation. Here, I have to admit, I have made a claim that I have tried to illustrate, rather than demonstrate. The claim is that moral argument is much better at making people feel guilty about what they do, rather than changing their behaviour, and if this is true it has implications about the type of structural change that is likely to be needed to meet social objectives. We will return to questions about motivation, though, in later chapters.

2
Gambling

INTRODUCTION

In the Introduction I mentioned a call from the Home Office, to ask me if I would be prepared to join a government committee looking into the regulation of gambling law. I was told it would involve around a dozen meetings and a similar number of trips to 'gambling establishments'. How could I refuse? I agreed right away. In the event it took up almost all of my research time for the next year-and-a-half. I visited dog tracks, a spread betting office, amusement arcades, and casinos, ranging from the tawdry to the unbelievably opulent. One casino employed more chefs than it would have gamblers most days, and redecorated its restaurant every two weeks to fit in with the theme of the London season. I visited during the Wimbledon fortnight. I also had to read thousands of pages of submitted evidence, as well as many research papers and reports. But it was worth it.

The committee, called by the unattractive name 'The Gambling Review Body', had the brief of looking at all aspects of gambling in the UK, except the National Lottery, which was outside our remit. As I understand it, the government thought a review was needed for several reasons. First, at the time — early 2000 — it was recognized that the Internet was going to change the gambling scene in a very significant fashion, yet there were no regulations in place. The gap needed to be filled. This was a challenge as we, as a committee, needed to predict how the Internet gambling industry would develop and grow. One prediction was easy. Internet business would gravitate to low-tax locations to avoid UK gambling duty and thereby make their offering more competitive and more profitable as well. At the time we started our deliberations, betting at bookmakers was subject to duty, which you could pay either on your stake or your winnings. However, there was no duty on stakes placed at the racetrack. Accordingly, professional gamblers would go to the races, as betting-office duty dug deep into their margin. But with new tax-free online betting opportunities from companies located in Malta and the Channel Island of Alderney, a good deal of business was switching offshore. Tax reform was therefore considered an urgent issue.

That, then, was the easy Internet development to call. The other was more difficult. What types of Internet gambling would be offered? There was little doubt that traditional horse and sports betting would be made available, but what else? We were worried about slot machines, and the possibility that every home or office computer could be transformed into a highly addictive gambling machine. As things turned out we seem to have been worrying about the wrong thing, and what has become probably the most popular form of Internet gambling – playing poker against other human beings – didn't even occur to us as a possibility. In a way it is rather comforting that people seek out human company even on the Internet, rather than playing against a machine.

The Internet, then, was an obvious gap in the regulations, and, in the event, one we found hard to cope with. A second problem was that the introduction of the National Lottery had led to the allegation that the government was not following rules it had laid down for others, and so, potentially, could be subject to legal challenge. The immediate problem was that gambling operators were very limited in opportunities to advertise their services. At this time, for example, it was not permissible to advertise betting shops or bingo halls on television. We will explore the reasons for this later. But the point is that while commercial gambling providers could not advertise, there were no similar restrictions on the lottery. A huge effort went into marketing the National Lottery, and other gambling operators felt that they were hampered by unfair competition, in possible breach of competition law.

In addition there were other aspects of the then current law which were possibly not compliant with generally understood ideas of fair procedure. For example, for reasons we will come to, the licensing authorities could refuse an applicant a licence to open a casino without having to explain the reason and without allowing the possibility of appeal. People were beginning to ask whether this practice was compliant with human rights legislation. Further, there were laws that seemed quite archaic. For example, if you wanted to go to play bingo, it was necessary to take out a membership of the club, which, by law, had to take forty-eight hours to process. This was to ensure that those who decided to go to play bingo had engaged in a sufficiently lengthy process of mature reflection before entering such a den of iniquity. Another strange quirk was that gambling contracts were not enforceable in law. If a betting shop refused to pay out you could appeal to a voluntary arbitration panel, but its rulings were not enforceable, and there was no further legal remedy. In the submissions we received, several letters were from people who claimed that they had been cheated on a grand scale, bookies refusing to pay out hundreds of thousands of pounds. Generally the bookmaking company believed that the claims were fraudulent, based on collusion with an employee who had falsified the betting slip, filling in the details after the races had been run. Who knows the truth? The claims were never tested in law.

In taking on the question of what sorts of reforms would be appropriate it was important to try to come to an understanding of why the law had developed as it had. It was also necessary to think more generally about the morality of gambling, and the reasons for its regulations. Given my background in political philosophy, and my general agreement with liberal principles, the issues, at first sight, seemed to me reasonably clear. A generally liberal approach to politics and public policy suggests that if people want to spend their time and money gambling, then, in principle, there is no difference between gambling and going to a football match or a restaurant. Like it or not, what people do in their own time is their own business. As the authors of the *Royal Commission on Gambling* (*Rothschild Commission*), a UK report published in 1978, put the point:

> The objection that punters are wasting their time is a moral or possibly an aesthetic judgement. As it happens, none of us is attracted by the idea of spending an afternoon in a betting office. But the people who frequent betting offices have chosen to enjoy themselves in their own way and we think that in a free society it would be wrong to prevent them from doing so merely because others think that they would be better employed in digging the garden, reading to their children or playing healthy outdoor sports.
>
> (RCG 1978, 50)

In passing it is worth mentioning that the authors of this excellent 1978 report were an interesting group. In addition to Baron Rothschild, the Royal Commission included the philosopher Bernard Williams, the football commentator David Coleman and the journalist Marjorie Proops, best known as 'agony aunt' writing the 'Dear Marje' column for the *Daily Mirror*, among others. Their report, however, was ignored by the government as it had the misfortune of being commissioned by the outgoing Labour administration and was of no interest to the newly elected Conservative administration of Margaret Thatcher. In Chapter 6 we will see that the same fate befell another report commissioned at around the same time: the Black report on the National Health Service.

As was true in 1978, and as it is now, gambling seems an ordinary part of life for many people. There are betting shops everywhere. British families used to do the 'football pools' and now they do the lottery. People have a fondness for a 'harmless flutter', entering sweepstakes for the Grand National or the World Cup, and having a go on the slot machines at the seaside. Indeed in the UK we are so relaxed about gambling we even let our children do it. The UK is one of the very few countries where it is legal for children to gamble, albeit for small stakes and small prizes, on slot machines, penny falls (also known as 'pusher machines') and cranes. Cranes are those machines where you might be able to pick up a furry toy by manipulating a crane mechanism in a glass box. They are often assumed to be games of skill, but in fact there is a gambling element as the grip of the crane varies according to a random pattern, so while skill is needed, it is never sufficient to win the prize. As it happened, seaside operators were worried that our committee might recommend further restrictions on gambling by children. Critics had pointed out that, while gambling by children on holiday with, and under the supervision of, their parents might be a harmless bit of fun, many children live near seaside towns and for them legal gambling could become a serious problem. In anticipation of criticism, a powerful lobby formed in defence of current practices, and the trade association organized a letter-writing campaign by seaside Members of Parliament, each of whom sent the committee an identical letter, arguing that to ban children from gambling would mean the end of the British seaside holiday, and that the practice was entirely harmless, adding 'spice to a bit of fun'.

There is, though, an interesting further angle to the debate about gambling by children. Sometimes it is argued that allowing children to gamble for trivial stakes and prizes under the supervision of their parents is rather like the alleged French practice of allowing children to drink watered-down wine at meal times. In both cases it is claimed to lead to responsible practices as an adult. However, the evidence, at least in the case of gambling, is less clear. One 'risk factor' for developing a problem with gambling later in life is to have been introduced to gambling by your family. Another, apparently, is having a large win early in your gambling career, which can give you the illusion that somehow you are good at gambling, and continual success is a legitimate expectation, almost a right (Bellringer 1999).

Thinking about how people can develop problematic attitudes to gambling can lead one to think about it in a quite different way. The occasional small-stakes bet is one thing, but hearing that someone goes to the casino every night makes us worried about them in a way in which we typically don't worry if we hear that someone goes to the theatre or to hear music every night. It seems, perhaps, sordid, or rather sad, even if they can afford to lose. We also worry that gambling can be addictive, or lead to a loss of self-control, at least for some people. Or perhaps we think it reveals a mistaken approach to how to get on in the world. Many people have at least some negative reactions to gambling; they regret that it seems to be on the increase in many countries. Recent attempts to experiment with a 'resort casino' in the UK, of the sort to be found in Las Vegas, met with hostility, perhaps even bewilderment about why this was considered a desirable change. It was the subject of massive press campaigns. Eventually the idea of a resort casino fell into a black hole, and there seems little appetite to revive it.

There are many different questions concerning the ethics of gambling. One, of course, is whether it is wrong to gamble. Here we can see that views are divided. Another is whether it is wrong to profit from gambling, and a third, quite distinct, is whether it is wrong to encourage people to gamble (Doughney 2002). It is possible, for example, to be very relaxed and tolerant about gambling, as long as people arrange it between themselves in their own homes, while, at the same time, strongly objecting to the commercial provision of gambling in which companies profit from other people's gambling. So, for example, in some countries gambling is, in effect, a nationalized industry with all profits going to the state. But even if one is prepared to tolerate commercial profit, it is possible to draw a line saying that there should be no encouragement in the form, say, of advertising. Indeed, as we will see later in this chapter, all of these distinctions have played a role in legislation in the UK.

However, an even more important distinction needs to be made between questions of morality and questions of policy. Is gambling perfectly legitimate from a moral point of view, or are there reasons to have moral doubts about it, at least in some forms? But we need also ask what we can achieve through regulation. Both of these questions will concern us in what follows.

THE CASE AGAINST GAMBLING

What is the difference between spending your evening in a casino and in a cinema? Some people will argue that gambling is, in itself, wrong – immoral. This is a judgement not about the consequences of gambling but rather about the activity itself. In the current age, we are somewhat losing the sense that an activity can be wrong in itself, irrespective of its consequences, but such things have been said, and in some cases still are, about masturbation, homosexuality or even dancing on Sundays. It is possible that gambling is simply immoral. Further, some will add, the state has a duty to stop people acting immorally. These are, of course, quite different claims. It is possible to think that Sunday dancing or gambling is immoral, but that the state has no business poking its nose into individual morality, at least when no harm is done to others. And it is also possible to take the exact opposite view: that the state should stop people doing what is morally wrong, but that there is nothing wrong with gambling. The combination of the premise that gambling is wrong, with the further premise that the state should prevent wrongdoing, leads to the conclusion that the state should prevent gambling (if it can). But does this argument have any plausibility? And if not, are there other arguments to justify state intervention?

First we must ask why might gambling be thought wrong? Many religions, of course, have taken a dim view of gambling, but we can still ask what, precisely, it is that they find so objectionable. One argument, which has resonance with the Islamic prohibition of gambling, is that there is something wrong with the basic attraction of gambling: that one might get rich without working (I was confronted with this argument from an Islamic cleric when appearing on the radio programme 'The Moral Maze' to defend the liberalization of gambling we had recommended in our report). The same thought underlies the Islamic prohibition on lending money at interest. One must earn one's living through honest work, and not by trickery or exploiting others, whether it is their gullibility or their labour. Gambling, so says the Koran, sets men against each other, and makes them neglect their prayers (Koran 5.91). Hence, on this view, gambling is to be prohibited, although even here we might wonder whether these are arguments that gambling is wrong in itself, or wrong merely in its consequences. The Islamic view, probably, is that it is wrong both in itself and its consequences. Early Christian views, both about gambling and money-lending, were, of course, very similar, and disapproval of gambling is still present among some Methodist and similar sects.

Yet it is one thing to say that those who accept a particular religious world view should also accept prohibitions on gambling, and quite another to say that the prohibition should be enforced by government against everyone, whatever their faith or private beliefs. To press this latter argument conflicts with the basic premise of liberal political philosophy: that the government must not intervene on the basis of its assessment of the morality of particular forms of behaviour. The state, it is said, should be 'neutral' between competing conceptions of the good. Private individuals can try to persuade others that their behaviour is wrong, but it is not for the state to prohibit anyone's chosen course of action unless it harms other people. A liberal state cannot ban action simply on the grounds that it is morally disapproved of by some people, or even by a majority.

That phrase 'unless it harms other people' is, of course, vital. Liberalism does not claim that literally everything should be permitted. John Stuart Mill, perhaps the most articulate and passionate defender of a liberal position, argued that if one person's action harms another, or threatens harm, then there is reason for the state to get involved. Mill claims: 'The only purpose for which power can be rightfully exercised over any member of a civilized community, against his will, is to prevent harm to others' (Mill 1962a [1859], 135). It is important to understand that Mill did not argue that the state has a duty to prevent all harms that one person may do to another, but that, at a minimum, if one person harms or endangers another the issue becomes the state's business. But if their action has no impact on others – if it is entirely 'self-regarding' – then the state should keep out. And, indeed, it is this thought – that if my behaviour affects only myself then it is none of the state's business – that seems so powerful.

This liberal response to the moral argument, therefore, suggests that if one person's gambling does not harm other people, then the state simply does not have the right to ban it. There are various obvious ways to react to this argument. One, of course, is simply to accept it. From such an acceptance it does not follow that gambling should exist in an entirely unregulated state. It can be taxed, to raise revenue, or restricted to certain parts of town, or certain times of day, to avoid nuisance – just as we have restrictions on where people can open glue factories or even restaurants. But if the liberal argument is accepted, gambling should not be prohibited or more heavily regulated than other similar economic or leisure activities, unless it can be shown that one person's gambling harms other people (a point to which we will return).

The opposite response is that if liberalism would not allow the state to prohibit gambling then what we must do is not to accept gambling, but to reject liberalism. After all, few people in the UK, it seems, supported the introduction of super casinos, and if anything many people wanted tighter restrictions on gambling. If their reason for this opposition was a belief that there is something wrong with gambling in itself then, it appears, many citizens have a rather weak commitment to liberal principles. This is a point that deserves reflection. At first sight Mill's harm principle seems incredibly attractive and powerful and it provides a key to solving a whole range of public policy dilemmas: don't interfere unless you can show harm to third parties. But the truth seems to be that many people feel very uncomfortable with these policy implications.

In the case of gambling many people who generally think of themselves as liberal in spirit are often happy with restrictions that sit uneasily with liberalism. For example, some might want to make gambling much less likely to happen than otherwise it would. The government could make it difficult for people to gamble, by restricting opening hours. It could engage in cautionary poster campaigns. It could refuse the gambling industry the right to advertise. At the same time it could subsidize activities it would prefer to see people take part in: perhaps art, music, or to revert to an earlier example, reading to one's children. Indeed, it is arguable that governments already act extensively in this way, in trying to encourage some forms of behaviour while discouraging others, but without fully banning, or requiring, any. In this way, then, such policies show an element of liberalism in allowing all types of (non-harmful) behaviours to take place, but also an element of anti-liberalism too, in which the government does make judgements about the value of different types of behaviour, and tries to wean its citizens away from some activities, towards others.

Liberals sometimes respond to this argument by suggesting that the government must engage in 'culture-preserving' activities in order to maintain a good range of future options. We must encourage fine art, music and literature so that future generations too have the chance to take part in and enjoy them. Yet typically few liberals will say the same thing about, say, wrestling or monster-truck racing. Despite their protestations to the contrary it does seem that non-neutrality has crept into the argument.

One form of disapproval of gambling is simply that it is not a worthwhile or attractive form of activity. However, this attitude is likely to shade into a more important observation: that gambling can be actively harmful. There are arguments that gambling harms the gambler. And there are arguments that one person's gambling can harm others, most notably the family of gamblers, but perhaps also society at large. Let us first consider the 'harm to the gambler' argument.

The argument, then, is that, whether or not gambling is wrong in itself, it can far too often lead to serious harm to the gambler. Gambling can be addictive, and it is fairly common for a gambler on a losing streak to start 'chasing losses'. This is the practice of placing increasingly large bets in the desperate attempt to recoup what one has already lost. Suppose in the casino you are on a losing streak. Rather than going home, feeling sorry for yourself, you might place a huge bet on red coming up on the roulette table (just below a 50/50 chance). If you win you have solved your problems (unless, of course, you decide that your luck has changed and you are now at the start of a winning streak). However, if you lose you are in serious trouble. What do you do then? One possibility is to place an even bigger bet – twice the size – on red again. To do that is to chase your losses, and on the roulette table it works in just under half of the cases it is tried. But it is highly dangerous. Doubling your bet each time you lose, but losing four or five in a row, could be absolutely catastrophic.

People in this situation become increasingly desperate. They might borrow money, perhaps on false pretences, lie, cheat and steal to try to win back lost money. Indeed, to quote the great liberal, John Stuart Mill, himself, from an article he wrote in 1823 (as a young man of 17, for the then newly introduced medical journal *The Lancet*, on 'The Effects of Gambling'):

> [T]he process by which gaming effects so complete a corruption of the character is two-fold. First, it reduces the gamester, not gradually, but suddenly, to that necessitous state where the temptation to crime is the strongest. Second, there is no practice capable of being pointed out, which so entirely roots out all good habits and plants in their stead so many bad ones.
>
> (Mill 1986 [1823], 78)

Problem gambling can be a very serious matter. These days, to decide whether an individual is a 'problem gambler' or even a 'pathological gambler' people are asked a series of questions about their life and gambling habits. There are different tests in use but typical questions include 'Is gambling the first thing you think about when you wake up?'; 'Have you ever lied about the extent of your gambling?'; 'Have you ever lost a job or a relationship because of your gambling?', and so on. Giving affirmative answers to enough questions tips one into the problematic, or more serious, pathological range.

A problem gambler risks losing his or her job, home and family, in a downward spiral. This, then, is what we could call the 'danger' argument: gambling has the danger of wrecking people's lives. It is important to see that the danger argument is quite different from the 'morally wrong in itself' argument. It would be possible to argue that there is nothing morally wrong with gambling in itself, but it does sometimes have very destructive consequences for the gambler. Gambling can wreck lives. Consequently it is harmful, whether or not it is morally wrong, and this gives the government a licence to intervene, so it could be argued.

An important response to this argument is that, once again, it conflicts with fundamental liberal assumptions, and so it may seem surprising to see Mill so apparently opposed to gambling. Liberalism permits governments to intervene to prevent one person doing harm to others. It does not, at least in Mill's official version, permit what is known as paternalism: intervening to stop people harming themselves. Now, Mill's actual attitude to paternalism is clearly more complex than it appeared at first, although he may well have changed his views between his precocious teenage years and his maturity, when he became highly influenced by the ideas of Harriet Taylor, whom he married late in life (Reeves 2007). But whatever Mill really thought about paternalism, and whatever politicians have said approvingly about Mill, governments have rarely worried about whether their action is paternalistic. They insist, for example, that all those who travel in cars must wear seat belts, and motorcyclists helmets, in each case for their own protection. These are perhaps the most obvious and conspicuous examples. But there is much more that they do to try to prevent people from harming themselves: health campaigns – anti-smoking, AIDS awareness, healthy eating – are all apparently paternalistic, but anyone objecting to such campaigns on the grounds of their paternalistic, anti-liberal character would likely be thought of as an attention-seeker, stirring up trouble for no good reason. (It should be noted, though, as I write, we have seen the start of a new debate in the UK, with the newly elected Conservative/Liberal Democratic coalition government raising the question of whether it is really for government to tell people how to live their lives. Whether action follows words, however, remains to be seen.)

But still, the paternalistic argument that gambling should be prohibited, or greatly restricted, would be fairly clear-cut if every gambler became hooked, and eventually ruined his or her life. That would give governments every reason to think that they had a duty to intervene. The truth is, though, that the vast majority of people who gamble even on a regular basis are not 'problem gamblers' or addicted to gambling, but find it an exciting and enjoyable way of spending an evening, and know how to limit their losses to what they can afford.

How, then, should the pleasures of the great majority be balanced against the harms – or risks of harms – of the minority? This is a difficult question, and in practice it has been sidestepped somewhat by the principle that one of the reasons for regulating gambling is to 'protect the vulnerable'. This has been interpreted as requiring regulations to keep children out of contact with serious gambling, to restrict access to the most addictive forms of gambling, and to put in other restrictions that will make it less likely that individuals will lose control, such as restricting the availability of alcohol in gambling venues, or prohibiting the use of credit cards. All of the restrictions on adults, however sensible they may be, are nevertheless paternalistic and run contrary to liberal principles. Again, it seems, one reasonable response would be to say 'so much the worse for liberalism'. The regulations suggested seem to strike a fair balance between allowing people to do what they want to do, but prohibiting the most dangerous forms.

Consider, for example, gambling in Australia, which has been used as a sort of bogeyman argument in the UK to warn us all of the possible excesses of gambling. Recent Australian liberalization of gambling allowed for the wide introduction of what are called 'pokies' or poker machines. These are slot machines which allow for rapid gambling, and are designed in a way that psychologists – including those employed by the gambling industry – have found to be most addictive and enticing. As a consequence, slot machine gambling is regarded by many as a serious problem in Australia, and there have been calls for much greater restrictions (Doughney 2002; and see P. Adams 2008 for similar arguments concerning New Zealand). To accommodate such restrictions, there may be a need to supplement Mill's liberalism with a principle that allows governments to interfere to stop people harming themselves, at least when the harm is to their health, safety or financial interest.

We have, then, outlined the 'morally wrong' argument and the 'harm to the gambler' argument. Both have been thought to justify restrictions on gambling despite their anti-liberal undertones, and at least in the case of the 'harm to the gambler' argument there does look like there is a reasonable case for some restrictions. A third argument, however, looks much more promising from a liberal point of view: that the problem that should concern government is not the harm individuals do to themselves, but to other people. Those who spend all their time and money gambling will neglect their families, and perhaps even rob and cheat family members or strangers. They will neglect their children. In the worse cases, in the US and Australia, there have been reports of children dying of suffocation in cars parked outside casinos in the summer heat while their parents lost all sense of time, caught up in the action. Mill, in fact, wrote to *The Lancet* because of a notorious murder case. The murderer, John Thurtell, Mill claims, had been thoroughly corrupted by his gambling habits, and the murder took place during a weekend's gambling. (A model of Thurtell was made and displayed for many years at the London waxwork museum Madame Tussauds.) But in more common and mundane cases, food will be short, school uniforms not purchased, and holidays never taken, as time and money are frittered away on gambling. Furthermore, those who become destitute through gambling will become a charge on the public purse. If gambling becomes a problem for an individual it then becomes a problem for everyone, although of course, generally the closer one is associated with the gambler, the bigger the problem.

However, even if problem gamblers harm their families and cost the taxpayer, the argument that prohibiting gambling is consistent with liberalism does not go through straightforwardly. Even conceding that gamblers are a danger to others, it does not follow that we should ban gambling. For if it did it would also follow that we should ban driving. As we will explore in more detail in Chapter 4, virtually every action that anyone does risks harming others. If we prohibited all risky action then we would be left with virtually nothing. The argument for banning risky action needs to take into account many factors, such as how risky it is, both in terms of probability and harm, and what we would lose if we were to ban it. In the case of driving, even though around 3,000 people die on the roads each year in the UK, we deem the benefits sufficiently important to allow it to take place, admittedly under highly regulated and supervised conditions. In the case of gambling, the third-party harms seem too diffuse and probabilistic to make a strong case for banning gambling altogether, although, as in the case of driving, there is good reason for restricting its most dangerous forms. Just as we do not allow people to drive drunk, or at very high speed, it appears that we can legitimately restrict the types of gambling opportunities made available.

Indeed, the best case for restricting gambling may well come, not from taking the arguments one by one, but by deploying several arguments together. When, in 2004, the *Daily Mail* launched its campaign against the UK Gambling Bill, it argued against the vision of:

> Trashy glitter and the lure of easy money, slot machines offering £1 million jackpots, roulette on tap and blackjack on every street corner – if ever there was a recipe for gambling addiction, poverty and the family traumas that inevitably follow, this is it. And this government knows full well what it is doing.
>
> (*Daily Mail* 2004)

Note that the strategy here is to present a particular vision of the consequences of allowing a proliferation of gambling. It is claimed that it will create a highly undesirable – trashy – form of social life, with dangers to the gambler and his or her family. This is a form of moral argument, suggesting that allowing the expansion of gambling would lead to other social changes that we have good reason to regret, and should try to resist. If we believe that the *Daily Mail* is accurate in its projections, and bearing in mind that many forms of gambling were already available in the UK at the time, then it is hard to muster enthusiasm for the liberal position that the prohibition of super casinos seriously violates liberal principles. This seems to be the sort of case where a decision can be left to the feeling of the majority. The broad consensus in the UK seems to be that within limits gambling should be tolerated, but that restrictions on gambling are perfectly justified.

I cannot, though, resist a couple of further comments. First, the *Daily Mail* seems to imply that if the UK were to allow slot machines with very high prizes, gambling addiction would increase. This is a natural thought, and something I had assumed myself. But to my surprise I found that it is not supported by the evidence. Rather, what makes slot machines addictive is the noise, and glitz, together with the constant reinforcement of winning regular small prizes and tantalizing 'near misses' of which the machines are said to be programmed to produce more than a truly random sequence would generate. A very large prize might tempt the punter to take a go or two, but not, in itself, to keep coming back (DCMS 2001, ch. 17, 85–96).

The second comment is something more of a cautionary tale. It was suggested as part of our work on the committee that we should produce a calculation showing the 'economic costs' of a problem gambler. Such an exercise is fraught with difficulties and it is very hard to get a neutral or objective view. Looking at the literature (all of which was from the US, rather than the UK) we found that studies sponsored by the gambling industry, often as part of a campaign to open a new casino, gave very low figures for the cost of a problem gambler. By contrast, studies sponsored by organizations offering treatments for problem gambling produced very high figures, in order to show that their services, though expensive, were cost-effective. Surveying this literature was rather depressing, as considerable intellectual firepower was being used to lobby for special interests, and to ridicule methodology used by others. As a way of subtly pointing out how absurd it all was we wrote:

Since we have no data on cost/benefit analyses in the UK, the best impression of costs we can give is by drawing on research from abroad. As we have shown, the range of costs per problem gambler covers a broad financial spectrum. The NORC [National Opinion Research Centre, University of Chicago] report provides the lowest estimate (of £373 per probable pathological gambler) and the Kindt study the highest estimate (of £35,300 per pathological gambler). If we apply these costs to the number of problem gamblers in Britain (estimated by the Prevalence Survey to be between 275,000 and 370,000 people) the annual cost of problem gambling in Britain would lie between £100 million and £13 billion.

(DCMS 2001, 96)

Our implied point was given such a range – £100 million to £13 billion – the exercise was in effect meaningless. But we were too clever for our own good. A couple of years later I was appalled to read on the front page of a Sunday newspaper lobbying against gambling reform, that 'according to an official government report' the economic cost of a problem gambler is 'up to £35,300 per year'. Well, yes, but …

ENFORCING THE LAW

Suppose that we conducted a poll and found that a majority of people in the UK expressed the view that gambling should be prohibited. I should say that such a result is rather unlikely as surveys show that around 70 per cent of the adult population do take part in some form of gambling in any given year (Wardle *et al.* 2007). This may seem high until it is realized that the National Lottery is a form of gambling, even if some of those people who take part don't think of it as such. But, still, it is possible that a majority feel that the current regime is too liberal and needs to be restricted. Let us suppose it was generally thought desirable if not to ban gambling outright, then to close betting shops, casinos, bingo halls and Internet gambling, leaving only horse and dog tracks as places where gambling could legally take place. In fact, that would be very close to the situation in the UK in the 1950s, before the introduction of betting shops and other liberalizations of the law.

Why was the law changed in the UK to permit more forms of gambling? Before the reforms, betting, at the course, on horse races and dog tracks, was perfectly legal, but legal off-course betting was highly restricted – limited to the 'turf accountants', who catered to a small group of affluent customers betting on credit accounts. This was a time when the great majority of British citizens didn't even have a bank account, never mind a credit account with a turf accountant. For most people who were interested in a flutter, it was the 'bookie's runner' – a stock character in many a gritty drama, being chased over garden fences by the rozzers (the police) – who took their stake. Bookie's runners were either agents of illegal bookmakers, or illegal middlemen between the ordinary punter and the turf accountant. Despite its illegality, off-course betting was extremely popular. By some estimates, in the late 1950s there were towns where about 25 per cent of the adult population gambled illegally on a regular basis (Davies 1991).

David Kynaston quotes the account of fifteen-year-old Fred Done, the son of an illegal 'street bookie':

> He traded in Knott Mill, one of the rougher areas of Manchester, under a tarpaulin in the back yard. He would open the shop from 11.00 to 3.00, and from 5.00 to 7.00 for the evening dogs. Bets were written on any scrap of paper, with a nom de plume on the back. We had runners in all the factories in Trafford Park, one of the biggest industrial complexes in Europe. We would send a taxi round every day, and the bets were handed over in clock bags [i.e. ensuring that the bets had not been placed after a race had started]. There were no books, there was no income tax, no betting duty. What you had at the end of the day was profit. The only payment you had to make was bribe money to the police, two or three quid a week to keep them off your back. If they were going to raid you, they'd let you know.
>
> (Kynaston 2009, 193)

Faced with lawbreaking on this scale, something had to change. The police did not have the resources to enforce the law effectively, and, as we see, often played their own angle. In any case they would have received minimal public cooperation had they tried to come down hard on gambling. So a new legal approach was tried. The starting assumption was that, while gambling shouldn't be encouraged, it cannot be stopped. Hence it is better to allow it to exist under highly regulated conditions. This approach yields the concept of 'unstimulated demand'. If demand can be shown already to exist, then commercial firms can cater – or should we say 'pander'? – to it, to prevent people breaking the law. But nothing should be done to stimulate demand. In this respect gambling was treated like prostitution: while the activity is legal, steps to drum up trade are not.

Recall that we made a distinction between three questions. First, should gambling be permitted? Second, should anyone be allowed to profit from gambling? Third, should it be permitted to encourage people to gamble? Initially the new UK legislation, introduced in 1960, gave positive answers to the first two questions and a negative one to the third. In doing so the legislation permitted off-course gambling on a significant scale for the first time. Primarily the intention was focused on permitting betting offices, although the legislation also allowed casino games under what were intended to be tightly restricted circumstances. However the details were not thought through and as it turned out there was an explosion in the numbers of casinos. From no legal casinos in the 1950s, by the mid-60s there were thought to be over 1,000. As casinos are businesses where large amounts of cash change hands it is not entirely surprising that they attracted organized crime on a grand scale, such as the notorious Kray twins, who owned a casino called Esmerelda's Barn. The connection between crime and casinos became intolerable and in 1968 a new Gambling Act was passed, which placed severe limits on where casinos could be sited and the conditions under which they could be operated. It was this legislation that required a licence to operate a casino, and included the provision that an application could be rejected with no explanation and no right of appeal. Essentially the point of this was to purge the casino business of 'unscrupulous' operators, and such draconian measures were thought to be the only way.

To return to betting shops, these were initially conceived of as somewhere to go and place a bet, but like the bureau de change, not somewhere where it would be fun to spend the afternoon. This is why they were seedy and hidden away, located down side streets with blacked-out windows, and at first were not allowed to broadcast sporting events or even to have toilets. Some had wanted even more restrictions. Here is how the Rothschild Commission described the situation regarding betting shops in 1978:

> The last Royal Commission [which took place in 1949–51] ... recommended that loitering in betting offices should be an offence, that no seats should be provided for punters and that winnings should not be paid out during betting hours. None of these recommendations was accepted by Parliament and punters are therefore at liberty to spend their afternoons in a betting office and to bet continuously on one race after another. On the other hand very little is permitted which might make this an agreeable way of passing the time. No television or refreshments are allowed and the rules about advertising and notices mean that the internal appearance of a betting office is usually bleak, functional, and depressing. This is perhaps a characteristic British compromise.
>
> (RCG 1978, 49)

The principle of unstimulated demand meant no advertising. Indeed often casinos were not allowed to put up a sign outside saying 'Casino'. As mentioned above, casinos, and, amazingly, bingo halls, had a 'cooling off period'. Unless you were a guest of an existing member you had to apply for membership and wait forty-eight hours before you could enter. It may still be the case that more Britons have stepped into a casino overseas than they have in the UK.

The basic motivation behind gambling law in the UK has, with one important exception, been one of social control. Virtually everywhere else in the world the prime mover has been raising of government revenue; gambling has been seen as a source of 'unresented taxation' and governments have restricted the issue of licences to open casinos so that they could sell them for a high price and share in monopoly profits. This has, in fact, led to arguments that governments have an intolerable conflict of interest regarding gambling (P. Adams 2008). In the UK, in recent times, the exception to the 'social-control' approach is the National Lottery which was introduced as providing a revenue stream for a series of discretionary 'good causes' and was allowed to advertise and promote itself in a way that was denied to other providers of gambling. (Surprisingly, the building of the British Museum was funded by a one-off lottery in 1753.) As already noted, the privileged position of the Lottery was challenged and this situation has now changed, partly as a result of the review of gambling law, and many forms of gambling can now be advertised. Gradually moves have been made to allow demand to be stimulated. This, in turn, appears to mark a change from a view in which gambling is considered a generally undesirable activity that we tolerate only because banning it is impossible, to a situation in which it is treated as one leisure activity among others. One mark of this is that during the period of the gambling review, responsibility for gambling moved from the crime-focused Home Office to the rather different Department of Culture Media and Sport.

The gambling regime in the UK, then, is now slightly more liberal than it was ten years ago. It is easier to gain entrance to casinos and bingo halls, gambling operators can advertise in a limited way, and opportunities to gamble on the Internet have grown exponentially. What effect, then, has such liberalization had on problem gambling? Our committee recommended that the industry should set up a charitable trust to fund research and treatment of problem gambling, and to our surprise the industry agreed, creating what is now called the GREaT Foundation (Gambling Research, Education and Treatment). Gambling addiction can be a serious problem. To quote the youthful John Stuart Mill again:

A mind which experiences the agonizing vicissitudes of the gaming table, soon becomes so habituated to strong excitement, that, like the body of the habitual drunkard, it is insensible to every stimulus of a gentler kind. It is totally and for ever unfitted to resume habits of

diligence and industry; and the habits which it has acquired are in
themselves, such as, above all others, tend to produce crime.

[Mill 1986 [1823], 79]

So were critics right that allowing greater opportunities for gambling would inevitably increase problem gambling? Just before the Gambling Review Body was set up, the government commissioned a 'prevalence study' of gambling, to try to understand who was gambling in what forms, and the percentage of people who had a problem with their gambling. As we noted there are different ways of attempting to measure problem gambling but the headline figure for 2000 was that between 0.6 and 0.8 per cent of the UK adult population could be classified as problem gamblers (Sproston et al. 2000). A second study was conducted in 2007 (Wardle et al. 2007). Given the rise of Internet gambling and some liberalizing moves in the meantime, government and industry were braced for a significant rise, and newspapers had already prepared their doom-laden editorials. After all, the papers had been full of stories of individuals who had stolen thousands from their employers to feed their gambling addiction, and so on. But when the results were published, to the great disappointment of the media it appeared that nothing had changed, at least at the level of the headline figures. The percentage remained the same. The newspapers had to spike their moralizing stories about the decline of British society. It is hard to tell why, but the result went against all predictions. A third study is in process as I write.

CONCLUSION: LESSONS FOR PHILOSOPHY

The first lesson is one, I hope, we have already learnt from the last chapter. Taking a philosophical theory and applying it to a public policy area is likely to yield consequences that are simply not publicly acceptable. In this case the example is Mill's liberty principle. It would seem to rule out all limits to gambling, but this is a position that simply could not be accepted in current policy discussions, and, as we saw, one that Mill himself found very easy to reject. A pragmatic compromise in which gambling is permitted but under conditions that reduce the chances of people developing problem gambling habits seems hard to argue against. Government should sometimes try to save us from ourselves, especially when, after all, we are talking about forms of entertainment rather than fundamental interests.

A second lesson is illustrated with the prevalence study. It may seem obvious that increasing gambling opportunities will increase problem gambling. Except that it didn't, just as higher-stakes slot machines are not necessarily more addictive. The lesson is that the world sometimes behaves in unexpected ways, and if an argument is to be based on empirical premises, speculation may well run ahead of evidence. Of course, one also needs to be critical about one's sources, as we will see in future chapters. The lesson, though, is obvious. Empirical claims need empirical support, not the support of common sense, however common and however sensible it may seem.

The third lesson is the most interesting, perhaps. The law on gambling was changed, in 1961, because it was ineffective. Not only did people gamble, they broke the laws prohibiting them from gambling. Putting this the other way round, if you think you can solve a problem by passing a law, but people don't obey the new law, then you now have two problems. Or maybe even three, for you also risk eroding general respect for the law.

3
Drugs

INTRODUCTION

Laws in developed societies regulate the production, supply, possession and use of recreational drugs – drugs taken for their effects on altering consciousness but not prescribed for medical reasons. Such laws present a puzzle both for liberalism and for public policy. For liberalism the problem is that while, as we noted in the last chapter, many liberals pay lip service to Mill's dictum that the only justification for interfering with the liberty of action of any individual is to prevent harm to others (Mill 1962a [1859]), it is very hard to identify significant harms to third parties caused by the use of many currently illegal drugs. This, of course, is to leave aside harms that are the result of the existence of an extensive illegal market, which cannot themselves be used in an argument to justify such prohibition in the first place.

We have already seen that public policy tends not to follow Mill's 'harm principle' and all governments take it upon themselves to supervise individual lives in various ways to reduce the risk of individuals harming themselves. It is here, though, that the problem for public policy strikes. It seems, prima facie, reasonable that the stringency of regulation should be related to the harms any action or substance causes or threatens. However, some currently illegal drugs do far less harm to the user, and to third parties, than some currently legal substances, notably alcohol and tobacco. Yet despite the ever-increasing restrictions on public smoking, the prospects of criminalizing the use of tobacco, or that of alcohol, or decriminalizing all drugs that are less harmful than alcohol, do not look bright. Hence it appears that societies do not in fact regulate drugs on the basis of the harm they cause. The actual basis of regulation is something of a mystery.

Lest it be doubted that some currently illegal drugs do far less harm than some currently legal drugs, consider the evidence presented by David Nutt in a short paper called 'A Tale of 2 Es' comparing the drug ecstasy (MDMA) and ethanol (i.e. alcohol) (Nutt 2006; see also STC 2006, ev110–17, and Nutt et al. 2007). David Nutt is now well-known as the former chair of the UK Advisory Council on the Misuse of Drugs, fired for his outspoken views and writings, including a comparison of the risks of taking the drug ecstasy and horse-riding (Nutt 2009). But his controversial writings pre-dated that episode, and a few years earlier he wrote a short paper claiming that, on average, alcohol causes 22,000 premature deaths in the UK each year while ecstasy causes 10. These figures are contestable but their order of magnitude is not. It is also true that there are many more users of alcohol than ecstasy, but even taking this into account alcohol is still, statistically, somewhere in the region of 200 times more likely to kill its users than ecstasy (and remember that one of the dangers of ecstasy is said to be that its illegal status means that it is sometimes 'cut' with other more toxic substances).

Alcohol is also known to cause brain damage, especially among very heavy users, yet the evidence that ecstasy has such effects is patchy and contested. The most notorious empirical study, in which it was 'shown' that injecting monkeys with MDMA led to brain damage (Ricaurte et al. 2002), was later retracted when, after failing to replicate their studies with an oral dose, the researchers discovered that the monkeys in the original experiment had actually been injected with methamphetamine (crystal meth) in error (Ricaurte et al. 2003). Despite this retraction, it is widely believed that there is clear scientific evidence that MDMA causes brain damage, although as far as I have been able to tell there is no study that actually shows this, as distinct from what scientists predict the studies might show if they had actually been done.

Nutt also suggests that alcohol causes a significant number of road traffic deaths, incidents of violence, cirrhosis and heart damage, while ecstasy has none of these effects, and we might add, is protective against violence, spreading affection rather than aggression. Comparable stories can be told for cannabis and even LSD, which are believed by many scientists to be far less harmful to health than alcohol. This may seem surprising for cannabis, as there is a well-known association between cannabis use and some forms of psychosis. Yet the nature of the relation between cannabis and psychosis remains disputed, and it is clear that alcohol abuse can also lead to mental disorder, both temporary and longer term (on the relation between cannabis and psychosis see W. Hall and Pacula 2003, W. Hall 2006, Fergusson et al. 2006, and Hickman et al. 2007). One team of researchers suggests that the most dangerous thing about cannabis is that typically you need to ingest another substance to take it: tobacco smoke (MacLeod and Hickman 2010).

To attempt to find whether there is a coherent basis for current regulations I will first consider the deeper assumptions underlying drug policy, and then explore the (surprisingly small) philosophical debate concerning the regulation of drugs.

CURRENT REGULATIONS IN THE UK

Just to provide some background, it is worth setting out a brief, somewhat simplified, snapshot of UK drug laws. At its heart is that 'controlled' drugs are grouped into three classes:

Class A: Includes cocaine, crack, ecstasy, heroin, LSD, methadone, methamphetamine (crystal meth), magic mushrooms containing ester of psilocin and amphetamine if prepared for injection.

Class B: Includes amphetamine (not methamphetamine), barbitu-
rates and codeine. Cannabis was recently also moved from
Class C to Class B.

Class C: Includes ketamine, anabolic steroids and minor tranquillizers.

The maximum penalty for possession of Class A drugs is seven years
plus a fine. Note that the offence for all categories is 'possession', not
'use', presumably as the standard of proof is much more certain.
For supply of a Class A drug the maximum penalty is life imprisonment plus a fine. Supply does not mean 'sale'; simply giving a
controlled drug to another person without payment is sufficient to
count as supply. These categories are not carved in stone, and
reclassification from time to time takes place, influenced by the
advice of the Advisory Council on the Misuse of Drugs, which,
notoriously in the case of cannabis, is not always followed.

Although it is very rare for maximum sentences to be imposed,
drug offences are common in the UK, and use up a good deal of
time and prison resources. For example, in 2004 a hundred-and-
five-thousand drug offences were recorded in England and Wales,
and about 10,000 people were sent to prison for drug offences,
primarily for dealing, with an average sentence of thirty-two
months (Mwenda 2005). US laws are more complex, and there
is often a difference between state laws and federal laws, with
the latter tending to be more draconian. Given how the criminal
justice system works in the US it is possible to receive effectively a
life sentence for possession of cannabis. (For examples see Husak
2002, 3, and for other background on drugs and incarceration in the
US see Barry 2005 95–108, although for a different perspective, see
Kennedy 1997).

SOCIETY'S UNDERLYING DRUG STRATEGY

The issue of the regulation of drugs is taken with such seriousness
in many jurisdictions that in addition to drug laws many countries

set out an underlying strategy to give a focus to those laws. In a paper published in 1989, Douglas Husak writes: 'Whenever this paper is read, America will doubtless be waging yet another round of its apparently endless "war on drugs"' (Husak 1989, 353). The US has stated, at various times, that it wishes to achieve a 'drug-free society'. It is not alone in the goal; Sweden has announced the same thing (W. Hall and Pacula 2003, 189). In the US this has led to a declaration of a 'war on drugs', which is being fought on a variety of fronts, but most notably severe punishment of users and dealers, and attempts to cut-off the supply chain.

It is not entirely clear how the idea of drug eradication should translate into policy. The central idea, however, seems to be that policy should be assessed in terms only of how effective it is in eradicating drug use: the fewer people using fewer drugs the better, whatever means are best to achieve this. Of course there will always be budget constraints, but notions of 'value for money' or balancing other costs against the costs of drug use are in some sense out of place. At best they could be side constraints on the pursuit of policy, rather than goals that should shape policy itself. But what should we expect the overall effects to be of a policy of striving for a drug-free society, if such an aim cannot realistically be achieved? Taken literally the strategy seems to imply that all drugs are to be treated as equally evil and in need of suppression. However this undifferentiated approach arguably could lead to more drug-related harm than another strategy. If, for example, possession of heroin and ecstasy are treated as of equal seriousness by the law, and heroin easier to obtain than ecstasy, then some users may be attracted to heroin when, under other circumstances, they would have been deterred by a greater penalty for heroin use, or by the message that it must be more damaging because it is in a higher category. For a real example, cannabis traces remain in the body for longer than those of many other drugs, and so in a regime of drug testing it is said that people prefer to use harder drugs, the presence of which is more difficult to detect by random testing.

An obvious alternative, therefore, to a drug-free society is the goal of minimizing harms from drugs. This has been adopted by some societies, including until recently the UK, which stated: 'The Drug Strategy aims to reduce the harm that drugs cause to society: to communities, individuals and their families' (Home Office 2007). This apparently permits the idea that some drugs should be counted as 'softer' than others, and regulations should try particularly to discourage the use of the hardest drugs, which is, therefore, a rationale for the differential treatment of various drugs we see in the UK law. Indeed it seems consistent with the idea of permitting a policy which will have the effect of increasing the total number of users, and drugs used, if as a consequence total harms from drugs fall. One possibility would be allowing easier access to the least harmful drugs as a way of trying to get users to stop taking more harmful drugs.

If the idea of minimizing harm from drugs also includes some harms that are the indirect, rather than the direct, result of drug use, then much more radical consequences may follow. For example, users who take their drugs by injection risk HIV and hepatitis from dirty needles. Consequently some societies have experimented with 'shooting galleries' and 'needle exchanges' so that addicts can be spared this risk. Other experiments have been undertaken, such as prescribing heroin to addicts so that they do not need to engage in crime to finance their habits.

Taking this idea even further allows the inclusion of the costs of imprisonment and a criminal record as an indirect harm of drug use, to be put into the balance. Quite possibly, at the present time, the two greatest drug-related harms are, first those following from imprisonment of offenders – the blight to the life of those imprisoned, and the associated public financial expense – and second, the social costs associated with a huge illegal market in drugs where contracts are enforced at the point of a gun. If so, then on the view that drug-related harm should be minimized there is compelling reason for reconsidering whether existing regulation serves its purposes.

In general such an approach goes along with the view that drug use should be theorized as more like a 'public health' problem, perhaps like a stubborn infectious disease, rather than as a problem that requires the intervention of the criminal justice system. Indeed, it has even been claimed that this is the current situation in England: Helge Waal, a professor of psychiatry in Oslo wrote, in a paper published in 1999: 'The English drug policy has traditionally been dominated by a medical model with doctors rather than the drug squad in central position, and addicts more seen as patients in need of treatment than criminals to be prosecuted' (Waal 1999). Perhaps compared to the US this is fair comment, but in itself it seems a slightly rose-tinted view. However, it may be a reasonable account of Portugal which reformed its drug laws in 2001 so that possession for personal use would not result in a prison sentence.

A further theoretically possible view, of course, is that not all harms are the proper concern of government, and self-inflicted harm through drug use is an example governments should ignore. So, for example, the radical psychiatrist Thomas Szasz argued that treating drug use as a public health problem, which many would see as a highly enlightened policy, is an intrusion on individual freedom. If people want to use recreational drugs, Szasz argued, why should they be considered ill (Szasz 1992)? A fair point, perhaps, although unlikely to convince worried parents and politicians.

Delineating possible underlying strategies, and their possible policy implications, settles nothing in itself. But it does help us understand the options available, and raises the question of what would justify adopting one strategy rather than another. To help think about this issue, it is worth comparing two other 'social harms': murder and pollution. We can, I think, quite understand why we would wish to try to achieve a murder-free society, treating murders as 'special' and not just one more cost to be placed in a cost–benefit analysis. Of course, there are budget constraints, but we would think it very odd – morally indefensible, most likely – if a Home Secretary announced that after a series of studies the authorities have decided that it is just not worth the cost of trying to prevent every murder, or detect every murderer, and some categories would no longer be deterred, investigated or lead to prosecution.

At the other end of the scale, the goal of a 'pollution-free society' could win votes but does not seem capable of generating sensible policy. Some forms of pollution may have very severe costs, and so there is every reason to try to reduce them, while others, so far as we know, are no more than a minor nuisance with only very small costs, and if the cost of removing them is very high we may feel that the best course of action is to tolerate a certain level of pollution in order to achieve the optimum balance of costs and benefits (which of course should not be restricted merely to financial costs and benefits).

What is the difference between murder and pollution? There are various possible answers. One is that murder is a violation of rights, and rights must not be traded off against other social goals. This, though, seems too general. Property rights can be subject to compulsory purchase, for example. Another possibility is that the value of life is immeasurable and so cannot be placed in a cost–benefit calculation (we will return to such issues in the next chapter). The details, however, are less important than the thought that preventing murder is in some way special, and silences ordinary claims about other costs and benefits. Preventing pollution is, in itself, not special, although when it creates a 'clear and present' danger to life it may become so. The question for policy makers is whether preventing drug use is more like preventing murder or preventing pollution. Are there arguments that can show that the harms of drug use are special and call for the goal of a drug-free society?

PHILOSOPHICAL ARGUMENTS CONCERNING THE REGULATION OF DRUGS

Libertarian self-ownership arguments

One apparently highly rigorous approach to drug regulation would be to start from libertarian principles of self-ownership, from which it would follow that one simply has the right to put whatever one wishes to into one's own body, and therefore drugs should be produced and sold on the free market like any other commodity. This is essentially Szasz's position, mentioned above. However, most libertarians will accept that self-ownership does not allow one to impose certain types of harms on others, and hence it is necessary to look at some of the likely consequences of drug use before declaring that people have a right to consume drugs. In essence, then, this view reduces to the Millian position which we shall consider shortly.

Consequentialist libertarianism

A different foundation for a libertarian, free market proposal starts from the observation that there is at least one sense in which current regulation has failed: its deterrent effects are far from totally effective. If we look at the statistics for drug use in the UK, according to government figures, 34 per cent of all adults have used illegal drugs at some point in their lives, 11 per cent did so the year before the survey and 7.1 per cent the month before (DH 2005, 187). For those between the ages of fifteen and twenty-four the figures are 45 per cent (lifetime), 27 per cent (last year) and 17 per cent (last month) (DH 2005, 38). Cannabis is by far the most commonly used drug for all age groups. Given also, first, the individual and social costs of imprisoning even the small proportion who are caught and prosecuted; second, the costs of the existence of the black market; and third, the problems of overdose and poisoning associated with unregulated supply – it is sometimes argued that legalizing the production and supply of all drugs (perhaps on the model of the sale of non-prescription drugs such as aspirin) would be far preferable. Furthermore, it is added, the government could raise considerable revenue through steep taxes.

However, there are many problems with the idea that we can reduce drug harm by legalizing drugs. First, even if this was a successful strategy in terms of eliminating the black market, it is unclear what the total effect would be on crime. If, to use an example from John Adams in another context, the former drug dealers spent their newly idle hours taking tea with their grandmothers, then the crime rate would go down, but if they decided to take up armed robbery, crime could go up (J. Adams 1995). Second, what would be the price of newly legal drugs? If they were treated as just another commodity then the price of drugs would be determined largely by their cost of production. A month's supply of heroin might cost the same as a month's supply of coffee or perhaps even of sugar. Those who suggest that consumption would rocket under such circumstances surely have a point. If, prices were kept high, perhaps by tax, as is the case with alcohol and tobacco, then prices would be high enough to recreate the conditions for an illegal black market to undercut the legal market. In sum, we really have no idea whether legalizing drugs would create more problems than it would solve. All we know is that the problems would be different.

A third problem was made apparent to me during a consultation with former drug addicts as part of my work with the Academy of Medical Sciences. I asked them whether they thought it would be better if drugs were legalized and sold in the way that over-the-counter medication is in ordinary pharmacies. They thought this a potentially catastrophic idea, not because of addiction, but because they thought it would increase the risk of dangerous crime. First, they said, the stock would be stolen by shop assistants. But more importantly, addicts would wait outside aiming to rob customers as they came out of the shops. It would be like the wild west.

Finally, a difficulty with legalizing drugs is that we have become so used to paternalistic governments supervising the marketplace for our own good, that if we were permitted to purchase drugs many people would naturally assume that the government has, after all, decided to give them a clean bill of health. These people would think 'if the government lets me buy them, then they can't be so bad for me after all', even if the government tried to convince us otherwise.

Millian arguments

Arguments starting from Millian liberalism would suggest the only reason for regulating the use of recreational drugs would be harm, or threats of harm, caused by drug use. There are, of course, claims that drug use causes harms of this sort:

> Drug use harms strangers by involving them in the collisions, shootouts and other catastrophes to which the impaired and overly aggressive drug users are prone. It harms family members by depriving them of the companionship and income of their addicted partners. It harms fetuses by exposing them to toxic and permanently damaging prenatal environment. It harms children by subjecting them to the abuse of their drug-addled parents.
>
> (Sher 2003, 12–13)

Now, whether or not there would be drug shoot-outs if there was no drug black market, we should at least concede that the rest of these harms can follow from some drug use, for some users, on some occasions. Yet in the last chapter we noted that the Millian argument is not that harm or threat of harm is sufficient to justify prohibition. Such a view would rule out most human activity. In addition to the example of road travel, given earlier, consider nuclear power stations, chemical plants, and even fireworks factories. Mill's own examples were those of economic competition, and competitive examinations, which harm the financial interests of people who lose out. We can see that there are many examples of permitted actions which threaten or cause physical harm, even death. And once again the third-party harms caused by drug use are relatively insignificant compared to the third-party harms caused by alcohol use and abuse.

In Mill's own framework it seems that the strength of regulation of a harmful activity depends on both the costs and the benefits of the activities. Thus, he says, if the only reason for buying poison was to kill people we could ban it, but as many poisons have other beneficial functions, such as killing rats, we should rather regulate the sale by requiring chemists to keep records of their customers so in the case of any human poisoning the police will have a ready-made list of suspects.

Can it be said that the difference between alcohol and illegal drugs is that the former has benefits which the latter lack, and hence in a Millian framework we can treat alcohol use on a par with driving and economic competition, but prohibit drugs absolutely? So, for example, it is often claimed that alcohol has modest health benefits for those who use it in moderation, but no such claim is made for any other drug. This is not to deny that in some cases people are said to use illegal drugs as a form of self-medication, to help overcome depression, pain, muscle spasm, and appetite loss (for much anecdotal evidence of self-medication among homeless drug users see Masters 2005), but there is, as far as I know, no claim that any currently illegal drug has any health benefit for ordinary users.

However it is hard to believe that any modest health benefits justify the contrasting laws regulating alcohol and illegal drugs. Furthermore, when considering the benefits of drug use, those who take drugs, excluding the relatively small proportion who are addicted, do so for the pleasure or other experience they derive from them. Peter de Marneffe, in part of a debate with Douglas Husak about the legalization of drugs, concedes that 'recreational heroin use provides relaxation and enjoyment, which are good things' (in Husak and de Marneffe 2005, 157). Recall, also, the very large numbers of people who have taken illegal drugs. For those who believe in a 'revealed preference' theory of well-being this is a very impressive set of figures, especially when we take into account that revealing one's preference in this way risks a criminal record, fine and imprisonment. But even on philosophically deeper accounts of well-being it is hard to deny the evidence that a lot of people gain enjoyment from using drugs, just as they and others do from using alcohol. It is very hard to make the argument that drugs can be prohibited because they cause a significant degree of harm to third parties without providing benefits to the users. Both sides of this claim look very weak when generalized to all drug use. Whether they are true of any particular drug is a further question, of course.

It is probably a fool's errand to think that there is a way of differentiating alcohol use and (some) drug use on some principled basis concerning their effects. Many illegal drugs are more like alcohol than each other. I will, therefore, put the issue of alcohol use to one side for the rest of this section, and return to it in the next.

Authenticity

A different line of argument against drug use is that it generates inauthentic experience. The drug user feels pleasure but has done nothing to 'earn' that pleasure; it is an escape from real life. There are, however, several responses. One is to say that this is common to many legal experiences, whether it is a trip to the opera, watching an action film, or any one of hundreds of other activities. Another is to say that while this may be a reason for not taking drugs, it is hard to see why it should be a reason for prohibiting them (see also Brock 1984).

Biological concerns

Some have argued that the way in which drugs typically work in itself provides the basis for moral condemnation. Essentially there is a 'reward' system in the brain, which, it is claimed, has evolved so that behaviour that is useful for individual survival or reproduction is given a positive reinforcement, whereas action with the opposite effect yields a negative result. Food and sex are rewarded with pleasure, physical damage with pain, for example. Drugs typically short-circuit these systems and produce the reward without its usual causes. Indeed they can reward behaviour that puts survival in peril. This alone appears to generate moral concern (Waal 1999).

However, philosophers will always be suspicious of arguments based on what is physically natural or normal, and this argument should not escape our suspicion. The fact that a natural system is not fulfilling its natural purpose should not in itself worry us: if it did then contraception would also be wrong. If drug use had no adverse effects on well-being then this 'biological' argument would be of no moral interest. Hence it is not the biological mechanisms but the effects of drug use, and especially addiction, that are worrying. Regular drug use can have adverse health effects, and can suck out people's interests in other aspects of their lives. Habitual drug use can lead to the neglect of family, friends, work and other interests, social networks, and so on. The fact that drugs disrupt biological systems is an interesting explanation of why they work so powerfully but is morally irrelevant.

Justice

Douglas Husak, in a relentless series of writings, has argued that 'the sheer scale of incarceration of drug users makes prohibition the worst injustice perpetrated by our system of criminal law in the twentieth century. Only the institution of slavery and the despicable treatment of Native Americans are greater injustices in the history of the United States' (Husak 2002, 2). Husak believes that claims of third-party harms caused by drug use (as distinct from the existence of a huge, lucrative drug black market) have been massively exaggerated and do not justify current policy. Rather, he argues, current US regulations violate individual rights.

Husak wants to distance himself from a libertarian view of self-ownership, in which people have a right to do whatever they want to their own bodies. Rather, he says: 'If many of the things people believe about drugs were true, our policies would probably be justified. We would be silly to allow anyone to use a drug that does to a brain what a fry pan does to an egg' (Husak 2002, 10). (This somewhat surprising analogy comes from a US anti-drug campaign.) Whether or not the word 'silly' is well-chosen, we can see that Husak does concede that avoiding extreme self-harm is a legitimate goal on which governments can legislate.

Husak's argument is relatively straightforward. It really comes down to the claim that it is morally indefensible to use the mechanism of the coercive law to attempt to prevent people from engaging in activity that gives them significant pleasure, rarely does them significant harm, and does not harm others any more than many legal activities.

There is, therefore, an empirical element that enters into the discussion: that drugs do not do as much harm as is often claimed. It is, however, surprisingly hard to get clear evidence of the harm drug use does. Of course overdose and infection from dirty needles are well-documented problems, but what are the physical harms of a regular, controlled dose of 'clean' heroin? The medical textbooks seem to be silent on this question, partly because it is very hard to study. Those who present at emergency rooms or addiction clinics, or find themselves in jail, can be studied, but this is only a very small proportion of users, and, for obvious reasons it is difficult to get a properly representative sample of all drugs users. The prospect of trying to get a randomized controlled trial through the ethics committee does not look promising. 'Natural' experiments are not much help. Almost all drug users use more than one substance (if alcohol and tobacco are included) and so it can be difficult to allocate particular harms to particular substances, especially when interaction effects between different substances need to be taken into account. Also, of course, to understand causation long-term studies are needed, but heavy drug users have a habit of not coming back for the second or third round of questions.

But still even if we are persuaded that governments have a duty to intervene to attempt to reduce drug use there are many strategies available that fall short of punishment, and these are commonly used for alcohol and tobacco (and analogous strategies are used for gambling):

- Issuing of health warnings.
- Imposition of taxes to reduce demand.
- Regulation of the quality of the good, prohibiting the sale of the most dangerous forms.
- Prohibition of production and sale.
- Prohibition of possession and use, but without penalty.
- Penalized possession and use, through fines or imprisonment.

Outside drug legislation, it is now rare for an activity to be penalized through a prison sentence if the point of its regulation is to protect people from self-harm. Although it was once possible to be imprisoned for attempted suicide, this law has been repealed, and its undesirability seems evident. Seat-belt offences, while driving, are punishable by fine only (DfT 2007, 126). Husak is surely right that the philosophical case for providing severe punishments for people who engage in activities which might harm only themselves remains obscure (in Husak and de Marneffe 2005). Of course, in harming oneself this may incidentally have effects for others, such as the cost of scarce resources used to help, and for this reason it is sometimes said that the idea that some activities cause only self-harm is a myth. At the very least, someone else has to clear up afterwards. However, stopping people acting in particular ways has costs too: law enforcement is expensive. We are stuck either way. But leaving aside such indirect effects the practice of punishing people who engage in self-harm appears to be the rather perverse one of harming people in one way for attempting to harm themselves in a different way.

De Marneffe makes the response to Husak that for some drugs at least, notably heroin, the risks to a flourishing life for children who take the drug (or whose parents are addicts) are so severe that this provides a reason for entirely prohibiting their production, sale and use (in Husak and de Marneffe 2005). Nevertheless, this still falls short of an argument for punishing adult users, as distinct from suppliers and dealers, and de Marneffe, despite writing as a critic of

Husak's argument does not attempt to justify punishing drug users (in Husak and de Marneffe 2005, 129).

Nevertheless, it is not impossible to find arguments to justify punishing people for harming themselves based on the idea of deterrence. If the form of self-harm is extremely severe, and it is thought essential to stop people from engaging in the activity, and only threatening imprisonment would be effective as a deterrent, then it may seem that under certain circumstances a prison sentence would be acceptable. However, the premises of this argument are each highly uncertain.

A different argument for punishment – or perhaps a different for-mulation of the same argument – follows a classic justification for the criminal law in general: that as individuals we are poor at following our long-term interests when short-term gratification gets in the way. If it is in no one's long-term interest to take drugs, especially those drugs with a heavy risk of generating addiction, then punishment could be needed, and justified, to align short-term and long-term interests. In sum, we need to remember Ulysses and the sirens. Drugs are special because of their addiction potential, especially when combined with the myopia of human long-term reasoning (Waal 1999, 143).

So there are arguments for prohibiting drugs, and even for punishing drug use. And there are arguments against. What should we do?

METHODOLOGICAL PROBLEMS

Many political philosophers are inspired by the opening words of Rousseau's The Social Contract:

> I mean to inquire if, in the civil order, there can be any sure and legitimate rule of administration, men being taken as they are and laws as they might be.
>
> (Rousseau 1973b [1762], 90)

This is often taken to be an enlightened thought, suggesting that we should not ask impossible things of people, given human nature. Laws, it is suggested by Rousseau, are much more flexible. But in response, lawyers, and philosophers of law, we might think, have to live by another dictum: not only do men have to be taken as they are, but so do the laws, at least for the time being. That is to say, it is one thing to set up laws for an ideal society of the imagination, but the task in hand is to deal with the world we have. Inevitably, then, for policy reasons what needs to be discussed is not ideal law and regulation, but change to existing law.

The relevance of this issue is that Husak opens his discussions of drugs policy with an attempt to convince the reader that the right question to ask is not whether we should advocate changes to the law, but whether there is a justification for criminalizing drug use. Is there a philosophical argument which can demonstrate that it can be right to punish people for engaging in actions which only harm themselves (Husak 1989, 1992, 2002, and in Husak and de Marneffe 2005)? Put like this, it is a severe challenge, and although I have sketched out a couple of possible arguments to justify punishing people for harming themselves they rest on empirical premises, which are uncertain and may, in many cases, be false.

Husak wants to frame the argument in the terms he does so that he does not have to justify decriminalization of drugs. After all, the effects of decriminalization are very hard to predict. To take just one issue, as we noted, there is the question of how existing drug dealers will respond to the loss of market opportunities. Will they start to engage in robbery with violence? No one can say with confidence that the world would be a better place if drugs were decriminalized. To argue about decriminalization, Husak suggests, gives the status quo an unwarranted advantage in the debate. So instead, he attempts to argue from considerations of justice, rather than from the beneficial consequences of a change.

The problem with this, however, is that the policy debate is not about ideals. It is about change. Those who refuse to grant the status quo a privileged position in the debate may still be able to make important and telling arguments (as we saw in the case of

Singer and animal rights), but are likely to be treated as background or marginal figures to the immediate policy debate. This is not to say that the status quo morally deserves privilege. Sometimes it will – it will be the accumulation of generations of wisdom (see Burke 2009 [1790]). Sometimes it will not – it will be the accumulation of generations of prejudice (see Mill 1962b [1863]). Rather, change is harder to justify than keeping things as they are, given that change is bound to have unanticipated consequences. This is the 'better the devil you know' principle.

To see the importance of the issue, let us return to the vexed question of the different treatment of alcohol and drugs. In recent studies, alcohol is considered more harmful than almost all drugs except heroin and cocaine (and their derivatives). How, then, can one justify differential treatment for alcohol on the one hand, and ecstasy and cannabis on the other? From the standpoint of philosophical theory, this is a real puzzle, and there seems no answer. There seems to be a real inconsistency in our laws. Alcohol and drugs that cause similar harms should obviously be treated the same way. But from the standpoint of public policy this argument cuts no ice: 'The serious problems created by alcohol and tobacco are in fact arguments against legalizing more drugs' (Waal 1999 159; see also Sher 2003). That is to say, the argument is that we are already permitting people to do enough – too many – bad things to themselves, and so why would we want to permit even more harms, even if they are smaller? Society has to draw the line somewhere. Perhaps one might concede that if we were starting again, knowing what we know now, the line would be drawn in another place. But we are not starting again, and we are where we are.

What place, then, is there for pure philosophical reasoning in such policy debates? It would be absurd to argue that there is no place for speculation about ideals – of course this is necessary, otherwise there would be nothing to inspire or direct change. However, speculation about ideals is the start not the finish, and if philosophers want to have an influence on the direction policy takes, then they need to engage with the policy debate as it is, not as they would prefer it to be. We have already seen one reason for granting the status quo a privileged position: the uncertain effects of change. A second reason, of course, is that people will have formed expectations based on current laws, and therefore change needs justification and issues of transition need to be addressed. But beyond that it has to be recognized that it is very rare for a policy to have been introduced for clear and principled reasons. Compromise, context and pragmatism are always in the background, and given that the introduction of policies is rarely based on pure principles, it is naïve to think that principled reasoning alone will bring about change. This is not to say that there is no room for debate about principles. Indeed such debate does take place – whether, say, we should aim for a drug-free society, or at something else, as discussed above, under 'Society's Underlying Drug Strategy', for example. There is room for discussion at the level of details: pointing out small-scale anomalies, inconsistencies and distinctions between cases. There is room for recommendations of changes of policy in line with other social developments. But to have any effect on immediate policy philosophers will have to swallow hard and accept that the discussion will often have to take place within the terms and space set by political and pragmatic concerns.

Starting from the status quo does not, though, mean accepting it as it is. But change is more likely if it 'goes with the grain'. For example, let us return to the idea that the overall social goal of drug policy should be one of harm reduction, and accept that the regime of allowing alcohol already creates a great deal of harm. If it is also accepted that some drugs – notably ecstasy and possibly cannabis – do less harm than alcohol, then an obvious conclusion follows: the legalization of these drugs could reduce, rather than increase, overall harm in society, by encouraging people to replace harmful forms of behaviour with less harmful forms. This, of course, is an empirical claim, but if teenagers drank less and took more soft drugs on Friday and Saturday nights it is likely there would be fewer acts of violence, and fewer people ending up in emergency rooms. Of course, empirical work is needed to see if legal availability of drugs would reduce alcohol consumption (it has been argued, conversely that cannabis consumption is associated with increased alcohol consumption (W. Hall and Pacula 2003)), and also the hypothesis that these drugs are 'gateways' to harder drugs needs careful examination. However, the merit of philosophical reasoning in this area is that it forces a clarification of the arguments, and allows the raising of what might otherwise be 'taboo proposals'. If the empirical claims are accepted, yet the proposal to liberalize is not, then it becomes apparent that 'harm reduction' was not the policy goal after all, and a clarification of the policy becomes necessary. Policy makers can be forced into further thought and reflection. When philosophers can make their contributions within the existing terms of the debate, rather than from the perspective of ideals, there is some chance that others with more influence will pay attention.

Nevertheless it is worth raising the question of whether substantial change might not, after all, be coming on to the agenda soon, and the wider the range of people who advocate change the more likely it is to happen. The status quo can be broken. There are very interesting parallels between drug use today and gambling in the 1950s. As we saw in the last chapter, off-track gambling became legal, in a highly restricted and controlled fashion, once it was conceded that the current law was being broken by a very large percentage of the population who were in other respects generally law-abiding. It was, therefore, unenforceable, and through attempts at prevention and prohibition the law used up a disproportionate share of police and court time. Sounds familiar?

CONCLUSION: LESSONS FOR PHILOSOPHY

Many of the themes of the last two chapters come up again here, but I will not repeat them. There are really just two new lessons I want to draw out. The first was already mentioned, though, in the

Introduction to this book. We must start from where we are. Rarely, if ever, do we make a 'fresh start' with all possible outcomes as equally likely. Debate has a 'status quo bias' and in policy terms we are stuck with this, however much we feel it is philosophically unjustified. This does not mean that radical change is impossible, but simply that in public policy debates the 'home team' has a significant advantage.

Second, and perhaps more surprising, is that the philosopher's favourite weapon is rather blunted in public policy. This is the appeal to inconsistency. In the seminar room the appeal to inconsistency is perhaps the strongest tool we have. If your opponent's position is inconsistent, and he or she admits this, you have won, and it is all over. No one should hold an inconsistent position. But in public policy this does not work so well. Of course the most blatant inconsistencies are problematic. If one law told you that you couldn't dance on Sundays and another told you that you must, then we have a serious problem that needs to be dealt with. But if we find out – as we seem to have – that the treatment of ecstasy and alcohol is inconsistent, then so what? You can still follow the law. Ideally, of course, there would be no inconsistencies, but many laws are compromises between competing interests, and different laws were made by different people, at different times for different purposes. While one can hope for consistency it would be foolish to expect it, and pointing out inconsistency is not a decisive argument. Here, once more, philosophy and public policy have different standards of argument.

4
Safety

INTRODUCTION

In 1996 I taught in a summer school in Beijing, to a group of actual and aspiring university teachers. One of these students was particularly friendly, and during a break, started to chat, asking me about my family. Soon we got on the topic of what my wife did for a living. My halting attempts to explain the secondary licensing market were cut short by his excited remark. 'Ah, your wife is in business! Like my wife'. Quietly, and with a mixture of pride and tactful sympathy, he added: 'But I think my wife is richer than yours'. Having already noticed that he was wearing very fine shoes, I was keen to hear more. He told me that his wife and mother-in-law owned a factory in southern China which manufactured 'low-standard car parts'. Explaining that many people in China drive old cars, he pointed out that when their cars need repair no one wants to be forced to waste money buying parts which will outlive their car. They know low-standard parts are less safe but they take this into account when they purchase them, and, perhaps, in their driving habits. Everyone knows the situation. The factory next door made 'one-week shoes': they look great on a big night out, but you throw them away when you get home. The only trouble is that, in both cases, middlemen buy in bulk, re-box them as the genuine article, and sell them abroad. At the time there had been a scandal in the UK about counterfeit car parts, and I had to wonder whether this man's wife was the only partially innocent source of the problem.

To hear that it is possible to manufacture and then sell something you yourself describe as 'low standard' is refreshing, but at the same time rather shocking, particularly when lives can depend on those items functioning properly. In highly regulated economies it would seem unthinkable. Certainly people can choose to spend ever more on the latest safety devices, such as cars with the best crumple zones, air bags, and advanced braking systems. They can spend on superior smoke alarms, or even safety mats for their baths. We all make decisions about how safe our lives are to be. Nevertheless, every household device, every workplace, possibly every product in every shop, has to be passed as meeting a minimum safety standard. Why?

This may seem a stupid question, and it is obvious that we should have safety standards. But what's so special about safety? In making a purchase you try to make the decisions that suit you best, given your tastes and pocket. It is for you, subject to your budget constraints, to decide whether to eat fine food or junk, to travel in a chauffeur-driven Rolls or take the bus. Yet, it seems, even societies that pride themselves on championing the free market stop when it comes to safety. A free market in safety would allow people to take into account the safety of what they purchase as one element in its quality. 'What do I feel like buying today? Low-standard car parts or premium standard?' Yet much of this is often taken out of our hands. We cannot purchase things below a certain safety level, that carry too high a risk of causing harm or death, and the like – not legally purchase, anyway.

There are, of course, some good reasons for regulation. Consider again low-standard car parts. A first, and very obvious, reason for prohibiting their sale is that, as we saw, they may be passed off to the unwitting as high standard. This is one version of a common problem that cries out for consumer protection. Typically the person selling a good has much more knowledge than the one intending to buy it, and can exploit this, by engaging in the common business practice of being rather selective in the information they pass on concerning the quality of the product offered for sale. For example, before the regulation of food standards in the UK, at the end of the nineteenth century, it was common to sell bread plumped up with chalk dust and, in ale houses, beer dosed with salt so that with each mouthful the drinker became thirstier. Defenders of the free market argue that competition tends to drive out those who cheat their customers, but the fact that legislation was necessary seems to show that theory and practice do not always line up. Consumers need protection to make up for their ignorance, and one way of helping is simply to make it illegal to sell goods that a knowing customer would not purchase, such as those that pose too high a risk of harm or death.

Still it can be argued that we do not have to ban the sale of dangerous products to solve this problem. A different response to consumer ignorance is to increase people's knowledge, as we see with the rise of consumer groups publishing magazines to expose poor products and recommend others. These provide a market in information, a sort of espionage on behalf of the consumer. Also the continuing development of labelling on food helps consumers inform themselves. Perhaps labelling would be just as effective as banning: who would buy bread if it was labelled '40 per cent chalk dust'? Well, those who cannot read, for one, and in the late nineteenth century this was not a marginal group. There are, of course, also those who couldn't afford any better, such as those who even in these days continue to buy ham that has been injected with water to increase its bulk.

The argument we began with – that ignorance can lead to exploitation and consequent harm – has begun to shade into a different one, that even if people had access to all relevant information they could not be trusted to make rational decisions. This second argument is a version of 'paternalism', which we encountered in the last two chapters: treating adults in the protective but fussy and interfering manner that a certain sort of father is thought to treat his children. Paternalism is often greatly resented, for obvious reasons, and is quite different from the argument that the consumer just doesn't have the time and expertise to acquire the relevant knowledge. But its practical consequences are the same: that we ought to make sure that all goods meet a minimum safety standard, exactly on the model of regulating other aspects of the quality of goods.

Beyond issues of exploitation of ignorance and paternalism, we have also to recognize that cars are a danger not only to the driver but to other road users who need protection. This is an example of what economists call 'exernalities' or 'third-party effects', and what the rest of us call 'effects on others'. One person's choices and behaviour can have consequences for others who have not had the chance to give or withhold permission, or even to approve or complain. Pollution is an evident example; it is a very common negative externality, something you get for nothing but would rather not have. Externalities can be positive as well. A positive externality is, in effect, a free gift for which you were never asked for payment. Those who walk through a pleasant neighbourhood receive the positive externality of a wholesome view. Sadly negative externalities are the more common, and for a very obvious reason. Creating negative externalities is the same thing as dumping your costs on others. Purchasers of low-standard car parts save some money and thereby increase risks, not only for themselves but for others too. It is not surprising, then, that many societies are particularly concerned to ensure that one person's behaviour – including consumer behaviour – does not increase risks for others, and this seems to provide a compelling further argument for regulation.

The cases so far have all focused on reasons for restricting choice. Sometimes, though, the issue is precisely that we do not have a choice. Think about travelling by train. A genuine free market here would offer people a choice between, say, a more expensive, safer journey, and a cheaper, more risky one. If there were ten completely independent operators running routes on different tracks between London and Manchester, offering differing levels of safety at different prices then each of us could choose our own price/safety trade-off. But there is only one line. Consequently the idea that safety can be left to the free choices of individuals cannot apply when there is no choice. Where there is a monopoly there is a monopoly safety level too. We all have to accept the same level. And here regulators cannot resist stepping in to say what that level should be.

SETTING A SAFETY STANDARD

Perhaps we should be persuaded that there are very good reasons for governments to set minimum safety standards. But how are these standards to be decided? The importance and the difficulty of the question were brought home to me when a former student asked if I was interested in looking at a problem worrying the organization he was currently working for, the Rail Safety and Standards Board. Having never quite understood, let alone shared, the British romance with the train, it seemed to me rather unlikely that this would have been of much interest, but I was curious and I agreed to look at a discussion note written by his boss. After the first couple of paragraphs I was hooked. At the time – around 2001 – the reputation of the rail industry in the UK was in shreds. There had been a number of high-profile accidents, including one at Hatfield where the track shattered as a high-speed train passed over it, killing four people. The industry claimed that it had never seen a track fail in this way before, and in consequence a decision was taken to test every inch of track in the UK. This was a slow process, and in the meantime severe speed restrictions were placed on untested tracks. It was months before the network was declared safe, and these were months of chaos. You would get on a train having no idea when it would arrive at its destination. There were stories of commuter journeys taking ten hours instead of the scheduled one hour. The industry was at its lowest ebb, and the general view among the public was that safety was a disgrace and the industry quite negligent. Many people thought that this was a consequence of the privatization of the railways conducted a decade earlier, which, it was commonly believed, was ideological motivated and ineptly executed, allowing many people to get rich quick at the taxpayers' and train-travellers' expense (Wolmar 2001; Jack 2001).

That, at least, was the common view, and as a reader of newspapers and watcher of television it was my view too. Safety on the railways was a scandal and something needed to be done. However the research paper I read put things rather differently. First, it explained the regulatory framework that applied to the railways, giving an account of when it is obligatory to spend money to improve safety and when it is not. I had no idea that there were rules about this, but in fact, in the UK, the core of safety regulation is a simple calculation, which I shall explain shortly. Second, this paper pointed out that railway travel was, in fact, statistically very safe indeed, even including the high-profile crashes. In an average year about 300 people die on the railways in the UK, which does sound a lot. However, about 200 of these, very sadly, are people who commit suicide. Most of the rest are trespassers, often drunk and sometimes trying to find their way home late at night by walking along the tracks in the unfortunate belief that the last train has already gone. On average there are only around ten deaths of people who are actual or intending passengers, and many of these are the result of slips and falls at stations (see, for example, RSSB 2008). On the roads at that time about 3,500 people died each year in the UK (which has one of the better records in the world for road safety) of which about 2,500 were occupants of cars (current figures are lower, around 3,000 die each year; see ONS 2009). All these figures were new to me. Given the prominence allotted to stories about train crashes in the media, you would assume that they were happening all the time, with massive loss of life. But in fact crashes are rare, and those with more than around ten fatalities are very rare indeed. In the last few decades, there may have not been in a week in the UK where more people died on the railways than on the roads.

The paper I had been sent set out the brute facts about rail safety. The next point follows with relentless logic. The money spent on some recent safety innovations for the railways massively exceeded the minimum standard. If very few passengers are dying, it is going to cost an absolute fortune to reduce the death toll even further. To illustrate, at the time I was reading the paper sent to me, government and industry, stirred by the media, were debating whether to introduce a new computerized signalling system called ATP (Automatic Train Protection). Even its defenders admitted that it could not save more than a couple of lives a year, on average. Yet it would cost around 6 billion pounds to introduce. That is 6 billion pounds to save two lives a year, for, say ten years. Now if you have 6 billion to spend and your goal is to save some lives, putting it into railway safety must be one of the most stupid things you could do. Road safety, the health service, or overseas aid, could use the money to save ten, a hundred, perhaps a thousand times as many lives. Consequently, rather than being negligent about safety, the industry had, it could be argued, been grossly extravagant in terms of the cost of innovations it had already brought in, never mind those under discussion. Overspending to this degree – the equivalent, perhaps, of putting in gold-plated fittings in the station washrooms – would normally have been criticized as criminally wasteful. Spending even more, as the public seemed to be demanding, would compound the problem. And so the industry simply didn't know what to do.

Seeing things in this light may make it sound obvious that we have already spent enough on railway safety, thank you very much, and there is no reason to do more. Yet as the paper I was reading made plain, when we look again at some of the accidents – a train going through a red light and crashing into another, or a track shattering – and we read about the people who have lost their lives, and how it has devastated their parents, partners and children, things can seem rather different. Any death, especially any death that could have been avoided, is a tragedy. Even one death is too many. It is tempting, then, to say that if we know how to improve safety then we must do so. But, then, we have already seen where this thought takes us: spending billions to make marginal improvements.

In philosophical terms, it is possible to see this dilemma as a conflict between two moral standpoints. If we want to spend our money in the most efficient way, we should look to see how we get the greatest benefit from it. In this case it means spending it on whatever will save the most lives. Such reasoning, we have noted, is likely to lead to the conclusion not to spend more on safety improvements on the railways, but to find a way of saving more lives with the resources at our disposal. This is a 'consequentialist' moral standpoint, which directs us to do the most good with the resources we have: to achieve the best consequences. Utilitarianism is the best known form of consequentialism. It instructs us to seek 'the greatest happiness of the greatest number', which is commonly interpreted as the demand to maximize the sum total of happiness in the world.

Utilitarianism was introduced as a humane and enlightened alternative to traditional and religious moralities, which suggest that the right thing to do is either what humans have always done, of what they are commanded by God to do. Jeremy Bentham, and his followers, who included John Stuart Mill, despaired of the conformity and oppression to which traditional moralities led, replacing them with the view that if a measure was not, all things considered, good for human beings (or other sentient beings) then it could not be morally required (Bentham 1996 [1781]; Mill 1962b [1863]). This is a liberating doctrine, which, if accepted, would require a thorough review of traditional eighteenth- and nineteenth-century moral restrictions, such as women's lack of access to professional careers and to the universities, or the prohibitions of homosexuality and contraception.

The problem with utilitarianism, though, is not that it bases morality on human happiness, but that it defines right action in terms of maximizing the sum total of happiness. This means that, in principle, it can allow the sacrifice of some individuals for the sake of others, and, even more tellingly, it can require a very large sacrifice of a small number for the sake of small benefits for the many. The greatest happiness might be increased by measures that cause great unhappiness, even death, to the few, if this is outweighed even by the small pleasures of the very many. And this, indeed, is what we see in the case of railway safety. It is not that the majority take pleasure in the death of the minority, but that we all place limits on how much we are prepared to sacrifice for the sake of improved railway safety, and this will inevitably lead to more deaths than it would otherwise have done.

To apply utilitarian reasoning to any area, including railway safety, we first must make a list of the potential costs and benefits of the available courses of action, and try to estimate how much happiness or utility (or their opposites) they will generate. Now, immediately you may wonder how it could be possible to put meaningful numbers on human happiness, which is a very fair point, and an important question. This is the problem of 'interpersonal comparisons of utility', but it would be distracting to get bogged down in it here. For the moment we will put this issue to one side, although it will reappear shortly.

But suppose we have estimated utility losses and gains for different policies as part of the process of deciding whether or not to introduce a new safety system into the railway network, paid for out of general taxation. If we do not make any change perhaps one or two people per year, whom the new system would have saved, will die. This, of course, is a very significant utility loss. If we raise the rate of taxation, to pay for the new system, however, this also generates a utility loss, in that anyone who pays more tax will have less money to spend on other things. This is only a small loss per person, but if many millions of people find that they have less money, then the total utility loss could be considerable. Assuming that all the quantities involved are finite, then the aggregation of enough small utility losses will eventually outweigh a small number of very large losses. So utilitarianism may well entail the judgement that, very sadly, introducing the safety measure is not justified as the benefits of raising the tax – the saving of a small number of lives – are not sufficient to outweigh the loss to utility it would cost. Hence in the case of safety, sometimes we have to sacrifice a small number of people for the sake of the greater good.

For many critics of utilitarianism this argument shows, not that sacrifice is justified, but that utilitarianism is utterly misguided as a moral theory. How can it be morally acceptable to allow the death of some people simply to save a small increase in general taxation? A position in moral philosophy to support this criticism of utilitarian reasoning is known as 'deontology' or 'duty-based' reasoning. Sometimes it is also called 'absolutism' which is the name we will adopt in the rest of this chapter. The basic idea behind this type of theory is that morality sets out some basic rules which at least in normal circumstances override considerations of consequences. Such theories come in various strengths, the most demanding of which is to say that the basic rules should never be violated, what-ever the consequences. To illustrate, it is not uncommon for people to argue that there are never any possible circumstances in which tor-ture would be justified. By contrast, the utilitarian position on torture is that it is justified in circumstances where, taking everything into account, including the very long term effects, torture is permitted when it would create better consequences than always prohibiting it. Something of a middle position is also possible: that while torture is generally ruled out, if there is a case where refusing to torture someone would have truly devastating consequences, such as the destruction of the entire world, torture can, regretfully, be acceptable.

The current example, of course, is not that of torture versus the destruction of the world, but saving a small number of lives, versus raising a small additional tax from very many people. The utilitarian, as we have seen, will say that there are cases where raising the tax causes greater total misery than a small number of deaths, and in such cases the safety measure should not be introduced. The absolutist, by contrast, is likely to respond that at least in these circumstances, even one avoidable death is too many.

Consider, for example, the things relatives of victims say after a train crash. In a sense, every crash is avoidable. Some combination of factors conspired to cause the problem and if any one had been different then it would not have happened. And very often the company in charge could have introduced some procedure or technology to make sure that such incidents could not happen. So, for example, if a train crash happened because the driver failed to respond correctly to a signal it is natural to wonder how on earth this can be allowed to happen in the twenty-first century. After all the technology exists to ensure that trains automatically obey the signals, and it is used in some other countries. So if the technology exists, why don't we just install it, and then we can stop this kind of incident once and for all. Surely there is something immoral about refusing to do so, just because of the cost.

The power of such reasoning seems very strong, perhaps undeniable. But the consequentialist may well reply that the cost of installing the new system is likely to be immense. In this case, we saw, it will run into the billions of pounds. Can it really be reasonable to spend so much money just to save one or two lives a year, especially when so much good could be done with that money if used for other purposes? The philosophy textbooks often line up the consequentialists against the absolutists, like the opposing sides in the First World War, each in their trenches, convinced of the rightness of their own cause, but clueless about how to bring about victory. In this case, though, the idea of two sides fighting each other gets things wrong. The struggle is inside each of us. It seems that most people will find themselves torn between both standpoints – flipping over from one to the other as different aspects come into view. There is, then, a very serious moral problem here.

In UK policy, as in many countries, broadly a consequentialist position is taken, at least as far as the regulations are concerned. Individual businesses, of course, for reputational reasons might want to exceed minimum standards, but let us look now at how the regulations are set out. Railway safety in the UK is treated as a branch of workplace safety, which falls under regulations discussed by the Health and Safety Executive (HSE) in a booklet entitled *Reducing Risks, Protecting People* (HSE 2001), cutely known as R2P2, like a character out of Star Wars. The approach taken is an application of what is known as risk–cost–benefit analysis (RCBA). This technique provides a way of comparing the costs of any possible safety measure against its benefits, so as to help us answer the question of whether it is worth introducing. To boil the approach down to its essentials, to carry out an RCBA we first need to think about the safety benefits that a measure might bring. Suppose, for example, every year five people die by falling out of open train doors while the train is moving – something, in fact that used to happen. Even more shocking is the fact that several people a year used to die while standing on the platform, being hit by doors accidentally swinging open as passengers, apparently desperate to get to work a few seconds earlier, tried to disembark from trains while they were still moving. All these types of accidents would eventually be avoided by devices making it impossible to open the door of the train until it had come to a halt in a station. The next question, obviously enough, is how much would it cost to introduce such safety measures?

With these two figures – the number of lives that are likely to be saved, and the cost of doing so – it is then possible to derive a figure for the cost of saving a life for the project under consideration. If, for example, the project will cost 10 million pounds, and can be expected to save twenty lives, then the cost of saving each life would be 500,000 pounds (ignoring any fussy issues about 'discounting' for future lives saved). In the end the issue seems to come down to this cold-blooded question: is it worth spending that amount of money to save each life?

It would not be absurd to think that this is a question without an answer. After all, how can we put any price on life? It seems to be the height of crudity, even immorality, to put a financial figure on the worth of a human being. On the other hand, a refusal to engage with this question may look like pure sentimentality. A decision has to be made, and on what grounds can we rationally make a decision except financial? That, at least, is the approach adopted in the UK regulations, which is the example we have taken. The value of saving a life is called 'the value of preventing a fatality' and, surprising though it may seem, there is indeed an official value of preventing a fatality (VPF). That value is currently somewhere around 1.4 million pounds. So we have an answer to the question: how much are you worth? Answer: according to the UK, about one million, four hundred thousand pounds! Readers from the USA will be interested to know their government thinks they are worth considerably more than this: something over 6 million dollars.

Once we have this figure for the VPF we can then check to see whether a safety measure is worth it. If the cost of preventing a fatality by introducing a new safety measure is higher than 1.4 million pounds, then it is too expensive. Of course, a company could decide to introduce it, but from the point of view of the law, the company would not be doing anything wrong if it did not. On the other hand, there is a requirement to introduce the safety measure if it provides good value for money – if each life it saves costs less than the official VPF.

Can it really be right to treat loss of life in this cold, calculating, financial way? But what is the alternative? Can we make sensible decisions about safety without this sort of calculation? And whether or not this is the right approach, where on earth does this figure of 1.4 million pounds come from?

Let us take these questions in reverse order, which means, first of all, looking at where the figure for the value of preventing a fatality comes from. At first one suspects that the argument is that public policy needs a clear, consistent approach, and while any figure is going to be arbitrary, something a bit above one million pounds has a nice feel to it. After all, it would be rather sad to think that a human life is worth less than a million pounds. But in fact there is much more to it than that. The basic thought is that actually, when a safety measure is introduced it is not quite right to think of it as saving particular lives. Rather what it is doing is reducing risks for a large group of people. For example, if it is true that building a footbridge over a very busy road makes the road safer to cross, this is a benefit to everyone who crosses the road, even if, actually, no one would have died had the bridge not been built (although of course this is not something we could actually know if the bridge is built).

There is, then, a subtle distinction between saving a life and reducing a small risk for a great number of people, and this is why when they are speaking carefully economists, engineers and regulators talk about the value of saving a statistical life, rather than saving a life. Suppose 1,000 people all have a one in a thousand chance of dying from a hazard this year, but then the hazard is eliminated. One statistical life is saved, but it may be that any number of actual lives, from 0 to 1,000, is spared. After all the probabilities are consistent with no one dying, 1 person dying (the most likely outcome), 2 people dying, or even, horribly and hugely improbably, all 1,000 dying. With the elimination of the hazard, all thousand people have had a small but significant risk reduced.

Seeing statistical lives as accumulations of large numbers of small risks is a major step forward, and the idea of putting some sort of price on the reduction of small risks seems less barbaric (Schelling 1984 [1968]). After all, as we have already seen, there are many steps we take in our lives to spend money to reduce risks. We buy smoke alarms and cars with air bags. We take taxis to avoid walking through dangerous parts of town. And, indeed, we avoid buying low-standard car parts. Noticing that we do indeed pay money to reduce small risks helps in two respects. First it makes us realize that paying for safety – putting a price on safety – is, in fact, a normal part of life. Second, and more controversially, perhaps the sums we pay can be used in some way to inform the value of a statistical life in our regulations. Perhaps the best way of getting to a figure that makes some sense is to base it on the types of decisions people make about safety in their own lives.

At this point in the argument some of the advocates of RCBA get a little misty-eyed about the democratic roots of their theories. In a democracy, they say, public policy should be based on the values of the citizens. And how better can their values be determined than by what they are prepared to spend their money on? Well, you might think, an economist would say that wouldn't they? But what would a theologian or an artist or a hippy, or even a moral philosopher, say? But let us first see where this approach takes us.

CALCULATING THE VPF

Theorists and lawyers have been grappling for some time with the question of how to calculate the financial value of a life. Thirty or forty years ago, the standard methodology was to base valuations on lost potential economic contribution. Human beings were regarded as 'human capital' and so a source of potential income, and the VPF as therefore equivalent to the cost of losing that potential income. The greater your potential contribution to the economy, the greater your value. Although there is some apparent logic to this, still it clearly has some unfortunate effects. On this method anyone who is economically dependent, such as the old and the unemployed, could have a value so low it could be negative, and if they are ill and in need of health care it could be significantly so (Mishan 1971).

Contemporary theorists point out that even someone who is old and has no productive contribution left to make to the economy may still be prepared to pay good money to reduce a small risk of their own death, and even if they are not prepared to spend money this way 'we' as a society may consider doing so on their behalf. Reducing their risks of death is a benefit to them, even if doing so potentially increases total social costs in terms, say of health care.

Instead of the 'human capital' approach, economists now typically use 'willingness-to-pay' models. In other words they try to work out the VPF by looking at purchasing decisions people would or do make, which is the approach briefly mentioned in the last section (for an early example that explains the methodology see Jones-Lee et al. 1985). The promise is that the valuation of VPF can be conducted in terms of willingness to pay: the payments people do, or would, make in the market. The payments people do make yields the methodology of revealed preferences, and those people would make yields the methodology of expressed preference. The former looks at actual market behaviour – what safety devices people spend their money on, how much extra pay they need to compensate them for dangerous jobs – as a guide to valuation. The latter uses purely hypothetical 'willingness-to-pay' methods, normally known as 'contingent valuation', elicited by economists and psychologists in the lab.

Both methods have their attractions and drawbacks. Consider, first, revealed preference methodology. This has the advantage of looking at actual market behaviour: the decisions people have actually made in real markets, spending real money that they could spend on something else. The disadvantage is something it shares with any attempt to deduce people's underlying attitudes from their behaviour: what in philosophy of mind is called 'the holism of the mental' (Davidson 1963). Given that both desire and belief play a role in the explanation of actions, it has been argued that every action is compatible with every desire if the surrounding beliefs are adjusted. A person's drinking the poison hemlock is consistent with that person's desire to die, but also to live a long life, if they believe that hemlock is some sort of vitamin boosting drink. In the present context, people might choose to buy a dangerous product, believing it to be safer than it is. Nothing, though, is revealed about that person's attitude to risk from this decision. Furthermore, it is rare for an action to be performed for the sake of a single desired goal. So, for example, it is very unlikely that the only difference between two complex products – two cars, say – is that one is safer than the other. The fact, then, that I have chosen to purchase a safer car does not show that I am prepared to the pay that premium purely for the risk reduction. It may be, for example, that I also prefer the image associated with one make of car rather than the other.

For these and other reasons some theorists prefer to follow the method of expressed preferences or, as it is also called, contingent valuation. The basic idea behind this methodology is that subjects are asked for their views of how much they would pay for a safety improvement, if one were available. There are at least two main advantages to this methodology. First, the experimenter can set up questions in such a way as to ensure that the subject must focus on the safety element alone in the choice. In a hypothetical example all other parameters can be fixed in a way that will rarely, if ever, happen in a real market case. Second, a given subject can, in theory, be asked many questions, and so a great deal more data can be generated.

In practice, however, such benefits are rarely seen. There are several limitations. First, there are what are known as framing issues. It is well known that if people say that they would pay a particular amount of money to avoid a risk, in general they will also say that they would need even more money in compensation if the feared event happened. This requires explanation, as many versions of decision theory predict that a given individual's 'willingness to pay' and 'willingness to accept compensation' should be the same. To get a sense of this imagine you are offered a pair of tickets to some highly attractive event: the World Cup final or a star-studded opera. What would you pay for them? What is the absolute most you would pay? A hundred pounds? A thousand pounds? Imagine you have just paid that amount for the tickets – if they were even a little bit more expensive you would have said no – and have them in your hand. Next, suppose another person comes up to you offering to buy them. Now you have got the tickets, what is the lowest price you would sell them for? If there is a significant gap between the two sums – as many people report there is – it shows that there is a difference between your willingness to pay and your willingness to accept compensation, and raises the question of what we should say is your 'price' for these tickets. (The classic account of framing effects is Kahneman and Tversky 1979.)

'Framing' was the first difficulty for contingent valuation. A second problem is that given that in contingent valuation no money actually passes hands, it is unclear how seriously we can take the figures offered. There is a legitimate worry that some people are simply plucking numbers out of the air, rather than revealing willingness to pay.

Third, and most seriously of all, human beings appear to be very poor at rational decision-making involving very small probabilities. Subjects can very easily be led to make inconsistent decisions: for example being willing to pay more if a risk reduction is broken down into two steps rather than one, even if the resulting outcome is the same, or paying the same for a larger reduction and a smaller one. In sum, when subjects are asked to express their preferences concerning paying to avoid risks with small probabilities, very little reliable data can be generated. If asked 'how much would you pay to avoid a 1 in 100,000 chance of death?' most people, I think, would not feel that they could give a robust or reliable answer, yet working backwards from a VPF of £1.4 million pounds, the correct answer should be £14! Furthermore, when asked a number of different questions it seems very unlikely that many people would give a consistent set of answers (Beattie et al. 1998).

These methodological problems are, of course, very difficult. But somehow or other the consequentialist must set a value. Let us suppose we are broadly happy with the figure of 1 million pounds for the value of saving a statistical life (rounded down from £1.4 million, just to make the calculations as simple as possible), and let us go back to the example, discussed above, of the old 'slam-door trains' where people were dying because train doors could be opened while the train was still moving.

In this instance it is clear that lives would be saved if doors on train carriages remained locked shut while the train was in motion. Ideally, existing carriages should be modified. But, it seems, this was not technically feasible in all cases. So the decision to be made is whether to phase out existing carriages, even though in other respects they are satisfactory, and replace them with new carriages with locking doors. For the consequentialist the decision procedure is straightforward. First, you need an estimate of how many lives the measure would save; suppose it is five lives a year for ten years (when the carriages would be replaced in the normal course of events), and so fifty lives. Next you need an estimate of how much the change will cost. Valuing the saving of a life at 1 million pounds, then the new carriages should be brought in, provided that to do so will cost less than 50 million pounds. But if the cost is more than that, and especially if it is substantially more, the benefits do not justify the cost.

As we noted, for the absolutist this is a morally outrageous way of approaching the question. A life cannot be valued in purely financial terms and if we know how to save a life we must do it, perhaps irrespective of the cost. The consequentialist response is that such a view is understandable but naïve. We could save all lives lost on the railways by closing the system. No one would die on the railways if there were no railways. Is that what we should do? But suppose that introducing new carriages will cost not 50 million pounds, but 500 million, or even 5 billion. Is it really true that it is immoral to draw the line somewhere on this scale? After all, with 500 million pounds we might be able to save not only 50 lives but perhaps 500 in factories and construction sites. Wouldn't that be a better use of the money? And for 5 billion pounds enormously more lives could be saved elsewhere.

This, of course, is the dilemma we started with. What should be done? In practice the railway industry did phase out slam-door trains early, saving perhaps five lives a year for a few years, and at a very high cost, perhaps as much as 5 million pounds per life saved. While the absolutist in each of us will approve, the consequentialist will raise the question of whether this really was money well spent. Indeed, on the consequentialist view it is probably morally wrong to have spent so much to save so few lives.

COMPARING DIFFERENT CASES

How can we make further progress? One way in which philosophers might attempt to address the issue is to find more and better arguments for either the consequentialist or absolutist position. But this is a debate that has been in process for at least two hundred years (on some views two thousand) and it seems very unlikely we can settle it now. A different way of proceeding would be to look at a wider range of real examples and see whether any clearer rules or principles appear at a finer level of detail. After all, it is not impossible that the correct answer to the question 'how much should we spend to save lives?' is 'it all depends'.

So let us start by comparing two notorious British train accidents, known as Hatfield and Great Heck. Hatfield, which happened in October 2000, has been mentioned earlier. A train travelling at high speed derailed when the track over which it was travelling shattered, due to a phenomenon known as 'gauge corner cracking'. Four people died and seventy were injured. Great Heck happened a few months later, in February 2001, when a trailer, being towed by a Land Rover on a road next to the track, came detached from the car and ran down the embankment on to the tracks. It caused a passenger train to derail, but, very unusually, the train continued its forward momentum at speed, and then hit a freight train in a head-on collision. Ten people died, of whom six were passengers and four railway staff, and a further eighty people were injured (S. Hall 2003).

The first thing to note is that although in terms of deaths and injuries the two accidents were on a similar scale, the responses to the accidents from the industry, public and media differed considerably. In the case of Hatfield the industry declared that there had never been an accident of this nature before – the track had degraded in a way previously unknown – and so the whole network had to be scrutinized for similar problems. The entire network was checked by ultrasound machine, and severe restrictions were placed on all tracks until passed by the inspectors. In consequence, travel on the railways became a nightmare. No one could know when – or even if – their train would arrive, as it was virtually impossible to run any sort of timetable under these conditions. The financial cost of the operation was immense. It almost certainly cost lives too. The chaos on the railways was so appalling that many people took to their cars instead. But travelling by car is much more dangerous than travelling by train. Although it is impossible to tell from the statistics, it has been suggested that perhaps fifty deaths were caused as a result of people shunning the railways during this period, and using their cars, motorcycles or bicycles instead (Sunstein 2002, 2).

The media, not surprisingly, found the whole business an almost unlimited fountain of stories. First, there was the tragic fact of the accident itself, and related human interest stories. And then there were the technical stories about how the accident happened, which allowed the press to revive comparative stories of previous train crashes in the UK. And then there were stories of legal challenges, and political stories about the legacy of train privatization. And then a whole host of stories of chaos on the railways, and commuter journeys taking ten hours instead of one. Surprisingly, however, what perhaps should have been the main story received little

attention. The track involved had, some months before, been identified as in need of replacement, but the attempt to replace the track
failed as a result of a series of errors. In the meantime no one had
thought to place a speed restriction on track known to be faulty.

But in summary, the industry adopted what is known as a 'precautionary' attitude to safety, placing extreme restrictions on the
network until it could assure itself there were no similar problems
elsewhere, and without consideration of the financial costs. This is
close to an absolutist approach. As far as the media was concerned, it
seems that broadly such an approach was regarded as required from
the standpoint of proper concern for the safety of passengers. The
public seemed to accept that the industry was doing the right thing –
it would have been wrong for them not to give this regard to the
lives of their passengers – while expressing very strong disapproval
about the state of Britain and its industries that could have brought
us to this pass.

In the case of Great Heck, media interest took a different turn.
There was something of a discussion about the details of the accident, of course, and the sort of safety measures that might have
made it avoidable, but on the whole attention was focused on the
car driver, and the circumstances which had led him to lose control
of his vehicle. It transpired that he fell asleep at the wheel because
he had spent most of the previous night chatting on the telephone
to a girl he had met on the Internet. And so the media had found
its scapegoat. It seemed that there was little, if any, public will to
vilify the railway industry. If anything there was some sympathy
towards the industry that had suffered another serious problem,
just as it was trying to pick itself up off the floor after Hatfield.

Of course, it would have been possible to adopt a precautionary
approach. All tracks that run close to roads could have been fitted
with strong safety barriers to make it much less likely that a car,
or trailer, out of control, could run on to the track, and speed
restrictions could have been imposed on all areas concerned until the
work was completed. Yet it seemed obvious that such a response,

which would have mirrored the response to Hatfield, would have been disproportionately costly in terms of money and disruption. In effect, then, something closer to a consequentialist approach was taken in this case, considering whether the benefits, in terms of additional safety, would be worth the costs. The general judgement was that they would not have been.

What makes the difference between Hatfield and Great Heck? The accidents were on a similar scale of injury and loss of life, with Great Heck being rather worse. Both were very unusual, perhaps unique, events, and there is no reason to think that one was more probable than the other. In both cases the accident alerted everyone to the possibility of further accidents of the same kind, although it is true that much more was made of this in the case of Hatfield than Great Heck. But the most obvious difference is that with regard to Hatfield the industry had nothing or no one to blame except itself, whereas for Great Heck the culprit was external.

To put this another way, when a disaster happens, all parties are very concerned with the question 'who or what was at fault?', or even 'who is to blame?'. Energy is spent uncovering what we could call the 'blame audit trail'. A key difference between Hatfield and Great Heck is that in the case of Hatfield the blame audit trail led back to the railway industry, but in the case of Great Heck it led outside. It seems much more problematic if the fault for an accident is internal to the industry than external, especially as it is the industry that has taken on the responsibility of ensuring safety (Wolff 2006b).

The difference in public and media reaction to the accidents can be explained in part by appeal to some sort of principle of special moral responsibility. Although it is not easy to express a precise principle here there seems a relevant distinction between those matters that should be of direct and immediate concern to the industry – the condition and maintenance of the track, for example – and those that are outside its direct concern, such as the degree to which car drivers act with due care and attention. Of course, the industry cannot abdicate all responsibility in the latter case, but in such cases our moral intuitions tend to be far more consequentialist, appealing to the idea of proportionate, cost-effective responses, rather than the more absolute, precautionary approach which seems to be appropriate for matters entirely within its responsibility. Of course even in these cases some notion of cost limits must be applied, but at least we can understand that the reactions are towards the opposite ends of the scale. In sum, the more directly under the industry's control the source of an accident is, the more absolutist it should be about safety.

For a further illustration, consider again the statistics about the categories of people who die on the railways each year. There are around 200 suicides, 100 deaths of trespassers, 1 or 2 workers and about 5 to 10 passengers killed, on average. The industry pays much more attention to some categories rather than others. Suicides, of course, are a difficult case. Although the industry does take steps to make it more difficult to commit suicide on the railways, presumably many people so deterred still simply find other ways of taking their own life. The case of trespassers is different, but here it is worth contrasting adult trespassers, who, one feels, should know better and share at least partial responsibility for their own death, and passengers, who, in general will be unwitting victims of circumstances entirely beyond their own control. The small number of passengers who die attract far more attention and expenditure of resources to prevent future deaths, than any other category. Why? Simply because the industry accepts that it has a far higher duty of care to those who have purchased the service, and have trusted the railway industry with their lives, than to those who are external to the system.

Of course, nothing I have said so far is a justification of the different practices; it is a matter of further debate whether the public, media and industry are correct in having the moral attitudes they do. But as we have seen, the vague principle which seems to underlie these judgements is 'the more an incident can properly be seen as the industry's moral fault if it happens, the more absolutist it should be in its attitude towards the prevention of incidents of that type.' Naturally, there is much to debate here, and perhaps it is closer to the starting point of the debate than its resolution. But the principle itself seems to have a certain obviousness. What is needed next, though, and will not be discussed further here, is what makes something an agent's moral fault.

CONCLUSION: LESSONS FOR PHILOSOPHY

As in all of the chapters of this book, I want to end with some reflections about the lessons for the methodology of the philosophical analysis of public policy that could be drawn from this discussion. Here, though, I can be brief, as the main points have been illustrated at length in the discussion.

First, although consequentialists and absolutists are often set out as opposing camps of theorists, most of us, when considering the cases, will find ourselves drawn both to consequentialist and absolutist reasoning. We need, therefore, to try to work out a position that accommodates both consequentialist and absolutist elements, rather than think that the issue is to make a choice between them.

Second, in order to make progress on policy issues, it will often be vital to look at a range of examples. In this case considering the contrast between the Hatfield and the Great Heck accidents aided the analysis in a way that would have been very difficult otherwise. Understanding real-life examples, and working out the basis of the dilemmas they create, is an essential part of the attempt to come to a resolution of the issues.

Third, in some areas of policy, even philosophers will have to get their hands dirty, or be consigned to irrelevance. In this case the practical question that policy makers face is when it can be right not to insist on a possible safety improvement. But what would be the reason for declining to make an improvement? Normally because it would be disproportionately expensive. This is, it appears, to put a price on safety, or human life. Who would want to do that? But what is the alternative? Philosophers can retreat, shaking their heads, and refusing to take further part in the discussion. Or they can grapple with the question either of what price we should put on life, or how we can make safety decisions without valuing life. None of these options is likely to be comfortable.

5
Crime and punishment

INTRODUCTION

Among the concerns of the British public, crime – or perhaps law and order – always features near the top of the list. Yet it is worth pausing to ask the question: 'what is so bad about crime?' This, clearly, is rather provocative. If asked in the spirit of an economist one would expect the answer that, when we look into it, crime isn't such a bad thing after all. Karl Marx ironically remarked on what would now be called the 'technology-forcing' aspects of crime. The need for secure locks led to developments in precision engineering which no doubt had many beneficial applications elsewhere. As Marx says: 'Doesn't practical chemistry owe just as much to the adulteration of commodities, and the efforts to show it up as to the honest zeal for production?' and 'Torture alone has given rise to the most ingenious mechanical inventions, and employed many honourable craftsmen in the production of its instruments' (Marx 1969 [1863], 387). Crime prevention – not to mention the academic study of crime – is a major enterprise and in this way contributes to economic growth and national wealth, albeit the growth of something that detracts, rather than adds to, human happiness.

Crime prevention, in fact, is an excellent illustration of the point that economic activity is not necessarily a good thing in itself. Crime, we know, is something we would rather be without even if it can have some consequences that are useful for some people. Crime is so bad that we punish people, often with imprisonment, if we find them guilty. In this respect crime is almost unique. Apart from severe cases of mental illness or infectious disease, in a liberal society there is no other reason that we take as sufficient to deprive people of their liberty, however irritating they may be. Many philosophers and legal theorists have looked at the question of the moral justification of punishment, and we will follow this up later on in this chapter. Yet to understand the point of punishment, and its possible justifications, we need first, presumably, ask why we find crime so troubling. And that is what we shall explore in the first part of this chapter.

WHAT'S SO BAD ABOUT CRIME?

Asking the question of what is so bad about crime, may seem very strange. Isn't it obvious? Especially for those who live in violent societies, such as South Africa or parts of Brazil, crime is an omnipresent fear and threat. Crimes such as murder, rape and violent robbery are so clearly devastating to their victims that one might think that only a philosopher, in a protected ivory tower, might raise the question. But nevertheless, I think that there are aspects of the issue here that need to be worked through. For one thing placing crime in a broader context may help not only with understanding what is so bad about crime, but understanding what is so bad about anything at all. That is to say, any philosophical account of human well-being will have to be able to give an account of what it is about crime which gives rise to so much misery. Hence crime is an important testing ground for a philosophical theory of well-being. But there are things to learn about crime too.

One standard answer to the question of what makes a human life go well or badly is that a good life is one filled with happiness or satisfaction. A different answer is that a good life is one that is well-resourced, in terms of income and wealth, allowing a good standard of living. The two accounts are, of course, related insofar as resources can buy happiness, but it is well-known that the correlation is imperfect. A life can be intolerable even though well-resourced, and happy though poorly resourced, at least by normal standards, for a whole range of reasons.

According to the happiness theory of well-being presumably what is wrong with crime is that it makes people unhappy. There is, no doubt, a great deal of truth in this. One has only to think of the misery, to the point of despondency, in which a mugging or burglary can leave people. A convicted housebreaker told me that he went straight after his parents were burgled and he saw, at first hand for the first time, how devastating it was for them, even though they hardly lost anything. He said that he had no idea that breaking into people's houses could have such an effect, and it shocked him to find out what he must have been doing to people. Perhaps this was because before he had implicitly held the second view of well-being − that a good life is a well-resourced one, or, more likely that there is a strong correlation between possession of goods and happiness. So if you steal from the rich, as he had been doing, or from the adequately insured, it should not affect their well-being in any serious way. Yet the experience of this burglar's parents convinced him, in effect, that this view was wrong.

The happiness view seems closer to the truth, yet it also seems in some way superficial. What it doesn't tell us is why crime makes people so unhappy. My own experience of having to deal with a minor break-in involving a broken window and the loss of some electronic gadgetry, is that, objectively, it is comparable to the hassle of having to assemble some badly made flat-pack furniture, while at the same time querying a utility bill and investigating the mislocation of a recorded delivery parcel. Very irritating, but, in itself, no worse than a bad day at the office, and certainly not worth getting yourself worked up about. I have had worse experiences with failing computer equipment. A mugging, in its purely physical aspects, is about at the same level as a mid-scale sporting injury. A character in Ian McEwan's *Saturday*, expecting to receive a severe beating in the street, has a flash forward to the months of convalescence and recovery that would follow. This would be to take a purely 'objective' view of crime. Yet these objective aspects hardly seem to capture what we worry about, as McEwan's novel brilliantly illustrates (2005). There is something about being a victim of crime that goes much deeper than this. Hence fear of crime is not, or at least not always, fear of the average expected objective effects of crime.

Jeremy Bentham, brings out the main issue in striking fashion:

> The great point is, to clear the country of those crimes, each instance of which is sufficient to awaken and keep alive, in every breast within a certain circle, the fear of boundless injury to person or property, as well as of destruction to life itself – in comparison of this widespreading – this almost universally extending mischief – this fear of boundless injury – the sum of the mischiefs resulting in each instance from losses and other injuries actually sustained would be found relatively inconsiderable.
>
> (Bentham 1843, 244)

Bentham makes two important points in this passage. First, he implicitly recognizes a point insisted on in contemporary criminology – crimes can be very different in their nature, and our psychological reaction to different forms of crime can be equally distinct. In a different context Robert Nozick makes the same point by contrasting two cases. Suppose that you know that sometime in the next year that your car will be stolen, and that, in a different incident, your arm will be broken by an attacker. The effect of these on your mental life is likely to be quite different. Knowing that you will lose your car is a nuisance. Knowing that you will have your arm broken makes you afraid. Some crimes generate much greater fear than others (Nozick 1974). For Bentham the crimes that affect us most are the ones which threaten 'boundless injury' to person or property. These can induce not just fear but terror, and Bentham plausibly argues that the total fear such crimes create may be worse than their total damage. The point is not that our fear is out of proportion to the likely harm, although this is likely to be true. Rather, it is that for any particular person the chance of being a victim of serious crime is low and so experiencing actual harm is unlikely. Yet the fear can be ever-present for a much greater number of people, depressing their lives and creating a wide and deep pool of misery. We can certainly see Bentham's point. And there seems something right about the idea that crimes that threaten 'boundless injury' are particularly feared. What seems especially terrifying is the idea of a situation escalating entirely out of one's control, even to the point of not being able to predict the likely consequences of one's action. Will an attempt to defend oneself or property frighten off the attacker, or just make things worse? How will it end?

An important insight into the way crime affects people can be gained from considering what was, for a time, a mission statement from the Home Office in the area of crime: 'Reducing Crime, Reducing Fear of Crime'. This is clearly inspired by the recognition that fear of crime can have a deeper impact on people's lives than crime itself, coupled with the thought that one way of reducing crime is to make people hyper-vigilant, which may make them hyper-scared too. So the two goals of reducing crime and reducing fear of crime have a complex relation. It is often noted that on average women have a greater fear of crime than men, but men are more likely to be victims of crime. It is likely that there is a causal relation here: women, being more afraid of crime, take greater precautions. The message, then, is that if we want to reduce crime, and are not worried about anxiety levels in individuals, then it would be better for officials to scare people stiff, so they don't go out on their own, and double lock every door and window even when home. If this seems unattractive one likely reason is that we value anxiety reduction alongside crime reduction. And there are at least two reasons to be concerned about anxiety. First it is unpleasant in itself; and second, it can have extremely undesirable further effects. If you are anxious about something, you might take all sorts of steps to prevent it. A particularly poignant example of this is documented in Eric Klinenberg's book *Heatwave*, which explores the Chicago heatwave of 1985, in which many people, especially the elderly and already sick, died of heat-related causes. As is often the case most of these deaths were in poor neighbourhoods. But Klinenberg noted that there were a disproportionate number of deaths in high-crime poor neighbourhoods. Those who died were very often elderly people, living on their own, in low-standard accommodation. In high-crime neighbourhoods people were less likely to keep their windows open at night, or go out to air-conditioned shops or cafes during the day, and so stayed home with the windows shut in literally stifling conditions. A fear of crime, then, can lead you to take steps which, in these cases, led to an increased risk of death or poor health (Klinenberg 2003).

Bearing in mind that people can be prepared to make such extreme sacrifices to avoid becoming a victim of crime, this returns us to the question of why it is that crime is so feared. So far we have Bentham's suggestion of the 'boundless injury', which I read as the concern to avoid a situation which chaotically spirals beyond one's control or even influence. Yet I cannot help thinking Bentham is missing something in this analysis. Boundless injury can be threatened by a tornado, a flash flood or a shark, and these are also terrifying to contemplate. Yet the fact that a crime is something one human being does to another seems to add a further moral and political dimension. And this can also make us disproportionately concerned about criminal incidents which do not engender such extreme fear: where the loss is known to be relatively insignificant or bounded. It is, then, necessary to take a deeper look at risk, anxiety and fear in relation to crime.

Is the problem that in picking on you as a target for his or her crime, another person treats you in a particularly undesirable way, showing you lack of respect, or contempt? This is a helpful thought, and, indeed, is something that struck Jean-Jacques Rousseau:

> As soon as men began to value one another, and the idea of consideration had got a footing in the mind, every one put in his claim to it, and it became impossible to refuse it to any with impunity. Hence arose the first obligations of civility even among savages; and every intended injury became an affront; because, besides the hurt which might result from it, the party injured was certain to find in it a contempt for his person, which was often more insupportable than the hurt itself.
>
> (Rousseau 1973a [1754], 90)

Do we fear crime, in part, because we fear the contempt of others? This may be getting closer but it still doesn't, though, sound quite right. To see why, it might be useful to start by thinking of the difference between being a victim of an attempted crime, which has been foiled perhaps by preventative measures, and being a victim of an actual crime. In both cases one has been victimized, but there is an important difference. In the failed attempt, one may be rather shaken but there may also be a rather triumphal feeling 'I got the better of him!' When the crime is successful, there is no such comfort. Victims of crime – and here we need to recognize that things differ case by case – report shock, anger and trauma, even for relatively small losses. People also report in some cases a feeling of violation, and even humiliation and shame. There is something about becoming a victim which is particularly upsetting. Contempt is shown even by an attempted crime. A successful crime cuts deeper. It seems to be an assault to the self, even to the point of putting one in a different category – that of a victim (which may go some way to explain why victims of crime are more likely to suffer repeat crime).

It would be wrong, I think, to say that people have a fear of becoming a victim: the fear is of loss or injury. Yet, as it were, on top of this there can be a very strong aversion to being made a victim. A minor example of the same thing might be those people who cannot bear being teased, or being duped by a street magician, in that, perhaps, it undermines their sense of themselves and their dignity. In the case of becoming a victim of crime one looses the sense of being master of one's own fate. Furthermore one can become the object of pity, which many people can find diminishing. But most all, another person has treated you with contempt, and has succeeded in doing so. As just noted contempt is expressed even through an unsuccessful attempt at crime. But when the attempt is successful perhaps one begins to harbour the thought that the contempt is deserved. If I am unable to protect myself, what sort of person am I? A successful crime seems, in at least some cases, to bring about a change in status and in self-respect. It is, in this respect, transgressive and disruptive of the social order.

PUNISHMENT

Of course what I have said about what it is to be a victim of crime is only one account, and it may capture only a proportion of crimes. I hope, though, that the analysis will ring true. For – and this is a point not always acknowledged in discussions of punishment – unless we know why it is we find crime so disturbing it may also be difficult to understand our practices of punishment, and especially imprisonment. As I write the number of people in prison in England and Wales is at near record levels, around 85,000, and the trends suggest that it will continue to rise (NOMS 2010), although the current government seems to be hoping to reverse the trend somewhat. A rising trend, however, is rather odd, as surveys suggest that crime is falling, or at worst, levelling off. However, over recent decades sentencing policies have hardened, with a higher proportion of custodial sentences, and longer terms, and this is enough to raise the prison population, irrespective of falling crime.

Is 85,000 people in prison a lot or a little? In objective terms it is hard to say. They would all fit into London's Wembley Stadium. At the moment the US has over 2 million in jail, which is not far short of 1 per cent of its population, proportionally about five times as many as the UK. On the other hand France, Germany and Italy all imprison a smaller proportion of their citizens than the UK (ICPS 2010). It may also be that they all have lower crime rates, but such comparisons are difficult as statistics are not all collected on the same basis.

Prison: what a strange thing it is. I can remember my shock as a child being told that some adults had done things which were so bad that they had to be locked away, for years, until they knew better. I could hardly imagine anything worse, and I still struggle with the idea. Prisons seem to belong to the age of the horse-drawn cart and the workhouse, not Eurostar and the Internet cafe. If anything, we should be trying to phase them out – converting old prisons into luxury apartments, like unused warehouses and deconsecrated churches – but instead we are building more and more, although, apparently, not enough to cope with the doubling of the prison population over the last thirty years.

Why, then, do we send people to prison? When philosophy students are taught about the justification of punishment, they are told that there are three main theories of punishment: deterrence, rehabilitation and retribution (see, for example, Honderich 1971). Society sends people to prison to deter others from the same act, to reform criminals into model citizens, or as an act of pure punishment to exact retribution. A fourth theory, sometimes called 'incapacitation theory', sometimes makes an appearance – we put people in prison because we are fed up and need a break from having to deal with them. We need to take criminals off the street. A fifth theory is also becoming better understood: that punishment is essentially a special sort of act of communication (Duff 2001). Ultimately I will defend a version of such a theory, but in the meantime, let us see how well we manage with the other approaches I have listed.

It is useful to classify approaches to punishment as either 'forward-looking' or 'backward-looking'. Forward-looking justifications see the point of punishment in terms of what it may achieve for the future: essentially less crime. Deterrence, reform, and 'keep 'em off the street' are all of this nature. Backward-looking justifications, such as retribution, pay attention to what has happened in the past, rather than the possible effects of punishment, and see punishment much more in terms of desert. On such a view those who have broken the law deserve punishment, irrespective of whether doing so will serve to discourage future crime.

We noted earlier that one of the reasons why the prisons are becoming more crowded in the UK is that as a matter of deliberate social policy, judicial action has been more punitive, with a higher proportion of custodial sentences, and sentences of greater length. The reason for this increase seems to be forward-looking, at least in part, which is to say to reduce the rate of future crimes. But of course, if imprisoning individuals is to have an effect on the future crime rate then at least one of the deterrence, rehabilitation and 'keep 'em off the streets' arguments would have to be effective. Of these, hopes must lie primarily with the deterrence argument. For only a very small proportion of those who break the law in the UK actually find themselves in prison. Therefore rehabilitation, even if effective, which it probably is not, could only have a marginal effect on future crime rates. For the same reason, our society manages to keep only a small proportion of offenders off its streets.

The theory of deterrence, quite obviously, suggests that a society should set its sentencing policy to put people off breaking the law in the future. As clever philosophy students point out, the obvious conclusion is that every crime should be a capital offence, or at least punished by the heaviest humane sentence possible. Here we might look to the US, where conservative commentators claim that the heavy sentencing filling their prisons is having a dramatic effect on the crime rate, which has been falling consistently from the early 1990s. (Readers of Levitt and Dubners' *Freakonomics* will be aware of another putative explanation: that legalizing abortion led to falling crime, by reducing the number of unwanted, neglected, children (Levitt and Dubner 2005).) But whatever the truth about the US, the salient point is that if a sentencing policy is put in place in order to modify future behaviour, then it presupposes an understanding of the springs and wheels of human motivation. Roughly, deterrence theory presupposes an economic model of human behaviour, and in particular that, if an action brings with it some probability of cost, then the higher the cost and the greater its probability, the less attractive that action will be. If I am thinking of stealing your car, then the higher the sentence on conviction, and the more likely I am to be detected if I try, the less likely I am to attempt to do so. This theory of motivation seems to be so obvious as to be banal. It is also at the foundation of the UK government's crime strategy, for without it, or something like it, changing sentencing policy will not affect the crime rate. The fundamental assumption of deterrence theory is that would-be criminals carry out a little cost–benefit analysis of their intended criminal action, and will refrain from it if the potential costs or risks are too high. A simple, elegant, theory. But is it true? It is, after all, both a philosophical theory of motivation and an empirical claim which can be tested.

Consider a study by Danny Dorling who made a detailed examination of the rising rates of murder in Britain in the 1980s and 1990s. During this period, in which rates of poverty and income inequality grew, so did the murder rate. The new victims, however, were highly concentrated among men of working age living in the poorest parts of the country, and whose death gave very little, if any, benefit to their murderers. Most of these murders were not premeditated but acts of sudden violence – scuffles, fights and chaotic incidents stumbling out of control. Dorling argues that the deeper cause here is inequality. Not simply poverty, but poverty and low status in a generally more affluent society (Dorling 2004).

But whatever the deeper causes, if Dorling is right about the nature of the new murders, then sentencing policy will not halt an increasing murder rate. Perhaps only contract killers conduct a cost–benefit analysis, and, possibly, better detection or heavier sentencing simply puts the price up. Murder, though, may be a special case. The conviction rate for known murders is very high, and the justification of punishment in such cases is much more likely to be 'keep 'em off the streets' rather than deterrence. Yet the message of the example remains: until we know why people are committing crimes we do not know whether changes in sentencing policy will lead to changes in crime rates. The crux is whether the economic model of calculation of consequences is really true of individual motivation.

It may help to make use of a distinction made by the legal philosopher H.L.A. Hart in his masterpiece *The Concept of Law* (Hart 1997). Hart argued that we need to distinguish two different attitudes people can have to the law – what he called the 'internal' and the 'external' attitudes. The internal attitude is held by those who identify with the laws of the land, and think of them, in some sense, as 'my own'. To have this attitude to the law is to see it as an absolute constraint on one's actions. Typically, those with this attitude do not weigh up whether or not to obey the law, and decide that the benefits of obedience outweigh the benefits of breaking the law. Rather they simply do not contemplate courses of action that involve a breach of the law. By contrast, the external attitude is quite different: essentially it is to see the law as attaching costs, or at least risks, to desired actions, and the higher the risks attached to breaking the law the more likely one is to obey it. This is, it seems, the economic cost–benefit analysis. Perhaps, indeed, part of the nostalgia for the past is for the thought that in the good old days many more people would have had the internal attitude to the law, but the cynicism of the current age has eroded it beyond repair.

We need, though, to add some further categories to Hart's pair. We have already seen, in the case of murder, that a third attitude is possible, neither internal nor external but chaotic – what we might call the 'disconnected' attitude. Disconnected actors act on impulse or anger or pride, without much, if any, thought to the consequences. Crimes of passion. Finally, arguably there is the 'anti-authoritarian' who takes pleasure or satisfaction in breaking the law; the excitement of taking a late night drive, with friends, in a clapped-out Ford Fiesta comes not from the thrill of the car, but from the fact that it is stolen.

It may be that no individual fits purely into just one of these categories. A successful middle-aged businessman might take the internal attitude to private property law: it just never crosses his mind to shoplift, say. At the same time he might take the external attitude to various aspects of tax and business law, and will cheat if, but only if, the chance of detection is very low. Yet, perhaps, he also loses control from time to time at home, and has been known to threaten his wife. Finally, maybe he has the odd puff on a joint, taking pleasure in reminding himself of his more bohemian youth and partly in protest at what he thinks are overly intrusive drug laws.

I won't speculate on how many people will recognize something of this in themselves, but we do need to consider one objection to the idea of the internal attitude: that it is really the external attitude in disguise. Consider a pillar of the community who is caught shoplifting. The scandal and reputational damage would be immense. One can imagine it leading even to bankruptcy and divorce in the most extreme cases. The cost, therefore, is not simply that of a fine or prison sentence, multiplied by its probability, but the cost of a possible criminal record, reported in the local newspaper and made known to family, friends and acquaintances. For those with a respectable life, the cost of a criminal record is so overwhelming that no benefit to be obtained by shoplifting could possibly outweigh it. Therefore the reason why the cost–benefit analysis is not done – that theft is never even considered – need not be that the person strongly identifies with the law, but that it is known in advance how the calculation will turn out, so it is not worth bothering with.

Let us, therefore, distinguish the 'pure internal attitude' from the 'impure internal attitude'. We are now in a position to consider the circumstances under which increasing sentencing and improving detection rates will deter crime. People with the pure internal attitude are not going to break the law in any case, so we can leave them to one side. Equally, sentencing policy is not going to have much effect on those with the impure internal attitude. Whether a prison sentence is a week or six months makes little difference, for reputational damage is done as soon as an alleged crime is reported.

It is those who have the external attitude who could be deterred by changing sentencing policy: the assumption, after all, of deterrence theory is that we all have the external attitude. Yet as we saw in our speculations about contract killers, potential criminals could change their behaviour without giving up crime. If theft is punished more severely, perhaps now is the time to change to fraud. Policy makers always have to consider that attempts to modify people's behaviour may do so in unexpected ways. Next, we must consider those with the 'disconnected attitude'. It is, however, more or less a datum that changing sentencing policy will not affect the incidence of crimes of passion, and the like, so we can move on quickly, to the final category, the 'counter-authoritarian', where matters are complex. If some people break the law because they enjoy doing so, what effect would an increase in the sentence have? Possibly it could increase the thrill; possibly it could make it too risky. Cases differ and it is hard to generalize.

We can see, therefore, that if the government wants to reduce crime by increasing sentences and the chances of conviction, it had better make sure first that a significant number of potential criminals really do behave according to the axioms of classical economics. This may, of course, be true of career criminals, white-collar fraudsters, and the like, but rather less so of drug-addled burglars, teenage vandals, and Friday-night drunks. Indeed it is worth reflecting on one of the most robust crime statistics: there are far more offenders among men in their teens and early twenties than in any other group. In other words, people grow out of crime. Why should that be? In the framework of this discussion we can make a plausible conjecture: as one gets older one is more likely to adopt the internal attitude, if not in its pure, then in its impure, form, where the costs of a criminal record are too high to risk. That is, there comes a time when many people have too much to lose, and no longer have to do an individual calculation of each potential crime to know that it does not pay.

These speculations, however, can be partially confirmed and partially corrected by the results of a survey of research on these issues, carried out for the Home Office (von Hirsch et al. 1999). Three findings stand out. First, it appears that if potential offenders believe that detection rates are improving, then crime does fall. This result applies across the board, including, surprisingly enough, crimes of passion. Perhaps those who know that they cannot control their passions can, at least, engage in a bit of personal cognitive behavioural therapy, and avoid situations where their passions might become inflamed. The second finding is that lengthening sentences seems to have little or no deterrent effect. Presumably few would-be criminals mug up on the latest sentencing guidelines before picking up their swag bags and setting off. Finally, the more extensive a person's social network – job, family, friends – the less likely he or she is to commit a crime.

All of this seems to reinforce the point that what seems to matter most is the impact a criminal record will have on other aspects of one's life. The nature of the punishment is barely here or there. As the bishops have told us for years: the best way to reduce crime is to 'give everyone a stake in society'. In the terms of this discussion, it means either making people feel members of a society in such a way that they strongly identify with its laws, or by changing their situation so that a criminal record, in itself, would be too damaging. Those with a decent job, a pleasant home, a supportive family and a flourishing social life are less likely to want to risk it all. But in the shorter term, these findings suggest that we would do more to reduce crime by switching resources away from prisons to police on the beat.

Punishment as deterrence, then, needs to be handled carefully. There seems little doubt that punishment acts as a deterrent, but oddly, as we saw, the claim that increasing punishment will increase deterrent values may not be borne out, as it presupposes an account of motivation that may not be true of many criminals. However, we have not yet looked at retribution, a backward-looking justification for punishment.

Retribution relies on the idea that criminals should be punished because they deserve it; they should be made to pay for their crimes. It is associated with the biblical 'lex talionis' of 'an eye for an eye'. As such, it has tended to make liberals extremely uncomfortable. Many people will reluctantly accept the necessity of judicial punishment if some future good will come of it: reform, deterrence or less crime. But imprisoning someone simply because we as a society seek retribution seems almost barbaric. Surely, it will be said, we are past that now, and if punishment serves no future purpose, then, it serves no purpose.

But the argument just given may be too quick. Think again back to the discussion of the first part of this chapter, where the question was asked 'what is so bad about crime'? Now, as far as the deterrence argument is concerned, there is not much need to answer this question. If crime is a bad thing then we ought to do what we (reasonably) can to stop it. It doesn't really matter what makes it bad. However, on the retribution argument, the issues are very different.

For consider that the main contention of the argument of the early parts of this chapter is that what is so bad about crime, or at least some crimes for some people, is the fact of being made a victim. It is not so much that others attempt to treat you with contempt, but rather that they manage to do so. This is why, we suggested, there is such a psychological difference between failed attempts and successful crimes. In succeeding in their crime against you, perhaps, they implicitly announce themselves as in some respect your superior. They have victimized you, and left you in a lowered status. Even when there is no identifiable victim – as in the case of vandalism of public property – the successful criminal implies that in some sense he or she is above the norm, or, at least, above the rules. Crime communicates a message.

Now, of course, there is little evidence I can present to demonstrate that criminals do view themselves in this way, but let me suppose that the description I have given has some sort of ring of truth. If so, then punishment appears in a new light. For at least part of the purpose of punishment then becomes to re-establish some sort of proper status between all the parties. If a criminal is caught and adequately punished he has no longer got away with something. He can no longer implicitly claim to be of higher status, and those who were victims may feel that their victimhood is expunged, and they have their previous status restored to them. What, though, of crimes where, at the time of punishment, there is no single identifiable victim – either because there never was (tax fraud) or because the crime involved their death (murder)? The analysis nevertheless still applies in modified form. In the standard case, where there is an identifiable surviving victim, punishment 'rebalances' status by raising the standing of the victim and lowering that of the perpetrator. In cases where the victim is dead, nevertheless the punishment can still show that we as a society take that life very seriously. Consider, by contrast, racist societies where murders of members of an ethnic minority are barely investigated, and so in effect, a powerful signal of lower status is communicated. In cases of victimless crime, all that can be done is lower the standing of the perpetrator, but this remains a significant matter. The echo of retribution is, presumably, the greater the crime, the more is needed to restore the moral balance.

Here, then, we see a connection with the communicative theory of punishment. If crime sends a message, so does punishment, standardly an attempt to send a counter-message, cancelling out the first message. Of course what counts as an 'adequate' punishment is very hard to define in this context, and is highly likely to be context dependent. For one thing, to return to the topic of imprisonment, we tend to forget how recently prisons were introduced for ordinary criminal punishment. After all, they are very expensive, needing guards, secure buildings, and a whole infrastructure. Prisons are a luxury. In earlier centuries forms of physical punishment, such as branding or flogging, were the norm, or execution for what would now be considered relatively minor crimes, or, at some points in history, transportation (Foucault 1991 [1975]). Given the massive historical range of punishments meted out for the same offence, it seems very unlikely that any particular punishment is 'natural' retribution for any particular offence. But the general point is that in any society some level of punishment will be recognized as adequate, and once a criminal has received their sentence, 'justice has been done' the victim's status restored, where possible, and the criminal's reduced.

In sum, retribution, understood in its communicative form, may be somewhat less barbaric, as a justification of punishment, than it is sometimes thought. Of course, the argument I have given depends entirely on the account of the badness of crime I offered being broadly correct, or at least in the right ball park. If not, then this particular defence of retribution disappears. But note too that there is no reason why one cannot offer more than one justification for punishment. Retribution and deterrence can be used alongside each other. And there is also a good moral case for rehabilitation, especially for younger offenders, although the sad truth is that it rarely appears effective.

CONCLUSION: LESSONS FOR PHILOSOPHY

What, then, do we learn as a result of this chapter? The lesson, I believe, may be very obvious. It is about the relation between philosophy and theory of human behaviour, and the danger of hidden assumptions. We can illustrate the point by considering the general approach followed by Jerry Bentham of the relation between philosophy, psychology and law. Philosophy tells us what goals we want to achieve. Psychology tells us what people are like. And law tells us how we must arrange our institutions if we are to achieve our goals, given what people are like (Bentham 1996 [1781]).

As with much of Bentham's thinking there is wisdom and a pleasing simplicity in these ideas. Yet we need to be careful. It doesn't seem true that philosophical thought alone can tell us what we want, or, rather, what we want to avoid. Psychology is needed for that too. Further, although Bentham was right that psychology tells us what people are like, the truth is often more complex than philosophers or lawyers might like it to be. In relation to this chapter we saw that psychological input was essential in several places. For one thing, in trying to analyse what is so bad about crime, it seems very hard to make sense of how badly we take victimization unless it somehow affects people's sense of themselves and their status, at least in some cases. (I do have to concede, though, that my account was speculative rather than research based, and therefore violates my own warning of the importance of seeking empirical support for such claims.) Further, while it may seem obvious that increasing sentences will have a greater deterrent effect it doesn't actually seem to be true. This can be explained when we start to break down the reasons why people obey the law, and notice how little difference severity of punishment is likely to make in many cases.

Coming to an understanding of human psychology very satisfyingly allows the theorist to link an account of the justification of punishment with one of what is so bad about crime. Boiled down, the message is this: applied political philosophy needs to understand human motivation, but a bad theory of motivation can very easily lead to deeply misguided social policies.

6
Health

INTRODUCTION

In 2008, before the US health-care reforms, a taxi driver in Florida told me that the United States had the best health system in the world. The only trouble, he said, is that a huge number of Americans can't get access to it. Does this mean that the US had a good system or a bad one? How can we tell? How can we know whether a society has a health system of which it can be proud?

There are, of course, many statistics that bear on the question of how to assess the quality of a nation's health system. The USA spends a greater proportion of its GDP on health care than any other nation. According to the World Health Organization (WHO), in 2006 it spent 15.3 per cent of GDP, compared with 8.2 per cent in the UK. The second highest-spending major country, as a proportion of GDP, was France, with 11 per cent (WHO 2009, 107–9). Even though it is largely a privately funded system, the US government even spends more money per citizen on publicly funded health care, largely through Medicaid, Medicare and medical support for veterans, than the vast majority of other nations (including even the UK on its National Health Service (NHS) in 2006) (WHO 2009, 110). Despite this, it is widely believed that there is something seriously amiss with the US health system. But what is the best way of revealing the problem? Life expectancy in the US, according to the WHO, was seventy-eight in 2007 which puts the US outside the top twenty of medium to large nations. The UK does better at eighty, with Japan, New Zealand, Australia, Canada, France and Sweden better still. The US, in fact, is at the same level as Denmark (WHO 2009, 38–45). The Danes, of course, are not happy to do so poorly, comparatively to the rest of Europe, but, nevertheless, there is less general sense in Denmark than there was in the US that its health system is in serious crisis, with a need for root-and-branch reform (Juel et al. 2000).

The obvious difference between pre-reform US and the rest of the OECD countries, of course, is that it was (and actually, still is) the only member without universal health care. Many millions lacked health coverage and many more had inadequate insurance – something they only discovered when they attempted to make a claim. Even those with high-quality insurance coverage could find claims exceptionally difficult to pursue and settle, and maximum limits of care could force very hard decisions. It seems clear that anyone designing a health system from scratch would not have dreamt of the US system; it probably would not even have occurred to them as a possibility to be rejected. It is still far too early to tell whether the recent reforms will provide a substantial improvement.

In some respects, and although we are living at a later time with many significant differences, the pre-reform situation in the US resembled the situation in the UK before the introduction of the NHS, in which access to health care was very uneven, and many, especially women, were left unable to afford routine care (Webster 2002). The introduction of the NHS had many beneficial effects. However it has not solved one of the problems it was introduced to address: inequalities in health. A series of studies have suggested that inequalities in health in the UK actually widened after the introduction of the NHS, and they remain a problem (Black et al. 1982; Acheson 1998). It is tempting to think that the problems within the US health-care system would be solved by universal health care. But, it appears, this was not so in the UK. Sixty years on we are still struggling. This, quite likely, should also raise questions about priorities for further reforms both in the UK and the USA and throughout the world.

Indeed, the debate on health-care reform in the US creates a dilemma for those who regard themselves, as I do, as 'progressives' about health and social policy more generally. On the one hand, it seems obvious that universal health care is essential to any civilized country; a universal human right to medical care appears in Article 25 of the Universal Declaration of Human Rights (United Nations 1948). On the other hand, many progressives also believe that the relation between health and health *care* is problematic. In general, what makes people ill is not the absence of health care. Poverty, poor nutrition, poor living and working conditions, and unhealthy behaviours, and so on, may be much more important determinants of health than access to health care. This is the thesis of the 'social determinants of health' (Marmot 2004, 2006). For some theorists, we have got the balance completely wrong. For example it was even suggested in the 1980s that the best way to improve health in the UK would be to divert spending away from hospitals towards social services. This seems to have been the view of sociologist Peter Townsend, one of the authors of the Black report, to which we will return (Berridge 2010). The argument has been made again very recently in the context of where government cuts should fall to do the least damage to health (Stuckler *et al.* 2010).

Other philosophers have understood the importance of the social determinants of health and have attempted to build them into their theories. Most notably, Norman Daniels rewrote his book *Just Health Care*, calling it *Just Health*, in explicit recognition that many of the most important determinants of health fall outside the realm of health care (Daniels 1985, 2007). But few philosophers have addressed what seems to me to be the central dilemma for progressives in the light of the social determinants of health. Why should we put so much emphasis on the issue of universal health care if it is likely to make relatively little difference to health and life expectancy compared to other factors? That question is the key focus of this chapter. We might ask why it is that a broad coalition of people have put so much energy into the issue of universal health care, arguing for vast resources to be spent, rather than pursue other progressive causes such as reducing long-term unemployment, or poverty? I'm not suggesting that we should abandon the goal of universal health care, but, assuming the critics are right that it makes relatively little difference to population health, why do we give it such emphasis?

Of course, in saying that health care makes relatively little difference I do not mean that it never makes a difference. For a given individual health care can be a matter of life or death, such as in the case of emergency surgery, or chemotherapy. It can provide people with the ability to manage a chronic health condition so as to live a relatively normal life (think of diabetes, or, now HIV/AIDS), and can provide relief from distressing conditions. But at the population level, health care looks like poor value for money in delivering health outputs.

HEALTH AND HEALTH SYSTEMS

Before looking in more detail at questions of policy we need to look at some background, definitional questions. In particular we need, briefly, to ask: what is health, what is a health system, and what is the relation between the two? The definition of health, of course, is a highly contested matter. Intuitively health is often thought to be the absence of illness, disease and disability (each of which then needs further clarification). The WHO continues to define health much more expansively as 'a state of complete physical, mental and social well-being and not merely the absence of disease or infirmity' (WHO 2006). In practice, however, the WHO has taken a more pragmatic approach to the understanding of health, as have national governments, such as the UK, when they compute the health benefits of various possible interventions. For example, when health economists from the UK National Institute for Health and

Clinical Excellence attempt to determine the QALY (quality-adjusted life year) value of an intervention, they evaluate health quality according to what is known as the EQ-5D instrument, which offers five dimensions of health: mobility, self-care, usual activities, pain/discomfort and anxiety/depression (NICE 2008). The idea is not so much that these dimensions provide an analytic definition of health, but rather if something is a significant health condition – and in the current international classification of diseases there are many thousands – it will show up in at least one of these dimensions. The advantage of EQ-5D is that it goes beyond 'absence of disease' in its incorporation of mental (pain, anxiety, depression) and some social elements (usual activities) while remaining fairly precise. Although debatable whether it is extensive enough, it will be adequate for the discussion in this chapter.

If the definition of health can be dealt with reasonably easily, what can we say about a health system? It is becoming a commonplace now to distinguish 'health' from 'health care', and so there is a question of whether a 'health system' is the same as a 'health-care system'. To explain, as we have already noted, there is increasing understanding that many of the determinants of health lie outside the province of medicine narrowly conceived. Nineteenth- and twentieth-century improvements in life expectancy have come at least as much from improvements in sanitation and basic hygiene, and from safer working and living conditions, as from medical developments such as the discovery of antibiotics and improved surgical techniques. Estimates vary about the contribution health care makes to population health. For example, in responding to scepticism about the role of science and technology in contributing to beneficial health outcomes, the WHO reported that 'scientific and technical progress explained almost half of the reduction in mortality between 1960 and 1990 in a sample of 115 low and middle income countries, while income growth explained less than 20% and increases in the educational level of adult females less than 40%' (WHO 2000, 9). Now there is a lot to discuss in these results, and we will return to similar issues, but here all we need to note is that other factors beyond health care can and do influence health to a very significant degree.

If it is clear that many of the determinants of health fall outside the health-care system, then it would seem wrong to identify a health system with a health-care system. Consider some of the major factors in the current assessment of the global burden of disease, such as lung (and related) cancers and road accidents, which according to the WHO are both in the top ten causes of death in the world (WHO 2008). Of course, medical professionals will offer care, to improve recovery and survival. Yet the main determinants of lung cancer and road deaths clearly fall outside of the health-care system. Should we say, nevertheless, that steps to reduce such deaths fall within a country's health system? Intuitively, some aspects fall more naturally into that classification than others. For example, public education about the effects of smoking seems a clear health initiative, whereas the design of a traffic system that makes overtaking safer would not normally be thought of as part of a health system. However, insofar as road safety reduces death and disability, it is arguable that an expansion to the notion of a health system is acceptable. For an even more difficult example, it is becoming clear that female literacy is an important factor in child health, as the WHO notes. Should we, then, say that a country's education system is also part of its health system? This may seem rather odd, in that as was pointed out during debates at the foundation of the NHS, if a child is ill, he or she cannot learn, and so by the same logic the health system should be part of the education system.

The WHO includes in a health system all the organizations and institutions within a society that have the *primary purpose* of improving health. This would include, for example, health-and-safety interventions in the workplace, but not routine education. But still, this may seem overly restrictive. After all many aspects of a society make a great difference to health – especially negatively – without that being part of their primary purpose. Instead, the following working definition of a health system will be adopted: a country's health system comprises those elements of a society which can be influenced by government action and are likely to have a significant impact on health (as defined by EQ-5D or similar measures). Clearly a country's health-care system will be included, as will other aspects of government action that impact on health, such as road safety, tax policy to influence the consumption of alcohol and tobacco, and environmental protection. And obviously such matters as the political decision to have a system of private health insurance, a state-funded system, or universal insurance will be part of a health system, on such a view. However this greatly expanded notion of a health system encompasses a huge range of activities, both by the government and by businesses and individuals. To keep the discussion within some bounds I have added the idea that the impact on health must be 'significant' if the activity is to fall within the health system, although I will not attempt to say any more about what counts as 'significant'.

INEQUALITIES IN HEALTH AND THE SOCIAL DETERMINANTS OF HEALTH: THE UK EXPERIENCE

Before the foundation of the NHS, health care in the UK was patchy, uncoordinated and enormously unequal. There were inequalities not only between the rich, who could pay for hospital treatment, and the poor, who at best had to rely on charity, but also between the insured working man and his uninsured wife and children, who were not covered by the policies provided with the National Health Insurance scheme running at the time. Part of the purpose, therefore, of the NHS was to address inequalities in access to health care between rich and poor, and to bring women and children into a universal scheme, free at the point of use. In this way the NHS was committed to equality, and every citizen, rich or poor, male or female, had the right to receive attention in proportion to need.

The Black report, published in 1980, revealed that even after three decades of the NHS, severe inequalities in health remained, and in some respects inequalities had widened (Black et al. 1982). The first message of the Black report is that equal access to health care does not automatically produce equality in health – far from it. The second message is that on just about every indicator there is a 'social gradient' of health, corresponding to social class. In 1980 the higher one's social class, the better one's health and the longer one lived. Members of the professional classes, both male and female, had fewer days of sickness and restricted activity than those even one step below them on the ladder. The pattern is replicated all the way down the scale of the occupational classes. The data paint an unrelenting picture of health inequality, and indeed, inequality moving in the wrong direction. It appears that the NHS had improved the health of those in the higher social classes, while making little difference to those of other classes. This is a surprising, even paradoxical result, as the professional classes had good access to health services before the NHS. The difference, it seems, is that the better-off made use of preventive measures and benefited from public health initiatives, while those of lower social and economic strata did not, or at least not in a way that significantly improved their health.

It has already been noted that access to health services has rather less effect on health than one might otherwise have assumed. But in a way the point is obvious. If you do a physically demanding and dangerous job and live in unsanitary housing, unable to afford healthy food, then while a health service might patch you up, as needed, its effects on your health will be fairly marginal. Doctors and hospitals can put you back on your feet; they rarely control the factors that put you on your back in the first place. The Black report argues for a shift in attention from intervention in the mechanism of disease after it has occurred, to the conditions leading to disease and illness.

What, then, are those conditions? 'Lifestyle' has to be a major cause of the social gradient: there is a social gradient in smoking, heavy drinking and poor diet, and that will exert it effects. Yet broadly unchosen working and living conditions also clearly have an influence. The Black report puts at the centre of its analysis the social determinants of health: the social and material factors which are causally responsible for ill health. It is hard to resist the conclusion that the causes and remedies of much illness, disease and disability lie outside the immediate scope of the health services. For this reason, the Black report, which had been commissioned by the Labour government, argued for massive public investment in anti-poverty action to address health inequality. Received by Margaret Thatcher's incoming Conservative administration, which was in no mood to increase public spending, the recommendations were rejected. Indeed, the government in effect attempted to suppress the report by releasing it with little publicity and in a poorly produced edition with a small print run. This tactic backfired when the newspapers treated the attempted cover-up as a story in itself, and so the contents of the report received unexpected attention.

The arguments were repeated, however, in the more recent Acheson report of 1998, which presents a very similar picture, making numerous recommendations for poverty reduction as a means to health improvement. What we can think of as the 'first wave' of the social determinants of health highlights the 'material social determinants of health', rooted in material poverty and life conditions.

Yet it appears that not all health inequality can be blamed on poverty or physically hazardous working conditions. The 'Whitehall studies' – large-scale studies of the health and mortality of British civil servants – were commissioned to investigate the phenomenon of 'executive stress': the hypothesis that those at the top of organizations suffered from damaging levels of stress, and therefore would be more likely to suffer from heart attacks than others in their organizations. The researchers, however, found the exact opposite. Permanent secretaries (the highest civil service grade) had better health than undersecretaries, who had better health than their deputies (on average, of course), and this gradient was replicated all the way down to the post room. Presumably the myth of executive stress is partly a result of the fact that when the boss has a heart attack everyone gets to hear about it, but the further down the hierarchy you are, the less impact your illness makes. It seems that not only is the gradient not the result of differential access to health care, it cannot be explained by poverty or hazardous working conditions. All those studied were well above the poverty line, and all worked for the same, considerate employer: the British civil service. There must be some other factor, or series of factors, at work.

One possible variable is pure status. Another is the control you have over your working life. Quite possibly the lower your position in the organization the less control you have, and this will greatly influence levels of chronic, unrelenting stress. The executive might suffer from acute stress, having to make a hugely important decision from time to time, but once the decision is made, relaxation is possible. Those under continuous daily low-level stress get no relief and no opportunity to recover. They may suffer lowered immune response, and problems with digestion and sleep. High demand, low control, low reward and low support are said to be the 'toxic combination' that causes chronic stress. Such arguments constitute what can be called a 'second wave' of the theory of the social determinants of health, where psychological factors, rather than material ones, partially determine health outcomes. The presence or absence of supportive social networks seems to be a further determinant of chronic stress, in that those with supportive networks will be able to achieve better relief from stress, and thereby, on this understanding, better health too (Marmot 2004, 2006).

HEALTH SECURITY

The sceptical argument about health care that we have sketched becomes clearer at this point. If health is largely socially determined, then health care is much less important to health than it may have appeared. In which case, one might wonder why there is so much fuss about universal health care? Why put so much money and effort into it if its effects are so marginal? The reply is twofold. First, the effects in terms of health may be highly significant for particular individuals, especially in terms of quality of life. Second, universal health care has other beneficial effects, even if they might not be in the most obvious places to look. To see this I need to introduce the notion of 'health security' (here I develop an account first set out in Wolff and de-Shalit 2007).

The term 'security' is widely used in contemporary political discourse and social policy. The term 'social security' has been used for decades, and more recently it has become common to talk of 'fuel security', 'food security' and 'water security'. Security, broadly, is the inverse of risk or vulnerability, and the effort to think through how it is that exposure to risk can make people worse off is a very fruitful one, especially in relation to thinking about health. Here we shall look at the adverse effects of what could be called the lack of 'health security'. Now at the present time when the term 'health security' is used, it is normally done so in a sense closer to 'national security' than 'social security', in relation to major public health threats: pandemics, bioterrorism and climate change are all threats to public health security. So the term has connotations that are not part of the present meaning. But here we are interested in what we can call health security at the level of each individual.

No individual can have complete health security. Whatever access someone has to medical services, no one can be guaranteed health. Indeed, even when receiving medical attention, all that an individual can be offered is a chance of recovery, whatever the procedure, however tried and tested. Of course, an individual's chances of recovery can certainly be changed by medical attention, generally, although not always, for the better (for ways in which doctors may do harm see Illich 1977, and Wootton 2006). But there is more to health security than health, and in particular four dimensions should be distinguished: vulnerability, control, resilience and anxiety.

To take the four dimensions in turn, the first, vulnerability or the probability of falling ill, is revealed through normal monitoring of health outcomes, which is the subject of epidemiology. Almost all health statistics that are presented to the public – the extent of a flu epidemic, cancer survival rates, the global burden of disease – are examples of statistics that will give some indication to individuals of their chances of suffering from various conditions, dependent on certain further facts about them. This dimension is captured by the normal work of epidemiology, and although there are numerous theoretical questions about the capture and presentation of such data, and puzzles about how to allocate individuals to groups in order to assess their risk, we need not pursue these issues here.

The second dimension of health security, which we referred to as 'control', is the cost and difficulty of mitigation strategies to reduce health risk. Within a society different individuals face different challenges in trying to reduce their health risks. For example, even though it is well known that smoking is a very significant cause of lung cancer, smoking is much more common among some social groups than others. For this reason epidemiologists want to know not just the causes of illness, but what they call the 'causes of the causes'. Why is it that low-income women smoke so much, compared to other groups? There are, of course, various hypotheses, which we cannot explore here. But the point is that variation between groups within a society suggests that people in different situations face different types of challenges in trying to control their health risk, and that there may be instruments or mechanisms within a government's control that can influence how costly or difficulty it is for people to adopt mitigation strategies to improve their chances of a healthy life. If it is very difficult or costly for you to change your health-related behaviour, then you have low control over your health. If it is relatively easy and cheap, then you have high control.

There are very obvious connections between the 'first wave' of the social determinants of health, and this second dimension of health security: the cost and difficulty of taking steps to control health. Those who live in poor housing (damp, unsanitary, overcrowded) performing demanding work in dangerous conditions, and with little income to buy expensive, healthy foods, or leisure to relax or take exercise, surely have less control over their health and hence less health security than others, in that steps they need to preserve their health are more costly or difficult than for other groups.

Those who become ill through lack of control will show up in standard epidemiology under the first dimension above (vulnerability). But what will not show up in health statistics is the cost individuals may have faced in order to try to control their risks. So for example, people who are frail typically are more vulnerable when walking in bad weather. As a result, such people who include many who are older, living on their own, and not possessing a car, will stay at home rather than risk injury from a fall. This reduces their opportunities for social interaction, and increases loneliness, which is a cost they suffer in order to preserve their health.

Now it might be said that it is rather harsh to consider loneliness caused by fear of injury when outdoors a failure of a health system. That point, itself, is arguable, but I use it for illustration. Similar remarks could be made about those who refuse to take a relatively well-paid job because of hazardous working conditions, and can find only poorly paid work. Or about someone on a low income who spends a high proportion of it on healthy food and thereby cannot afford other sources of enjoyment. Or someone who prefers not to join in a heavy-drinking culture and has difficulty maintaining a social network with colleagues. These are all ways in which an individual's attempts to reduce their health risk add non-health costs to their lives.

Some of these elements are under greater government influence than others. For example the Acheson report of 1998 argued that the EU Common Agricultural Policy made certain healthy food choices more expensive. If this is so, we can see it as a defect in a health system, broadly conceived. Similar remarks can be made about exercise. The configuration of towns and cities can make it more or less easy for people to build exercise into their normal daily lives. So, for example, it is all very well to encourage children to walk or cycle to school, but if education policy results in children attending school far from home, such policies are unrealistic. The public health mantra of making 'the healthy choice the easy choice' – renamed by Thaler and Sunstein 'libertarian paternalism' (2008) – reinforces the point that the second dimension of health security (an individual's ability to control their health risks) is very often under the influence of governments, in that it can make certain choices easier or more difficult. This is not to say that health considerations should be decisive in all public policy decision-making. But such things should figure in what could be called a health security audit.

The third dimension of health security was termed above 'resilience', which in this context essentially means people's ability to 'bounce back' after an adverse health event. It has two aspects that could be represented as separate dimensions, but are so close that to do so may seem artificial: these are the consequences of ill health, and the costs and difficulties of taking steps to mitigate those consequences. The consequences of illness themselves can be divided primarily into three categories: medical, social and financial. Medical consequences include the physical and phenomenological aspects of illness and recovery, including the standard of care one receives. Social consequences include the attitudes of those around you, including family, friends, workmates, shop assistants, and so on, which can make illness harder or easier to bear. Finally, the financial consequences include not only potential loss of income, but in some societies, the expense of medical services themselves. Each of these three elements, even the attitudes others hold towards you, can be greatly influenced by government policy.

In terms of an individual's ability to mitigate the consequences of illness, once more we can distinguish medical, social and financial aspects. The medical aspects include one's ability to access care and to take advantage of it. Social aspects include government initiatives to educate the public about illness, in order to reduce the stigma, say, of cerebral palsy or mental illness, but also steps it might take to help (or hinder) individuals' ability to form a supportive social network, whether in terms of support groups or more generally. Financial aspects include the cost and availability of medical and unemployment insurance. I will say more about these financial aspects under the final dimension – fear and anxiety – and for the present will concentrate on access to, and use of, care.

A good deal of work has been undertaken exploring de facto inequalities in provision of health-care services, and, by implication, differential health security. There are concerns about access in rural areas, and concerns about the supply of female doctors among some immigrant communities where women are reluctant to consult male doctors about, for example, cervical screening (Acheson 1998). There are concerns about striking the right balance between large centralized hospitals with highly specialized services and small, less well equipped, local hospitals making visiting much easier. There are concerns about the take-up even of free services when to do so means missing a day's work and pay. This is all well-trodden ground, and all affect health security by making it more costly or difficult for some individuals to influence their health by seeking cures. Here, though, I would like to highlight what appears a less well documented aspect: ability to follow doctor's advice.

I rely on the somewhat disarming observation that before the introduction of antibiotics, doctors had few tools in their armoury. Often advice would be: to put heat on it, put cold on it, take some exercise or take some rest. This, it has been said, is not far from the ancient theory of the four humours. Even these days, unless you have a condition that is amenable to surgery or to antibiotics or to counselling, very often there is little the medical profession can do for you except to advise you to rest so that the body's natural recovery mechanisms can do their work. On the basis purely of conjecture, it seems to me likely that one important determinant of health is the opportunity to take time out of work and domestic duties in order to let physical systems recover. Someone on minimum income with no sick pay, or a young mother with no one else to look after her children, can hardly follow doctor's orders to rest. The point was very well-made more than a hundred years ago by George Bernard Shaw, in his play The Doctor's Dilemma. Here Blenkinsop, a doctor with a practice in a poor neighbourhood, says to his old friend Ridgeon, a fashionable high-society doctor: 'My patients are all clerks and shopmen. They daren't be ill: they can't afford it. And when they break down what can I do for them? You can send your people to St Moritz or to Egypt, or recommend horse exercise or motoring or champagne jelly or complete change and rest for six months. I might as well order my people a slice of the moon' (Shaw 1946 [1906], 109–10). A little later Blenkinsop reveals that he himself is unwell and, being of very low income remarks: 'If a fortnight's holiday would save my life, I'd have to die' (Shaw 1946 [1906],134).

Quite clearly a health system can influence people's ability to rest, through provision for sick pay and for domestic support for mothers and other carers who otherwise cannot escape their duties. In fact here we might see why social networks are so important for health. Those with good social networks, with family or supportive neighbours, are more likely to be able to take a complete break from domestic duties in order to recover. How important this factor is remains to be seen, but it may have been relatively neglected to date.

Finally, to turn to the fourth dimension, we must add the more subjective element of fear or anxiety. In many cases people fear or become anxious about falling ill. Sometimes the fear or anxiety attaches to the illness. Many people, for example, have a particular fear of cancer. Sometimes fear or anxiety attaches not to the direct experience of illness, but to its adverse consequences. This can include how it would affect one's relations with family or workmates, but also its potentially ruinous financial consequences. One of the arguments for the UK National Health Service was precisely that it took away 'money worries'. People on low income simply had no idea how they would be able to pay for a doctor's services. Not only did this mean that such people often delayed treatment until it was too late to do anything, but also they 'worried themselves sick'. That is to say, worry about the consequences of illness can be a cause of illness, both mental and physical. As we saw, it has been argued that chronic stress suppresses the immune system, making stressed individuals more vulnerable to illness (Wilkinson 2001). Hence a system of universal coverage, free at the point of use, is good for individual health even if no one takes advantage of it. (Note that systems with significant 'co-payments' – contributions from patients – lose this advantage.) A system in which medical bankruptcy is a possibility – especially a common occurrence – is one that does poorly on the 'resilience' dimension of health security; and if people live in fear or anxiety of such outcomes, does poorly also on a further dimension, fear and anxiety.

Anxiety, is, in fact, important in three different ways. First, as we noted at the beginning, the standard 'instrument' for measuring health – the EQ-5D – includes depression/anxiety as a dimension of health. So where there is significant anxiety this in itself counts as detrimental to health. Second, even if the anxiety does not reach 'measurable' levels nevertheless it can induce chronic stress, and suppress the immune system, leading to other health problems. Finally, even when anxiety has no adverse effects on health, it can be a significant reduction in well-being. Here, then, is another effect of the health system that would not be captured in straightforward health data.

CONCLUSION: LESSONS FOR PHILOSOPHY

Health-care reform has been extensively discussed in the US. As an issue it is politically highly charged, emotional and criss-crossed with the vested interests of those who would lose out if the system was reformed. After all, huge amounts are presently being spent, and they must be going somewhere. Those who advocate universal health care take its importance largely for granted. Yet experience in the UK suggests that, in terms of health improvement, the results of universal health care may be disappointing. But this is not a reason for abandoning the goal; rather it is a reason for being clear about what the policy can reasonably be expected to achieve. In the terminology of this chapter, universal health care will significantly improve individual health security especially in one important dimension at least: anxiety. Health worries are bad enough; coupled with 'money worries' they can be stultifying. Universal health care can improve the quality of people's lives, of which improvements in health may be only part.

From the point of view of this book, the methodological lesson is, once more, the necessity to look at evidence. It is amazing how often the obviously true turns out to be false, on inspection, or at least problematic. In this case it seems obvious that the main value of universal health care is the health benefit it brings. But the evidence suggests that access to health care is but one, and possibly not the most important, determinant of health. Yet, it seems, it is also a determinant of other things, especially ease of mind. Understanding the notion of health security enriches our understanding of the casual frameworks in which health and health care stand. We can begin to see how other types of government action can impact – positively and negatively – on health, and how the availability of health care can impact on well-being. But the route from goals to policy reforms is a tortuous one, and many types of evidence must be brought to bear on the questions.

7
Disability

INTRODUCTION

What is it to be disabled and what should society provide for people with disabilities? This, quite clearly, is a topic of great importance in the real world. In the UK at present there are over 10 million people with a 'limiting long term illness, impairment or disability' (DWP 2010), and a huge amount of financial resources and other forms of support and effort are devoted towards making the lives of people with disabilities better than they otherwise would be. Of course we might wonder whether all these people really are disabled in any significant sense. But obviously very many people do suffer from some form of disability. But do we do enough for people with disabilities? And do we do the right things?

It is, of course, well known that until fairly recently it was standard practice for people labelled as disabled – especially, but not only, those said to have mental disabilities – to spend their lives in special institutions, often in semi-rural settings or on the edges of towns, where they lived with other people in similar conditions, and with those who were there to take care of them. Unless they had first established a life elsewhere they would have been unlikely to have friends outside the institution, and visits from family members would typically have been special occasions, such as weekend afternoons, rather than built into the fabric of everyday life. Such places were often called 'asylums' as if they were places of special retreat and protection. In the analysis of some critics, though, the reverse is true: they allowed members of mainstream society to take refuge from those people who were disturbing to deal with. Thus, it is claimed, the main function of homes for disabled people was to ensure that the rest of us need have little to do with them. In the worst cases they were likened to prisons, with inmates having no rights to leave.

This changed during the 1980s with the Conservative government policy of introducing 'care in the community', strengthening individual rights, and closing down many such facilities. No doubt there were economic motives behind such changes, but whether intended or unintended, they have done a certain amount to bring disabled people into contact with broader society. Yet the transition is only half made. In many cases disabled people see few people other than family members, service professionals, and other disabled people at day centres. To some degree, day centres have taken the place of homes for the disabled, in that they keep disabled people occupied, but away from non-disabled people (Duffy 2010). Imagine yourself in the shoes of a person who attends a day centre. It is likely that you will be collected by a coach or minibus, which then winds round town for an hour or two picking up others. On arrival at the day centre there may be a visit from reluctant school children, required to help out as part of a social education programme, or from volunteers or others who will engage on a variety of levels, but often tending towards the patronizing end of the spectrum, while watching television fills the empty spaces. You would be fed a meal of a quality you almost certainly would not have paid for, followed by an afternoon of cursory activities, under the heading of 'occupational therapy', which is halfway between nursery school and the hospital ward. Then back into the coach for a couple of hours, before being dropped off to watch some more television in your parents' home.

Are we doing the right things? What else might we do? The treatment of people with disabilities appears to be a question of justice, and, one might think, contemporary theories of distributive justice should put the question of what society should do for people with disabilities at the forefront of concern.

That is what one might think. The reality is somewhat different. The topic of distributive justice in contemporary political philosophy takes its lead from John Rawls, and, especially, his *A Theory of Justice*, first published in 1971. But in order to present and defend a compelling general theory of justice Rawls had to restrict the scope of his theory in several ways, making a number of simplifying assumptions. For example, he assumed that there was no immigration or emigration (and hence no question of the wealthy selling up and leaving if they did not like the tax regime). He also ignored all questions of foreign relations, including war and trade. But, more importantly for present purposes, he assumed that everyone in society is within the normal range of health, and he took this also to mean that no one is disabled (Rawls 1971, see also 1999b, 259, and 1982, 168). He assumed this not because he thought it true – it is obviously false – but because it would allow him and his readers to concentrate on what he took to be the central cases of justice. Once we are clear about the central cases, argues Rawls, we can drop the simplifying assumptions and extend the scope of the discussion to cover other cases.

Of course, one can argue about what the central cases of distributive justice are. If one thinks that distributive justice primarily concerns what society should do for those who are unable to look after themselves, then concerns for people with disabilities should be right at the core. On the other hand, if, like Rawls, the subject of distributive justice is how to share out the benefits and burdens of social cooperation, then those who are not part of the scheme of social cooperation – including many disabled people – will not be central to the topic of distributive justice. Their needs, claims and rights will have to be dealt with as some sort of special topic.

Although Rawls later on in his life discussed some of the cases excluded by his simplifying assumptions, such as global justice in his late work, *The Law of Peoples* (1999a), he never did address issues of disability in any detail. However, the challenge was taken up by other theorists, including Ronald Dworkin. In his writings on equality, Dworkin begins by contrasting two quite different approaches to the understanding of equality, which he calls 'equality of welfare' and 'equality of resources'. Equality of welfare is the theory that the goals of equality will be achieved when everyone has achieved the same level of (subjective) welfare, by which Dworkin means happiness or preference satisfaction. Equality of resources, by contrast, supposes that equality requires everyone to have equally valuable packages of resources, suitably understood. Dworkin raises a number of powerful objections against equality of welfare, including a detailed discussion of some of the difficulties in formulating a plausible account of what equal preference satisfaction would even mean. For this and other reasons, equality of resources is Dworkin's favoured approach (Dworkin 1981a, 1981b).

Within Dworkin's theory there are two types of resources: what he calls 'external resources', such as money and wealth, and 'internal resources' which include skills and talents. To simplify, Dworkin's view is that those who are disabled lack *internal* resources, and so need to have extra *external* resources to compensate them for the lack, if everyone is to have an equally valuable 'bundle' of resources. Much of his discussion concerning disability consists in setting out – by means of a hypothetical insurance market – a proposal for determining the right levels of tax and transfer to compensate for disability.

Dworkin's proposal is extremely ingenious, and beautifully worked out, although the details need not concern us here. Yet there is something doubly troubling about it. First, he does not provide any analysis of disability, and appears to assume that disability consists purely of a physical or mental impairment, now often known as the 'medical model' of disability. This contrasts with a 'social model' in which disability is, at least to a high degree, 'socially constructed', in the sense that the way we have fashioned the world, both physically and conceptually, makes it more suitable for some groups than others. On the social model, at least in its radical form, 'society disables people'. While it is true that people are born with different physical and mental capacities, what one can do with those capacities depends on a whole range of social, material and cultural factors. A number of philosophers have taken this approach to these issues, often through their own experience of disability either personally or through family, and these philosophers have greatly influenced my own thinking on these issues (Asch 2001; Bickenback 1993; Kittay 1999; Silvers et al. 1998; Tremain 1996). However, the philosophical mainstream of thinking about distributive justice has taken a while to absorb their insights.

To see the importance social, cultural and material factors can have for the experience of disability, consider a study comparing paraplegia in urban Sydney and rural Cameroon. Sydney is well-adapted to the needs of people who have severe mobility difficulties, who consequently suffer relatively little hardship. In Cameroon, physical immobility is experienced as a humiliating nightmare, leading to exclusion from virtually all aspects of life (Allotey et al. 2003). One can even imagine society becoming adapted to such an extent that the difference between those who use wheelchairs and those who do not becomes one of the same order as that between those who wear correcting lenses for their eyes and those who do not. Conversely, imagine what the world would be like now if correcting lenses had never been discovered.

The first difficulty with Dworkin's discussion, then, was the assumption of the medical model of disability. The second is that Dworkin's approach to disability appears to consist of transfers of cash from the able-bodied to people with disabilities. While this may well be part of a useful set of social policies it hardly seems complete. Indeed, we can now see that it might have been inaccurate, after all, to describe Dworkin as holding the 'medical model' of disability, for if he had held this view one would expect his remedy to be concerned with research and therapies of various sorts to cure, or at least reduce the impact of, disability through medical and other professional means. But in fact he seems to regard medical need as just one of any number of factors that make disability expensive and that make it reasonable to think of dealing with disability in terms of increasing the income of people with disabilities. This, we might say, is to adopt an 'economic' model of disability. Being disabled makes life economically harder: your expenses increase and your earning power typically falls.

As noted, cash transfers of this sort are likely to be welcomed by those people with disabilities who do find themselves with high expenses and/or low income. And one can also imagine a society where medical services and other forms of therapy are provided entirely on the free market, either by 'out-of-pocket' expenses or insurance, and so the use of such services requires extra income. Yet there remains a great deal of current social policy that cannot be dealt with by individual purchase. In the medical field, for example, research typically requires public, collective investment, unless it can be supported by a business model that will show how, eventually, it might turn a profit. Casting the net more widely, much disability policy now focuses on accessibility of workplaces, changes to building codes, specialized computer software, inclusive design, and other measures that reduce the impact of impairment. Cultural changes involve such things as the abandonment of stigmatizing language, such as the terms 'cripple' or 'spastic', and educating schoolchildren into more enlightened attitudes towards people who are different from themselves.

With these examples we can in fact, see the two criticisms of Dworkin coming together. If there is more to disability than increased economic expense, then it is not unreasonable to think that solutions focused on each disabled individual might go about matters the wrong way. If the source of disability is 'the world' rather than 'the person' then intelligent social policy may well aim to change the world, rather than compensate the disabled person.

Dworkin bases his approach to disability, we noted, on the theory of equality of resources. Would he have done better to adopt equality of welfare rather than equality of resource? If anything, this might make things even worse. Dworkin himself puts forward the objection that the condition of people with disabilities might be so grim that vast social resources might need to be spent to bring them up to a level of equal happiness or preference satisfaction. Indeed, this may be true in some cases, although individuals will vary greatly in this respect. Equality of welfare seems to mean that we should transfer everything we can to people with low welfare, provided that doing so brings them closer to everyone else in terms of happiness or preference satisfaction. But there is also an opposite difficulty too. Insofar as it can be quantified, people with physical disabilities have, in some studies conducted in the developed world, tended to report a similar level of satisfaction with their lives, at least in some types of cases, as people without disabilities (Albrecht and Devlieger 1999). If this is so, then the approach of equality of welfare would seem to have the most counter-intuitive consequence: that justice does not require any special treatment for people with disabilities. Of course if they were particularly unhappy or lacked preference satisfaction then there would be a case, but this would be in virtue of their misery or dissatisfaction, just like anyone else, rather than their disability. Here, then, is a problem. If we restrict our attention to theories of justice that measure well-being in terms either of resources or of subjective satisfaction then it is not obvious that they provide a sound justification for what are generally considered to be enlightened forms of disability policy, those of making the world more accommodating to people with disabilities. These are policies that, in effect, try to change the world to make disability disappear. It is not that resource- and welfare-based theories rule out such approaches, but rather they do not give them any special prominence. We will return to this below.

And there is a quite different problem too, not just for Dworkin's theory but any theory of justice which is critical of the existing social order. For illustration, suppose we agree that a just society is one that achieves equality in some respect. Yet existing societies are very far from doing so. We still observe inequalities due to race, gender and social class, and differential earnings that do not seem to be defensible in terms of any theory of justice. This then raises the question about how to deal with a special topic of justice such as disability. How can we expect to be able to achieve complete equality in distribution between able-bodied people and disabled people in a world where there are many other unjustified forms of inequality? Many would argue that these inequalities are quite unjust, yet we are far from eradicating them, even though most theories of justice call for the abolition of these social and economic equalities.

Of course as theorists, we can set our sights high, and insist that society should aim to remove all injustice. But if that is so, it is hard to work out how to make policy recommendations about disability. Should policy makers first attend to the inequalities that are most pernicious? But how do they decide which they are? And once they are identified should they ignore all else? In particular, those who have a special interest in achieving equality for people with disability may then find themselves on the sidelines. For perhaps racism, sexism and extreme poverty could be determined to be more important. How can theorists of disability formulate a goal of equality for disabled people without giving priority to campaigns to eliminate all inequalities?

We are considering, then, disability activists who are especially concerned about disability, but are prepared to concede that the problem of inequalities between those who do and do not have disabilities is not necessarily the most urgent problem of injustice that society faces. How should they then attempt to influence social policy? There would be something unappealing about attempting to hijack social policy to give priority to those who, in the broader context, might not have the most urgent claims. Yet it would also seem wrong to abandon the claims of people with disabilities until they became the most urgent social priority. Those who wish to take on such a role of special advocacy seem, then, to face a difficult dilemma. In practice disability activists have tended, implicitly, to occupy a middle ground. While accepting that the world at present is unjust, and it will take a great deal of time, energy and resources to come close to justice, and also accepting that other claims could possibly be more urgent than those of people with disabilities, nevertheless it seems possible to argue that the world should not be *especially* unjust to people with disabilities.

To explain, even if we may have to accept that it may be impossible, at least in the short to middle term, to eradicate all injustice, it may be possible to remove special injustice such as that towards people with disabilities. One way, then, of embedding the discussion within a realistic context is to adopt, for practical purposes, an approach that we could call 'pragmatic equality': that justice for people with disabilities requires that disability does not add to the other injustices in the world. On such a view, although theorist and policy maker very reluctantly accept that inequality exists, at least for the foreseeable future, injustice should not be made worse still by the existence of disability. Another way of thinking about it might be to say that a world that is (pragmatically) equal in respect of disability should contain the same degree of inequality between disabled people as there is between able-bodied people. Disabled people should be able to do as well as non-disabled people, given their race, gender, talents and social group. It might seem rather uncomfortable, perhaps even cynical or hypocritical, to acquiesce in other forms of injustice while insisting on justice for people with disabilities. However, first, even achieving pragmatic equality would be a terrific advance for many disabled people, and, second, ideally at least this is offered as a short-term goal rather than a model of a just society.

DISABILITY, INDEPENDENCE, INCLUSION

I suggested in the last section that the mainstream egalitarian literature, represented by Rawls and Dworkin, does not generate a promising approach to disability. Even Dworkin's position does not provide any obvious justification for social policies that go beyond transfer of financial resources. Yet if we look to see the social policies we have in place, they are very varied. They include, at one end, forms of surgery and other therapy to improve physical or cognitive function, through personal support, such as carers or extra income, to changing the material and social environment, such as making the workplace accessible and prohibiting subtle forms of discrimination. Within the disability-activist movement key concepts are 'inclusion' and 'independence' (Shakespeare 1998, 2006, but also see MacIntyre 1999 on the role of dependence in all human lives). On the face of it these ideas might seem to push in different directions, in that inclusion emphasizes taking one's place alongside others, whereas independence seems to have the opposite connotation. But in fact, both of them have a common root: the idea of being able to live a normal life, which, generally, has elements both of inclusion in society and independence in the performance of the tasks of normal life, in a complex balance. On this analysis people with disabilities simply want to take part in the life of society, on the same terms as others.

Our immediate problem, however, is that, as was implicit in the earlier discussion, the philosophical conceptual vocabulary derived from Dworkin's work on equality does not take us as far as we need to go in thinking about these issues. To make progress we need, somehow, to construct a bridge between philosophical theory and real social policy, if we are to be able to think about policy options in philosophical terms. To begin, let us accept that the current, relatively modest project of pragmatic equality is, in effect, one of assimilation: to make the world just in respect of disability is to ensure that people with disabilities have a similar package of opportunities to those who have similar talents and attributes but are not disabled. To make progress on such a project, we need to ask what it is that determines any individual's opportunities. Crudely there are two sorts of factors we need to enter into the calculations: what the person has and what they can do with what they have.

Dworkin's language of resources is a helpful first step in the right direction. As we saw, for Dworkin this includes both external resources – money, control over parts of the external world, etc. – and 'internal resources', such as talents and abilities. However, resources on their own are not enough to determine an individual's opportunities. For as Dworkin would be the first to admit, you also need to know facts about the structures operating within that society: laws and customs, the influence of tradition, religion, language, culture and other social norms; the configuration of the material and natural environment, and perhaps other things too. Slightly misleadingly, we can refer to all of this as 'social and material structure' (sometimes 'social structure' for short). Thus the overall formula comes to this: your opportunities are determined by what you can do with your internal and external resources, given the social and material structure within which you find yourself. Together, resources and structures create paths of varying cost and difficulty. Your resources are what you have to play with; the structure provides the rules of the game.

Accordingly, we can see that if someone is thought to be lacking in opportunities, then, in principle, there are at least three spheres in which we might try to address this: internal resources; external resources and social structures. An attempt to remedy disadvantage by means of adjusting internal resources means, in effect, acting on the person (which, of course, is something agents may do for themselves in some cases). This would include education and training as well as medical and surgical intervention. This, for obvious reasons, we can call 'personal enhancement'.

Action focused on external resources can take at least two main forms. One, of course, is cash compensation, in which individuals are given money to spend as they like. Yet, to introduce the second, individuals can also be provided with resources with strings attached. For example, some students with learning disabilities are given cash to spend only on computers, or are given a computer. But this is not intended as a grant of a piece of private property, with all the rights normally associated, but rather the use of an object for a particular purpose and not for others. They cannot, for example, sell the computer and use the proceeds for buying beer, or even food and books. There are many similar examples, including loaning disabled people wheelchairs, or the provision of state-funded carers who are employed to perform some services but not others. So for example, a disabled person cannot order his or her carer to work for someone else or hire them to the highest bidder. Granting people resources with use restricted in such ways we can call a 'targeted resource enhancement'.

Finally there are ways of improving an individual's opportunities without changing his or her resources. We can, in effect, change the rules of the game so that people can do better with the resources they already have. This could be the result of a change in law, or social attitudes, or a change in building codes to replace stairs with ramps or to widen doorways. Perhaps no term is perfect for this, but here we can call it a status enhancement. Status enhancement is, of course, the remedy favoured by those who advance the social theory of disability. Consequently there are at least four distinct strategies for attempting to address lack of opportunity: personal enhancement, cash compensation, targeted resource enhancement, and status enhancement. All of these are possible strategies that can be used in helping to overcome the disadvantages of disability. But are there reasons to use one, in particular circumstances, rather than another?

CHOICE OF STRATEGIES

Deciding between strategies will sometimes be easy and sometimes difficult. Sometimes it will be obvious that one strategy is not feasible or its cost is prohibitive. So, for example, although personal enhancement in the form of a medical cure will often seem the obvious approach, there are always limits to medical science and therapy, and there will generally come a point where personal enhancement has nothing to offer, or even where attempts to improve someone's life will be counterproductive by requiring lengthy and intrusive intervention for negligible benefit or even risk of harm. For this reason some people with physical disabilities prefer to get on with their lives as they are, rather than go through medical intervention. But status enhancement also has its limits. For example, it may be that rendering a historical town centre accessible is impossible with current technology, given the configuration of buildings, and the only option would be to demolish everything and start again. Refusing to do so would seem reasonable, although it would not be reasonable to refuse to relocate important public services to accessible locations. Considerations of cost – financial and social – will often rule out some possible strategies.

Yet even among feasible options cost may not be the only factor. Sometimes it is not impossible that we might prefer what appears to be a more costly strategy to a less costly one. For different strategies seem to have quite different underlying assumptions and can send different messages. To see this, consider the contrast between the strategy of personal enhancement and the strategy of status enhancement. The medical model of disability, in proposing that we act upon the person normally through surgery or other medical attention, provides a good example of personal enhancement. Disability, wherever possible, should on this view be 'cured' by medical attention. Opponents of the medical model, however, often point out that it appears to suggest that there is an 'ideal' way that people should be, and that those who do not meet that ideal are 'defective' and need to have those defects removed, as far as possible, through medical attention. Hence people with disabilities often find the assumptions of the medical model deeply disturbing, for it has the implication that they are defective or abnormal and need to be fixed before they can play a full role in society.

In contrast, the social model of disability proposes that we modify not the individual person, but technology or laws, the built environment or public understandings – in the terminology of this chapter, to attempt status enhancements. Status enhancement seems much more tolerant of people in their differences than policies of personal enhancement and so sends much more of a pluralist, inclusive message. Hence those who accept the social model of disability suggest that society needs to adapt itself to accommodate people of all types. If it is successful in doing this then the concept of disability can be rendered obsolete by making different body types (and perhaps, although this is more problematic, levels of cognitive ability) irrelevant to people's ability to pursue their opportunities in life.

The social model is, therefore, humane and optimistic. It is an extremely welcome corrective to the thought that disability is, above all, a medical matter, requiring surgery or other forms of medical treatment. Let us provisionally (for we will see some difficulties shortly) assume that status enhancements are generally to be preferred to personal enhancements. Can we understand why this is so in the terms of philosophical theory discussed so far? The answer, I think, is that both theorists of equality of welfare and of equality of resources can show that their theories are consistent with such social policies. But a third theory – known as the capability theory – is often thought to do better still.

To show this, assume, then, we favour the theory of equality of welfare. If we also accept the goal of 'pragmatic equality' – that people should not suffer further disadvantage on the basis of disability – the idea would be to ensure that people with disabilities do not suffer welfare losses relative to others in virtue of their disability. One obvious source of welfare loss would be the frustration of not having access to roles in society, such as in the workplace or in politics, that are open to others. Status enhancement, where successful, will equalize the playing field in this respect. It removes forms of effective discrimination, whether deliberate or the unintended consequences of other decisions – such as the decision to have stairs at the front of a building – taken for what are otherwise good reasons. Opening opportunity reduces a potential welfare deficit for disabled people, and so moves society closer to pragmatic equality of welfare. Accordingly those who favour a welfare measure should support status enhancements. Therefore, it seems, welfare theory can provide a philosophical foundation for enlightened social theory after all.

Now, it would be possible to end the search for a philosophical foundation at this point. But it would be a pity not to pursue things further, as it seems that resource-based theory is in an equally good position to provide a philosophical foundation. For consider someone who cannot work, because physical immobility prevents them – literally – from entering the workplace. They suffer, in Dworkin's terms, from reduced internal resources. But what would happen if modifications to the workplace mean that they are now able to work? At first sight this seems to be a social improvement that leaves their resources untouched. But it could equally be represented as a change that has revalued their internal resources; indeed this is how Dworkin would view the matter. Without access to the workplace their skills and talents are worth little. Once access is granted, their skills and talents are suddenly worth much more – as much as anyone's who has similar training and so on. Accordingly anyone who accepts pragmatic equality of resources has reason to support status enhancements too: in the best case it brings the value of the internal resources of people with disabilities to the same level as those who otherwise have a similar background. Again, it can equally provide a philosophical foundation for status enhancement. Now we appear to have more than one.

This may seem a surprise. I suggested above that both welfare theory and resource theory are inadequate to conceptualize disability. The reason for rejecting these approaches, we saw, is that the problem that people with disabilities face is not that they have less welfare than others, for they may or may not. Equally, it was said that disability is much more than a matter of economic loss. These criticisms often lead to the further insight that the main problem with being disabled is the inability to do things that others take for granted. To be disabled, on such a view, is to lack the capability to function as others do. And, to follow on, those philosophical theories that concern themselves with capabilities – most notably in the contemporary literature the views of Sen (1980, 1999) and Nussbaum (2000, 2006) – seem much more appropriate to ground the type of social policies that would be generated by the 'status-enhancement' approach. Those who are unable to take part in the economic or political life of their community lack a capability to function in particular ways, and this is the best way of theorizing their loss, so it is often argued.

The key insight of capability theory is that what matters to human beings, at least as far as the government is concerned, is what they can 'do and be'. Of course, it is important that human beings have high levels of welfare, and adequate resources, but resources are only a means to do things, and welfare levels are too uncertain to be directly distributed by governments. By focusing on capabilities, government can do its best to ensure that all citizens have a rich range of opportunities, which they can then use as they choose to pursue their own ideas of what is worthwhile in life. On this view disability policy should be designed to improve the capabilities of people with disabilities. Status enhancement – removing obstacles – is an important way of boosting capabilities.

How, then, do we reconcile the objections to welfare and resource theories with their apparent success in providing a foundation for policies of status enhancement? The link between the theories is this. If one lacks capabilities to function then, very typically, one will have lower welfare, because of the frustration and the lack of access to sources of satisfaction. Equally one may also lack resources, because of reduced access to the labour market and thus reduced ability to earn a living, as well as – following the argument used above – lowered value of one's 'internal resources'. Hence both welfare and resource theories are consistent with policies of status enhancement. But the problem is that they are also consistent with other approaches too. Suppose we are primarily interested in individual welfare. It appears, though, that welfare can be increased, not by giving people a capability to function by a reconfiguration of the workplace, but by leaving the workplace as it is and compensating disabled people for their lack of access with more welfare by other means: more holidays, better entertainment, and so on. If there seems to be something objectionable to that approach (at least when status enhancement is possible), then it seems we do not accept welfarism, at least in simple forms.

And, of course, a parallel argument can be made for resource-based theories, such as Dworkin's. Although Dworkin could support policies of status enhancement as a way of improving the resource share of people with disabilities, it appears that this approach to disability theory, as he used it himself, more naturally leads to policies of cash transfer. If we feel that this is problematic, and that status enhancement is to be preferred, then once more it appears that capability theory, rather than resource-based theory, provides the best foundation for status enhancement as an approach to disability. If these arguments are successful then an important move has been made. For what it means is that by looking at better and worse policies to deal with complex, real-world cases, we have found reasons for preferring one philosophical approach over another. And, in turn, philosophical theory can help us articulate the reasons why one approach is preferable to another. Apparently we have discovered a perfect marriage between theory and practice.

REMAINING PROBLEMS

But before we get too pleased with ourselves, we must continue to ask whether we have, in fact, answered all the problems. Capability theory, we saw, naturally concentrates on giving people the ability to function in the world. But there are many 'capabilities' and there could be hard choices between them. And while we can understand what it would be to give people equal resources (equal welfare may be harder) what would it even mean to give people equal capabilities? This is a serious difficulty for capability theories of social justice, considered generally. However, for present purposes we can sidestep it. For, recall, our project is one of 'pragmatic equality': in effect trying to describe a world in which disability does not add to other sources of inequality. For this we only need to know when disability reduces someone's capability compared to other people who have otherwise similar talents and so on. It does not require a theory of complete equality of capability, although for 'ideal theory' it is an important question as to whether this could be defined.

So let us accept that the philosophical theory is not complete, but also recognize that we do not need a more complete account for present purposes. But still, there remain difficulties. For one, while the social model of disability has been a liberation for many thinkers and activists, even its defenders are beginning to become more aware of its limitations. The way in which it conceptualizes matters is, essentially, to say that human beings are born (or develop) a range of physical and mental types, and social structures 'validate' some, rather than others, by making the world a much easier place to live in for some types than others, and labelling the ones that fit in less well 'disabled'. The thought, then, is that by sensitive social change it should be possible to make the world equally hospitable for all. However, there are obvious questions as to whether this picture is not, after all, too optimistic. Consider someone who is blind, and is unable to enjoy visual experience. Now, it is often claimed that blind people find that their other senses – aural and tactile – become more sensitive as a result, and hence there are 'natural' compensations for blindness. This may be true, although it has nothing particularly to do with the social model of disability, for it states that disability in one respect leads to personal enhancement in another.

Rather, theorists applying the social model would need to argue that society can make other adjustments so that blind people can function just as well as those who can see. So, for example, screen readers for computers, the availability of books in Braille, and guide dogs provide blind people with access to much of the world that others inhabit, but in a different way. And presumably many further innovations are possible. Yet it is hard to accept that this leaves no deficit. Not to be able to experience visual beauty, in its natural, human and artistic forms, is a lack that cannot be made good by verbal descriptions or tactile substitutes. It seems simply to be the case that although social change and material change can improve things considerably for blind people, it remains that there are many valuable experiences that they simply cannot enjoy (Terzi 2004; Shakespeare 2006).

One response to this argument is that what is true of blind people is true of all of us to some degree. Who can claim to be able to experience all kinds of pleasure? Many of us will never gallop on a horse, attempt a ski jump or run a marathon. Whether it is cowardice, lack of ability, lack of effort or lack of opportunity, every human being will fail to have some experiences that others find valuable.

This is an important point. Yet it is unclear whether it rescues the social model. What it does is erode, to some degree, the distinction between people labelled 'able-bodied' and those labelled 'disabled', which is useful and important. And it also reminds us that where we draw the line is, in practice, rather arbitrary and hence, in that sense a 'social construction'. Nevertheless there are limits to what can be achieved by status enhancement, in that social change cannot eliminate all aspects of disability.

However, there are further limits to the role of status enhancement, and thus to the social model of disability. It is worth noting that all the examples that have been used so far have been of physical disability. And in such cases it is often the case that changes to the material or social environment can make particular physical functioning difficulties less 'disabling'. However, cognitive limitations are another matter entirely. Consider someone with a cognitive disability that leaves them unable to read or to understand some complex forms of reasoning. In earlier, largely manual economies, this may barely have been a disadvantage, but in modern societies differences in cognitive ability are much more important than they were. The social model, it appears, would recommend changes to the social environment that would render such cognitive limitations 'differences' rather than 'disabilities'. As noted by Daniel Wikler this might mean various changes to such things as contract law, so that there are no permanent commitments (for those with mild cognitive disabilities are likely to have great difficulty understanding contemporary contract law). But as Wikler plausibly points out, the total social cost of the change of such practices would be astronomical, leading to the end of commercial relations as we know them. Similarly, rearranging the world so that there is no disadvantage in not being able to read would appear to rule out a great deal of our most important cultural achievements (Wikler 1979).

Status enhancement is not, then, a plausible approach in all cases. For cognitive impairment, personal enhancement is surely a very likely 'first resort': forms of education and training to bring everyone to a 'normal' threshold of cognitive functioning where possible. But if this is not possible, then what? It is unlikely that there is one single answer, but the capability view helps. All theorists within the capability tradition emphasize not only the capabilities of health and life, but also autonomy and affiliation. An approach to justice for people with cognitive disabilities requires thinking through how to overcome the passivity and separation from mainstream society that people with cognitive disabilities often suffer even to a greater extent than those with physical disabilities. Some recent innovative social policies have seen those with cognitive disabilities involved in making decisions about their own care, how they will spend their time, and who they will spend it with. This is a welcome contrast to earlier social policies which saw such people institutionalized, either in full-time care, or in day care, as we noted above. More recently it has come to be appreciated that such approaches have tended to view people with cognitive disabilities as problems to be dealt with, rather than people with potential for a range of enjoyments and achievements. But it is likely that status enhancement in this case will be a matter of changing social attitudes. Other forms of support – personal enhancement, and targeted resource enhancement, in the form of social and financial support – will be important parts of any approach that focuses on the capabilities of people with cognitive disabilities.

CONCLUSION: LESSONS FOR PHILOSOPHY

What, then, have we learnt from this chapter? As a matter of personal autobiography, I started to work on issues of disability as part of a general project on equality. Without thinking very deeply about it, I had assumed that something like Dworkin's approach – in which disability is conceptualized as a lack of resources for which compensation is needed – was broadly right. But then I had the idea of looking at some writings by people who were themselves disabled, and was knocked sideways. No one seemed interested in the issue of compensation. Some seemed to have come to terms with their disabilities, to the point where they refused further medical attention, fed up with hospitals, pain and little improvement in their condition. In some cases their frustration was often partly that the world as it was configured stopped them from doing what other people could do easily, and that the attitudes others held towards them was both objectionable in itself and a barrier to progress. For a small example, people in wheelchairs often found that shop assistants spoke to them via the person pushing the wheelchair rather than to them directly (nicely captured in the title of a radio programme for people with disabilities and their carers 'Does He Take Sugar?'). To my horror I found that some academic writing on disability was completely irrelevant – possibly even harmful – to the needs and aspirations of people with disabilities. So, the first lesson was that attending to real cases, and the writings of people outside philosophy, is indispensable if we want to arrive at a sensitive understanding of problems of injustice, and to develop the right tools to understand them. And the pay-off for philosophy is considerable, in that it can help, as we have seen in this chapter, not only formulate theories, but provide arguments for and against them. The pay-off for the policy area is that it can help conceptualize, order and prioritize claims, and understand the compromises and trade-offs that might be necessary.

Following sharp on the first point, however, is the second lesson that, as we have seen in previous chapters, real-world cases come in many varieties and they might not all fit the same pattern. As Wittgenstein warned in quite a different context, it is important not to rely on a 'one-sided diet' of examples (Wittgenstein 2009 [1953], 164). In case of disability there has been a lot of focus on physical immobility, and in particular the situation of those who use wheelchairs. Arguably the radicalization of the disability movement, at least in the United States, was the result of the return to the US of many conscripted soldiers who had become disabled as a result of injuries sustained in the Vietnam war. Previously fit young men who had suffered injuries in the service of their country are a very powerful lobby, and it is no surprise that eventually they achieved sufficient public sympathy for their case to be listened to, and, to some degree, acted upon. Better accessibility in transport and public buildings has been a welcome result. Yet wheelchair users, though most noticeable, are not the only group of people with disabilities. Others have insufficient muscle tone even to sit in a wheelchair. Others have sensory disabilities but no motor problems. Others have cognitive disabilities. And so on. Just as we must pay attention to examples of people with disabilities we must also not allow the debate to become completely dominated by those with the greatest public presence or sympathy or strongest lobbying group. In particular we must avoid a 'one-size' solution. Here philosophical thinking can help. In understanding why a policy is desirable in some cases, it will also be possible to understand why it is not in others, and to gain some idea of what else should be done.

Thirdly, policies can seem more firmly based than any particular reason for them. Let us return again to the status enhancement policy of accessibility of the work place for people with mobility difficulties. As we saw, welfare theorists, resource theorists and capability theorists can all show how their theory provides reasons for this policy: typically it will improve the welfare, resources and capabilities of people with disabilities. Although, in the end, I think that the arguments in favour of capability theory are decisive, from the point of view of defending the general policy of improving accessibility it may not be necessary to settle the philosophical debate. Of course, it may be that when we look at fine details, the different philosophical approaches will entail somewhat different policies, and set out different limits and constraints. But building a wide coalition of support for the general policy is arguably more important for policy purposes than showing why one philosophical foundation for the policy is more appropriate than another.

Finally, we noted that the task of arguing for equality for people with disabilities is a problematic one. It may be possible to set out an ideal of what a just world would be, and to advocate moving to such a world. Such a world would consider everyone to be an equal, and all economic and political institutions and policies would be aimed at creating and sustaining a society of equals. Yet however attractive one finds this vision it is very unlikely that, politically, a great deal of progress can be expected. This in turn raises the question of whether justice for people with disabilities should wait until there is justice for all – a day that might never come. Instead I suggested that for practical purposes we could accept what I called 'pragmatic equality' in respect of disability, just as many societies are aiming for in the case of race and gender. That is, we should try to achieve a world where race, gender or disability do not add to the inequalities in the world. In other words, even if there are regrettable inequalities of wealth and opportunity as a result of accidents of birth and privilege, these inequalities should not be magnified by differences in race, gender or disability. Adopting pragmatic equality, at least in the short to medium term, allows one to present a political programme which is both realistic and radical, while at the same time being very hard to resist, at least by means of argument.

8

The free market

INTRODUCTION

In Chapter 4 we looked at the regulation of public safety. One reason why regulation can be necessary is that the free market cannot always be trusted to deliver outcomes that will seem to be socially acceptable. In the case of safety we noted that there are at least three reasons why the free market may go astray. First, in many cases one person's purchasing decisions will have effects on others. This is the problem of 'externalities'. An example was 'low-standard car parts' where my purchasing decisions can make me a danger to others. Second, where there is a monopoly, as for example with railway travel, there is no free market. Those who don't like what is on offer cannot find another supplier. A monopolist has huge market power and it seems generally accepted that the public interest calls for independent scrutiny and regulation. Finally, and this is a common problem with virtually all markets, there is an asymmetry of knowledge. Typically the seller of a product will know much more about it than the purchaser, and if the transaction was completely unregulated might be able to get away with selling goods that don't actually match the purchaser's expectations. As we can see these problems are not exclusive to the issue of safety; they could affect many types of products.

Critics of the market – especially capitalist forms of the market – can find other ammunition too. For example, market relations are often said to lead to injustice in labour relations. Capitalists, especially if acting in combination, have a powerful bargaining position which they can use to impose low wages and harsh conditions especially on non-unionized, low-skilled workers, for whom the only alternative is unemployment. This, of course, is a version of the classic Marxist argument that capitalism leads to the exploitation of workers. Of course a lot has changed in the 150 years or so since Marx presented his forceful case, and as a generalization it no longer seems to hold. It would be absurd for many well-paid salaried workers in the developed world to claim that they are exploited in anything like the sense Marx had in mind, even if they may have other complaints. Yet one can hardly deny that there are large pockets of the economy – and especially the world economy – where the accusation rings true. But I want to put questions of justice between worker and capitalist to one side here – important though they are – and to look at some less-discussed controversies about the free market.

The point of this chapter is to look at the wide variety of situations in which we try to protect areas of life from the encroachment of the market, and the reasons why we might limit, or, at least, try to regulate market transactions. Rather than asking the question, 'the free market: for or against?', it seems more reasonable to ask, 'the free market: when and when not?' That is our question in this chapter.

FOR AND AGAINST THE MARKET

A market transaction is a miraculous thing. If all goes well it creates what is called in economic theory a Pareto improvement (named after the economist Vilfredo Pareto). A Pareto improvement makes at least one person better off and no one worse off. A market transaction, if entered into freely and with a reasonable degree of knowledge on each side, will typically make both parties better off, and, unless there are externalities, no one else will be affected either positively or negatively. If I buy a can of drink from a corner shop, both my position, and the shopkeeper's, has improved. We are both better off than we were before, pleased to be able to do business with each other. Put this way, market exchange is almost a piece of magic, conjuring mutual benefit out of thin air.

Defenders of the market point out that it has this effect whatever the intentions of the traders. For, it is said, the market actually works best if everyone tries primarily to seek their own profits and further their own interests. The argument is that, in the long term, the only way in which it is possible to make a profit in a sustainable way is by giving people what they want. One inspiration for this argument is Adam Smith's famous observation that 'It is not from the benevolence of the butcher, the brewer, or the baker, that we expect our dinner, but from their regard to their own self-interest. We address ourselves, not to their humanity but to their self-love, and never talk to them of our own necessities but of their advantages' (Smith 2003 [1777]: ch. 1, bk 2, 119).

More recently the Austrian economist Friedrich Hayek extended Smith's argument to emphasize the benefits not just of market transactions but of the entire profit system. Hayek wrote at a time when there was keen debate between economists as to whether the free market would be more or less efficient than the centrally planned economy, of which the Soviet Union was the primary example. In the planned economy the government takes complete control, down to every last detail, of organizing the production and distribution of goods. The academic debate was generally conducted in the context of assuming perfect knowledge: that everyone knows everything relevant to the functioning of the economy. Hayek argued that such a debate was rather sterile and unimportant. Under conditions of perfect knowledge both the market and the-planned economy could be efficient. But in the conditions of the real world, where knowledge is much more limited, things are very different (Hayek 1937).

Governments have relatively little information about the needs and preferences of their citizens. Of course, the government knows that people need food, clothes and housing. But what types do they prefer? For example, do they want to live in houses or apartments? And would they prefer larger room sizes to a second bathroom? Preferences will vary between individuals, and if production and distribution is to be efficient, detailed information about preferences is needed for every person in respect of every one of the hundreds of thousands of goods produced in the economy. Yet without such knowledge a centrally planned economy becomes close to impossible. If the government doesn't know what people want, how can it plan production and distribution?

Faced with this argument, it might fairly be asked how the free market could do any better. How does a house building company know what to build? Of course it could conduct market research, but Hayek's response is that the free market, by means of the price system, has its own way of spreading information. Suppose that the building company builds a mix of houses and apartments. And suppose that the houses sell much more quickly than the apartments, to the point where the company has to drop the price of the apartments to sell them, while competing purchasers bid up the price of houses. In its future plans the company will adjust its production to maximize its profit. Other building companies will observe the situation and adjust their plans, noting that the price of houses is rising and apartments falling, and so, for the time being at least, better profits are to be made from selling houses.

Of course, things can change, and if too many companies start producing houses then the market will be oversupplied and prices will start to fall. Perhaps at that point some building companies will switch back to apartments or experiment with building offices or sports facilities. What is so interesting is that while changing prices reflect changing patterns of demand, no one needs to know that demand is rising or falling, still less collect in all information to plan the economy. All capitalists need to do is observe movements in prices and profits, and to try to maximize profit in the face of changing circumstances.

Now, it is true that over a very wide range of cases Smith's argument, expanded by Hayek, holds. Free competition and profit-seeking behaviour should drive out poor-quality goods, keep prices low, and match supply to demand. It can be an excellent way of providing value for money for consumers. However, as Smith himself was aware, there is a question of how far this argument generalizes. We have already noted that opponents of the free market allege that consumers are likely to be tricked and cheated by ruthless capitalists in an insufficiently regulated market. The mis-selling of financial products, such as subprime mortgages, is a particular recent bugbear, but the concern is much older. As we noted in Chapter 4, it seems that it took the Adulteration of Food and Drink Act of 1860 to stop publicans putting salt in beer and bakers chalk dust in bread in the UK. Competition between brewers, or between bakers, seeking their own self-interest, did not do the trick.

Both defenders and critics of the free market assume that capitalists on the whole pursue their self-interest to a high degree. Where they disagree is in their claims concerning the likely effects of such behaviour: the invisible hand, or the slap in the face. Both sides are both right and wrong. In other words, cases differ. For some goods the market will tend to drive up quality and drive down prices, but there are other goods where the market provides no such inbuilt tendencies, and, indeed, the incentives of profit-seekers will be detrimental to the interests of consumers. In these cases, assuming that we are concerned about such effects, we will need to explore alternative ways of pursuing the interests of consumers, such as common provision or highly regulated markets, rather than the free market of classical economics.

To appreciate the problematic cases, consider again buying meat from the butcher. The butcher might try to sell you an inferior cut, passing it off as the highest quality. But if you are disappointed you might try a different butcher tomorrow. The point is that the butcher wants your continued custom, and while he needs to make a profit, he has to find a way of pursuing his self-interest in a way that keeps you satisfied. In a market where people make repeat purchases, and consume the good they buy very soon after purchase, the producer has every incentive to make sure that the product is of decent quality. In fact, it is very unlikely that he will stay in business for long if he tries to deceive his customers, assuming that he has competitors.

But suppose next door to the butcher is an office selling pension plans. And as for so many of these products, the agent selling them is on commission. Suppose various different pension schemes are available, from different companies. If the companies are driven by self-interest they are likely to offer the greatest commission to the agent for the products that make them the biggest profit, rather than those that are best for the consumer. And if the agent is driven by self-interest then he or she is likely to try to steer you to the pension that gives the highest commission. As a consumer you will be able to gather a certain amount of information about the pension plan, but not very much. And you certainly won't be able to know how well it will perform in future years. You cannot even be sure whether the company providing it will still be in business when your pension is due to start paying out. In the case of the meat, if you make a bad deal you would know very soon, and take your future business elsewhere. In the case of the pension plan, you won't know for many years whether you have a good plan or a bad one, and by then it is too late to change, for you would have already sunk your money in an inferior product. With a pension plan there is a long delay between being committed to purchase, and consumption, and it is a purchase you will intend to make only once, in normal circumstances. Consequently there is no opportunity for the kind of 'evolutionary learning' by the customer that kept the butcher honest. In other words, if we assume that everyone acts out of self-interest it appears to follow that the agent will have an incentive to sell you the product that produces the highest commission and not the one that is best for you. The inexorable market logic of the pursuit of self-interest is beneficial in some circumstances but potentially very harmful to the consumer in others, especially where the purchaser makes a very significant purchase but does not consume the product for many years. Many, perhaps most, financial products are of this nature, and this is why there have been so many problems with the provision of long-term financial products for the ordinary consumer.

It appears to follow that, at least sometimes, the market cannot be left to itself to protect the consumer. Regulation is necessary, in order to ensure that producers and agents are somehow punished if they put their own interests too far ahead of the consumer. Punishment is a form of change to incentives, although as we saw in an earlier chapter, it doesn't always work as smoothly as some theories might suggest. Here though, we can take away a conclusion. At least in some cases substantial regulation, or modification, is necessary to protect consumer interests. The Smithian and Hayekian arguments are much more limited in their scope than is often assumed.

BLOCKED EXCHANGES

So far we have seen what I believe to be a powerful argument to the conclusion that at least in some cases market regulation is highly desirable. But some people go further. In some cases, they argue, there are goods that should not be sold on the market at all. This has become known as the theory of 'blocked exchanges': that there are some things that simply shouldn't be bought and sold. In recent years, this criticism has been especially associated with Michael Walzer (1983) and Michael Sandel (1998). But of course it goes back to Marx (1975a [1844]), and through Marx to Shakespeare's *Timon of Athens*, and Goethe's *Faust* from which Marx takes inspiration.

But can it be wrong to sell things between willing parties? Certainly some people think so. There are many common examples. See if you can find some plutonium on the open market. The permissibility of selling one's own kidneys has been under discussion for some time now; selling oneself into slavery for much longer. The morality of selling one's baby is an occasional theme on soap operas. But in real-life there are genuine examples of things that used to be sold which now seem amazing to us. In the nineteenth century, for example, it was possible to buy and sell a commission in the British Army (Bruce 1980). Officers were people who had bought their posts, and would sell them again. Now this is no longer the case, and the suggestion to reintroduce it would be treated as some sort of parody of free market economics. But why?

The practice was, it seems, perfectly acceptable during peace time, but not so good during wars. The army was reformed presumably because it was thought that this practice had pernicious externalities. The British started losing battles, or, at least, large numbers of people. Instead of selling commissions, the army now makes appointments on grounds of fitness for the role, which now generally permeates the entire world of work. Here, then, the argument seems to be that a market in which people can purchase posts will so clearly lead to bad consequences that this provides sufficient reason to prohibit the practice. Nowadays we may talk about equality of opportunity for its own sake, but its initial justification appears to have been to allow the rise of the meritocracy for the sake of the general good.

But can all blocked exchanges be understood in this way? Would selling kidneys or babies have disastrous consequences? Do we know this? And do such beliefs explain the positions of those who want to keep the exchanges blocked? If so, presumably, were we able to devise forms of regulated markets to ensure good outcomes only, then the opposition should drain away. Yet this does not seem likely. The undesirability of third-party effects does not seem to me to explain why so many people are resistant to a market in organs from living donors. However the more I think about it, the more convinced I am that our – or at least my – intuitions in this area are unreliable. By this I don't mean that they are wrong, but that it is rather hard to understand why we have them. In what follows I will argue that there are many different reasons for questioning particular exchanges and thus, potentially, many types of blocked exchanges. Although I do think there are moral limits to the market, the moral reasons for the limits are not always so obvious.

The most straightforward type of case is where strictly it should be impossible to purchase what is offered for sale, as the nature of the good is, for some reason, incompatible with the idea of a trade for money. Love, friendship, moral praise and salvation are common examples. Of course it is possible to buy services which superficially resemble love and friendship, and so on. Michael Walzer, for example, has discussed the practice of 'selling indulgences' in the church as a way of purchasing salvation (Walzer 1983). But, understood strictly, goods such as love are, conceptually, not available for sale. Consequently, anyone offering love, friendship or salvation for money is trying to pull off a fraud. This means not so much that we as a society must block these exchanges, but that there is a sense in which the exchange is naturally ruled out, for it is simply not possible.

But is it so straightforward? Marx writes the following:

> I am ugly, but I can buy myself the most beautiful women. Which means to say I am not ugly, for the effect of ugliness, its repelling power, is destroyed by money.
>
> (Marx 1975a [1844], 37)

Although on a first reading one might think that Marx's point is about prostitution, he seems to have something else in mind. Marx seems to be suggesting that money makes an ugly person genuinely attractive, and he may well be right, if the ugly person is sufficiently rich. Yet, he seems to suggest, this is morally problematic − as if one shouldn't become attractive on the basis of one's money. Indeed it seems implied that only one's looks should be relevant in how attractive one is to others (a view one would not normally think of associating with Marx). But the implication appears to be that anything else is a subversion or corruption.

Now whatever we think about this example, the interesting thing about it is its form. The idea seems to be that there is a proper ground for finding someone attractive. An attempt can be made to replace this ground with money, but whether or not this is successful, it is, nevertheless, problematic. We have already seen two variants of the alleged problem. First it could be conceptually impossible, or second it is possible but corrupt. How, though, can we understand this notion of corruption? The problem is made more difficult by the thought that it would now seem deeply corrupt to sell a commission in the army, yet apparently it was once common practice.

Michael Walzer, who was already mentioned with regard to selling indulgences, argues that there are several distinct 'spheres of justice' each distributing goods specific to that sphere, and regulated by its own principles. It is a form of corruption to try to use principles appropriate to one sphere for the distribution of a good in another sphere. One prominent example from Walzer is the relation between political power and money. Walzer points out that in many societies, including his own American society, not only can money help you towards political power, political power can help you towards money. Such interference between the spheres Walzer describes as 'tyranny'. This may put it a little strongly, but certainly we view it as corrupt. It seems easier, however, to say that to use politics to become rich is a misuse of political power than to say that to use money to gain political office is a misuse of money, even though we may well object strongly to people using their money in this way. Ideally it seems socially beneficial for politics to be screened off from commercial matters, even if we have happened to be rather unsuccessful in this respect. And perhaps this turns out to have some things in common with the army case after all. We don't want a political system which may lead to disaster, or even disregard of the citizens' interests, and letting politics and money mix too closely is going to be bad for almost all of us. Perhaps, then, the desire to keep politics and money apart could be explained in terms of third-party effects. Consequently it is not impossible that even this paradigm example of blocked exchanges has less to do with the intrinsic nature of the good – political power – and more to do with the pernicious effects of letting it be sold.

It is not surprising that many of the examples used in the discussion of blocked exchanges concern important social goods, such as love, or political power. But in fact there are examples of blocked exchanges everywhere. When I first started working at my university in 1986 it sold parking permits at a very cheap price to anyone who wanted one. Unfortunately, though, there were far more permits than parking spaces, and to get one required getting to work before the scientists – that is, around 7.45 – which is what I used to do. If you missed one, the only alternative short of returning home was to park in a commercial car park for what was, at the time, the astonishingly high central-London price of ten pounds a day. At that time I was reading a certain amount of economic theory and it struck me that by getting my space early I had gained possession of a scarce resource. Consequentially there could be money to be made. Suppose I let it be known that at around 9.30 I would be willing to give up my space to another, for the price of, say, five pounds. Possibly when they had got over the shock of the offer, I would find a willing buyer. This would be a Pareto improvement – I would be better off, the purchaser would be better off and no one, it seems, would be harmed. But if I had actually done this, and the university authorities discovered it, I would probably have been warned or perhaps even fired for misconduct. Hence in practice, even if not by formal regulation, an exchange – a potential Pareto improvement – was blocked.

When we start to look around, we can find many similar examples. Suppose in the rush hour you are on a crowded Tube train and a businessman in a handmade suit offers you a fiver for your seat. What would you think? Or suppose it isn't you who is offered the money, but the person next to you. And suppose the transaction is completed to the apparent satisfaction of both parties. What would you think of that? One can almost hear the murmurs of disapproval going round the carriage.

Or consider ticket touting or 'scalping'. Many find this a highly dubious activity, and it is true that it is often mixed in with various forms of deceit. But where no deceit is involved it can be hard to say precisely what is wrong with it, at least without thinking about the possible long-term effects of the practice in terms of externalities. The curious thing about the 'blocked exchanges' I have just mentioned – car-parking spaces, seats on trains, concert tickets – is that the goods involved are mundane. It is hard to say that there is anything in the nature of these goods themselves that leads us to wish to block their exchange. Do we really want to say that market transactions corrupt the social meaning of parking, sitting down on the train, or going to entertainment events? This would be nonsense. All of these goods are sold for money; the point seems to be that we accept some markets for them but strongly resist others. Why?

Now a curious thing about the car-parking example is that a few years after I joined my university the management decided to change to a new scheme, issuing permits for particular spaces at market price. The space I used to park in turned out to be one of the premium ones (well it was in the front quad, just by the portico) and was up for 1,500 pounds a year. By that time I had changed my habits anyway and was not interested in a space. Of course there was a lot of grumbling, and some insistence amongst the highest-paid staff that they should receive an increase in pay to compensate for the cost of parking. But within a year or so, paying a lot of money for a space became the established system and as far as I know it was accepted as a reasonable, if somewhat opportunist, policy.

Consider, too, the seat case. Many forms of public transport offer more than one class of comfort where more money buys you a better seat, or a better chance of a seat. It is true that there could be reasons for wondering whether such provision violates some principle of equality, expressing and reinforcing unjustified social privilege. Yet the disapproval likely to attach to making a private additional payment for a seat on the Tube train seems to go further than any disapproval about differential ticket pricing. Rather it goes to a sense that such things just shouldn't be done.

One explanation of these cases starts from the observation that where a good is scarce, any society needs a rule for its distribution. Often we use a rule which has an element of 'first come, first served'. But this is not the only possibility. Charging a market-clearing price is another. What we see in the car-parking and seat cases is that when a rule is in force, we do not take kindly to someone who tries to operate according to a different rule. It is not that parking spaces and seats should not be distributed on market pricing principles. Rather, when another rule is in place it is unfair, or possibly exploitative, to subvert it for your own ends, even if it does no one any harm. This is a third-party effect of sorts, but very different to the other examples we have seen. Were we to replace the rule wholesale with another one, then once we have got over transitional effects, we would get used to it easily enough, as we saw in the parking case. My conjecture is that the non-market rules we have in place for the distribution of scarce goods, such as 'first come, first seated' on trains, only survive because we have such strong intuitions that anyone who breaks them is doing something wrong, even outrageous. In other words we have somehow evolved a type of taboo status around the rule. Probably the rule is intrinsically fragile and so needs to be supported by taboo if it is to survive. The taboo is exemplified in the form of 'strong moral intuitions'. The rule's survival is precarious unless breaking it is regarded as almost unthinkable, for moral reasons. But, it appears, there is nothing about the nature of the good that requires the rule; it is simply how we have chosen to regulate scarcity. The taboo – and hence the strong intuition – attaches to the rule, not the good.

By way of further illustration, consider again the practice of ticket touting. Tickets for some very popular sporting events are sold at well below market-clearing price, as they tend to be sold at a price established by custom, rather than one based on the attractiveness of the particular fixture. Consequently allocation is based on first come, first served, subject to paying the required price. Tickets sometimes sell out early and the conditions are ripe for a black market, which comes into being. Consider, for example, rugby internationals at Twickenham. Tickets often change hands at much above face value, and touting is commonplace, which generates both approval from anyone prepared to pay over the odds for a ticket and disapproval from others.

One good thing about the current system is that keeping ticket prices relatively low means that the event is affordable to a wider section of the population than would otherwise be the case. In effect, there is a strong element of distribution by lottery. But suppose Twickenham decided to outdo the touts or 'scalpers' by putting all tickets up for auction on eBay, with the auction closing the day before the game. Although there would be protests at first, we might come to think that this is a reasonable way to allocate tickets. After all we are used to auction pricing in many other contexts. Sotheby's and Christie's are not expected to give the sale item to the first bidder. If this is right then we could easily flip from one allocation rule to another. If so, this further illustrates the point that there is a species of blocked exchange that has little or nothing to do with the nature of the item traded. Rather, we have a rule for allocating a scarce good, and we sometimes treat this rule as unquestionable – as we noted, almost as a sacred taboo. What strikes us as corrupt is trying to break the taboo for one's own benefit. Yet after a while we would have no difficulty in switching to a new system with a different allocation rule, provided it is generalized and applies to all, as actually happened in the parking case. This is a type of conventional, or contingent, blocked exchange. It reveals one type of moral limit to the market, but not one rooted in the nature of the goods.

The confusion between blockages being rooted in the nature of certain goods, and being rooted in other social factors, is a common one. And allocation rules are not the only social factors in play. Here is a quite different case, from the sphere of compensatory justice. Many years ago I read a detective story which featured an elderly American couple who were extremely proud of their new black Cadillac. One morning they came downstairs and went to their locked garage only to find a dead body in their locked car. Naturally they called the police who took away body and car for forensic tests. A week later, the couple wrote to the Police Department saying that because of the unpleasantness surrounding the car they couldn't face having it back, and suggested that the Police Department replace it. Only this time they'd like one in white with a red trim, please, which shouldn't cost any more. The Department replied with a curt note saying that they could have the car back when the tests were finished. But imagine now that the tests did indeed destroy the car and the police accept that they have a duty to replace it. And suppose that the white one is actually cheaper, so supplying it would be a Pareto improvement; everyone would be better off. Still, it seems to me, there is a duty only to replace it with one of the original colour. Somehow it seems wrong to ask for anything else — as if it is a misunderstanding of the situation. Of course once the request is made, it would be rather churlish of the police to decline it. But that doesn't mean that they have any duty.

But again it would be absurd to conclude that this shows us anything about the proper grounds for the distribution of Cadillacs. Rather it seems to be an application of a little-noticed axiom of what is known as deontic logic — the logic of moral statements — which we could call the inalienability of duty. If A has a duty to provide B with x, and B would rather have y, and y is cheaper or easier for A to supply, nevertheless A has no duty to provide B with y.

In all of this we have come no closer to the idea that some goods should be protected from the market because of the nature of the goods themselves. The most plausible cases are those where there is something in the nature of a good itself such that selling it destroys the good. Love and friendship may remain the best candidates.

Beyond that, we have noted that some limits to exchange are needed to avoid adverse third-party effects (selling commissions in the army). And further there are also limits to the market in order to avoid a form of exploitation or subversion of a rule, but many of these rules are entirely contingent and could be changed.

MARKETS AND THE VOLUNTARY SECTOR

Another important form of argument that there are areas of life which should be kept free from the market starts from the observation that much of what we find of value in our lives comes not from the market, or from the state, but from voluntary associations: things people do for themselves and others but for non-commercial reasons. Clubs, associations and less formal groupings of friends and family networks fall into this area. In our own time the Internet is the perfect example. Although there is now a great deal of commercial use of the Internet, and it is also used for state and other governmental purposes, there is still a huge amount of material put on the Internet simply because people think it is worthwhile to do so. Why do people think it worthwhile? It is hard to say in other terms, but clearly it is of great value to many people, giving them a sense of purpose and connectedness with others.

The argument here is that there are values intrinsic to voluntary associations, or, in MacIntyre's terms, practices (1981). Russell Keat has made this argument about the limits to the market. Practices have their own traditions, excellences and virtues. Keat is particularly exercised by the market's role in supplying cultural goods. Once the market gets a foothold, Keat suggests, commercial values will corrupt the practices, the traditions will be forgotten, and the virtues will wither in pursuit of money (Keat 2000). This argument has often been made, recently, on behalf of two state organizations masquerading as voluntary associations: the BBC and the universities.

As a more general question, why should we think that cultural goods are more appropriately left to distribution by voluntary associations? Possibly one argument is that they should be made available to all, but the market cannot guarantee this. This is important and I will return to it. But is the point so clear? In recent years certain areas of life have changed their status from voluntary associations to commercial organizations. Think of the Olympic movement. Not long ago you would have been banned for life if you accepted payment. Now top athletes earn huge amounts of money. Has this made sport worse? We can argue about the details, if we were so minded, but it is hard to make out the case that sport is now corrupted. Changed, yes, with both advantages and disadvantages, corrupted no. Might we not say the same thing about cultural goods? Has the art market destroyed art? Or has it made it possible for people from modest backgrounds to pursue their artistic ambitions if they have the talent? It is looking harder to mount an argument that anything in particular should be excluded from the market. There are likely to be considerations on both sides.

Does this mean that everything should be supplied on the market? This does not follow from what I have said. From the fact, if it is a fact, that it is not the case that anything in particular should be excluded from the market, it does not follow that everything should be supplied on the market. In fact, I think there should be a rather large non-market sphere. But rather perversely, I am coming round to the view that, a few key elements aside, it may not matter so much what is in the market sphere and what is not, as long as the non-market sector is significant in size.

Let us ask, first of all, why we should have a non-market sphere? Let us approach this by considering what is probably the most famous example of all: Richard Titmuss's blood-donation example. Titmuss compared the British system of the 'gift relation' where blood is given, not sold, with the US system in which a substantial amount of blood is purchased from individuals who can make money by selling it (Titmuss 1970).

Titmuss saw two advantages in the donation system. First, he claimed, you got better blood. Why would anyone donate blood if they felt it might be infected? But you might sell blood you suspected was infected if you needed the money enough. Second, the practice encouraged feelings of social solidarity. Now whether or not we get better blood is contingent, and has been contested. It is said, for example, that commercial blood banks responded much more quickly to HIV infection, as they were worried about legal liability. But the point about social solidarity seems undeniable. For example, after a major crisis, such as 9/11, you may find blood-donation drives even in countries without such a tradition, as a way of expressing grief and solidarity with the victims. And it seems appropriate that blood should have such a role, as it is a 'good' with such symbolism and resonance. Nevertheless is it so clear that we could not have chosen some other good, either as well or instead? In some countries people take on the duty to keep the roadside that borders their property immaculately clean, as a civil duty. Is that better or worse than blood donation?

These cases look primarily at the supply side of the transaction, in terms of the quality of good and the implications of supplying it on a voluntary basis. Yet we also need to look at the consumption side too. Here I want to look at two arguments for reserving a range of goods from the market. The first is perhaps the more obvious. If all goods are available only on a market basis, those who have not made an economic success of their lives will be excluded from almost everything else too. Allowing non-market provision can make a normal range of fulfilments available to a broader range of people. From free concerts in the park, to free medical care, an economically unsuccessful life can still be relatively secure and full of enjoyment, even if choice is more restricted. Some of these goods will be provided by the state, some by voluntary associations, and some by individuals out of a sense of civic duty. What, then, should be in the package of non-market goods? Several are obvious candidates, such as education, and, as discussed earlier, health care.

But others are more optional. Many societies offer free use of libraries and admission to art galleries, but not free food or housing. There are, no doubt, good reasons for this, but we can imagine society being organized on rather different lines.

A second argument is especially concerned with the contrast between principles of supply in public and private sectors, and compares two types of economic relation. The first, in the market, is what we can call 'the deal-making society', in which you go into each transaction looking for the best deal you can. If you do not get what you expected, or are given poor value, you have a right to complain, and perhaps, go to law. The second is less easy to characterize but might be thought of as 'taking the rough with the smooth' or the 'swings and roundabouts' society. In this case the idea is that there are general rules or policies of distribution which sometimes yield good results and sometimes bad, but rather than judging each transaction on its merits we should judge the practice as a whole.

This 'rough with the smooth' attitude is, in general, the attitude we are encouraged to take with respect to public services. For example, someone may know that some of her taxes go to pay for public libraries, which she never uses, and so in that sense is getting a bad deal. She would never join the library if it was a private service. However perhaps she has an ailment requiring expensive medication which she gets on the national health system, and thereby receives a subsidy. So by the standards of the deal-making society she is being 'overcharged' for one good and 'undercharged' for another. In the 'rough with the smooth' society she just never does the calculations. The idea is that it is possible that we can all be better off if we take the rough with the smooth and goods are supplied publicly. In some cases we win, in some cases we lose, but we win overall in two ways. First, the administrative costs of individual pricing would make a private system more expensive, and second we gain in social solidarity.

Now the first of these is a contingent claim and one many will think false, believing that individual pricing encourages efficiency in other ways. However it is likely to be true for some goods and false for others, and where it is true this is a good reason for having public provision in that area. But social solidarity – a sense that we are all in this together – is encouraged by keeping the public sector large. However, the positive effects of this will drain away if the sector as a whole is thought to be inefficient and wasteful: there needs to be at least belief in net gain.

Of course some individuals will not gain materially. And if they dwell on their material losses and let it affect them too much, they will not gain in other ways. So we need to maintain a difficult balance. If society is to achieve the best results, we need to be able to ask whether, as a whole, public services give good value, while not asking 'do they give me good value?' What is even worse is the question 'do I get good value from each public service?' Once this last question is commonplace, public services will be vulnerable, and our potential loss will be very great. Hence we need to preserve a public sector and subject it only to some sorts of scrutiny if we want it to be a vehicle of social solidarity as well as efficient provision.

CONCLUSION: LESSONS FOR PHILOSOPHY

My task in this chapter has been to explore arguments both for and against the use of markets to produce and distribute goods. My general approach has been to look at a range of examples and to try to understand our different reactions to different situations. My tentative conclusion is that although we often have strong intuitions about the rights and wrongs of cases, we don't always understand why we have them. Very often we don't appreciate the ways markets can fail, especially in the supply of goods that will not be consumed until the far future. Equally, very often we object to the intrusion of the market into an area of life not because there is anything special about that area of life, but because we currently have a different, non-market rule in place for the distribution of a scarce good. But, I think, often we could perfectly well get used to a new rule. Despite this, I do not advocate a free market in everything; far from it. It is, I think, important that large areas of life are fenced off from the market, but less important where exactly the boundary is placed.

The methodological conclusion of this chapter is rather troubling. Much theorizing in moral and political philosophy, as well as in public policy, begins from a clear appreciation that some practices are obviously right or wrong. But can we always be sure that our moral intuitions are firmly based? To put my point in its least contentious form, the strength of our convictions that something is right (or wrong) is not a clear guide to whether, in fact, it is right (or wrong). What, then, is a better guide? I wish I had a quick and easy answer. All we can do is try to think about the issues as clearly and imaginatively as we can, while being as self-critical about our own assumptions as we can bear.

9

Conclusion

Connecting philosophy and public policy

Inscribed on Karl Marx's tombstone are the words: 'The philosophers have only interpreted the world in various ways, the point is to change it.' This slogan, the last of Marx's *Theses on Feuerbach* (Marx 1975b [1845]), has been an inspiration to many people who think that philosophy should not be confined to the academy, but should get its hands dirty by engaging in the real world. And it is a stirring thought, aimed against the German philosophy of the 1840s. In our own time, though, as I have said before, and no doubt will say again, there is a sense in which this gets the problem backwards. On the whole moral and political philosophers have not been short of suggestions for how the world can be changed. Political philosophers compete with each other to come up with the best models of a good and just society. Moral philosophers tell us why or why not practices such as abortion, euthanasia and the eating of animals are right or wrong, and what we should do instead. Accordingly there is no shortage of philosophers who hope to change the world. But what they sometimes have failed to do is to interpret the world they live in. Often they fail to investigate why it is society does the things it does. What approach do we actually have to abortion or euthanasia? What does the law say? What do doctors actually do in practice? Do they find ways round laws that, they think, stand in the way of compassionate outcomes? Would changing the laws really lead to improvements, or would there be unwelcome side-effects? How would the courts interpret new laws in the light of existing legislation and common law? Would a hostile press wreck attempts at law reform? And so on. Philosophers have been known to write as if the entire issue is an intellectual one, and once the best reasons are set out for the best policy the philosophers' work is done. Of course no one thinks that somehow the world will miraculously conform itself to the intellectual ideal, but philosophers sometimes fall short of taking up the challenge of thinking hard about questions of the process and, even more importantly, consequences of implementation.

The challenge is, of course, multifaceted. First of all, we need to heed Bernard Williams's advice. At least as far as applied moral and political philosophy is concerned, the important question is not 'what is the best form of society?' but rather, 'what is the best form of society we can get to, starting from here?' (Williams 2005, 23). This, in turn, leads to two constraints on ideal-building. First, given our history, it may simply be impossible to achieve a particular ideal. So, for example, much as some people would prefer to live in a world without nuclear weapons, or genetically modified organisms, there is no way of eliminating the accumulated knowledge. Second, and just as obviously, without understanding where we are we will not know what needs to be changed to bring about the world we seek. Blundering in, and trying to make improvements without as comprehensive an understanding as we can achieve of the situation, can lead to all sorts of problems. Change could be ineffective, or, in the worst cases, do unexpected harms. To take a case not discussed in this book, foreign aid is often said to lead to such problems. Consider the vast amounts of money currently being spent in sub-Saharan Africa in the attempt to mitigate HIV/AIDS infection by the use of antiretroviral therapy. A huge amount of benefit results from these projects, and hundreds of thousands of lives are being, or will be, extended as a result. Yet the programmes need medical staff to run them. Many of the project directors have an understandable, perhaps even commendable, goal of using local staff wherever possible. But it is not as if there is a surplus of trained medical staff in Africa – quite the reverse. This means that to employ a doctor or nurse in an HIV programme is to take them away from whatever else it was they were doing: vaccinating children, or attending births, perhaps. An unintended consequence of pumping large amounts of money into HIV programmes appears to have been, paradoxically, to weaken health systems (Haacker 2010). And this is a consequence of appreciating only a small part of the picture before acting. Of course, it is easy to make such observations with the wisdom of hindsight, but it is a good lesson to try to acquire as much foresight as possible.

Seeing cases like this may make one despair of being able to recommend changes that are unreservedly to the good. What can a philosopher hope to understand about health systems in the developing world, or the complex economics of foreign aid? Without a comprehensive understanding of where we are, will we not act blindly, making recommendations that are dismissed as naïve, or, even worse, accepted and then found later to do more harm than good? Is the lesson of this book that philosophers should leave public policy to other people, and go back to safe topics like the metaphysics of value, or the nature of time? That, in fact, might be the right response for some philosophers, but I don't think that is all we should do. At the end of this chapter I will make some suggestions about what I think is the right way for a philosopher to approach issues of public policy. But to build up to that point, we need to draw together the conclusions from the chapters of this book.

The first lesson, we saw, was presented in the Introduction. Despite the obvious promise of moral and political philosophy as areas of thought with an important bearing on public policy, there is something, nevertheless, about the discipline of philosophy that makes the connection with public policy much more difficult than it would seem in advance. Philosophers, on the whole, are individualists and controversialists, who prize originality over agreement, which they tend to find dull and uninteresting. Compromise is not a concept familiar to philosophers. Philosophers don't have to compromise because they are under no pressure to agree to produce a practical outcome. This leads to a flowering of ideas and the pursuit of novelty. I used the Freudian notion of 'narcissism of minor differences' to bring out the difficulties. Philosophers are much more interested in the ways in which their views differ from that of others than what they have in common. Of course this is not an absolute bar on philosophers contributing to public policy discussions, but it does mean that they will need to guard against some of their natural tendencies in order to do so.

The further point in a sense naturally follows from the first, in that it indicates one way in which a philosophical approach to policy can go wrong. Taking a philosophical theory or dictum and then applying it 'neat' to problems in public policy typically leads to views that have little chance of adoption, and, indeed, may leave practical people incredulous. So, for example, Peter Singer's argument that 'all animals are equal' has very radical consequences for how human beings should treat non-human animals. But it is a fantasy to think that policy makers might read Singer, realize that our practices are wrong, and then, on that basis, completely revise what we do, eliminating everything that on Singer's view discriminates against non-humans. Similarly John Stuart Mill's liberty principle, which states that the only justification for interfering with the liberty of any adult human being is to prevent harm, or risk of harm, to others, appears to recommend policies regarding the regulation of drugs and gambling that are far more liberal than any society has ever permitted, at least in the modern world. This is not to say that Singer and Mill are wrong, or that their work has no value. Quite the reverse. Their ideas provide very important contributions that help define the debates in which we are engaged. The point is simply that while such contributions help start the debate, and perhaps will influence others either to modify their positions or to take opposing views more seriously, they do not settle anything. If the philosopher insists that truth has been found and the debate is finished, he or she is likely to find the debate continuing without them. Some have said that the task of the philosopher is, in the words of the old Quaker slogan, 'to speak truth to power'. That's all very well, but are you really so sure you have the truth, and the means to make those in power listen?

One way of putting the general point is that we can distinguish two roles for philosophical input into policy debate. At the sharp end of policy, when an issue is being discussed and a practical outcome is being sought, philosophers have to operate in a pragmatic mode. For if their recommendations do not respond to the values people actually hold, then they will be left out in the cold. But a longer-term project is also possible, and arguably more valuable: to set out arguments and visions of other ways of doing things that might hope to shape the values that people hold. If successful then for future generations the policy context, and the debate, will be different. We might, for example, see the contributions of thinkers such as Mary Wollstonecraft in this light. From a policy point of view, attempting to vindicate the rights of women in 1792 was a hopeless, laughable project. But in the long term, it has been of immeasurable value. She has helped shape the values behind public debate, so that, in the twentieth century women won many of the battles that Wollstonecraft and others fought for. My point here is not at all to disparage long-term contributions of this sort. It is rather to make clear if philosophers are to intervene successfully in short-term policy debates they need to understand how this sort of work differs from ideal theory.

One difference between the philosophers' context and the policy context can be brought out by developing a point that has been only implicit in the earlier chapters, that of 'moral realism'. This has been an important issue in moral philosophy in recent decades, and many philosophers now defend views that reject forms of moral relativism and subjectivism, arguing that there is truth, or at least some form of objectivity, in moral values (see for example Sayre-McCord 1988). But some philosophers go further and suggest not only that there can be true moral principles but that they, the philosopher in question, know what these principles are and can tell you. Well, they might be able to tell you, but it is far less likely they can convince you. The attempt to suggest that public policy ought to be shaped a particular way because that follows from a true moral principle is likely to meet with the response 'who says?' More progress is likely by appealing to values that are widely shared, and in the public policy arena there seems little to be gained by asking whether values are 'objective' or 'subjective'. If we can achieve intersubjective agreement then we have all we can reasonably hope for.

Intersubjective agreement can be achieved in many cases. As we saw in the chapter on disability, it may be much easier to gain agreement on policies – in this case policies to change the material and social world to make it more accommodating to people with disabilities – than it is to get agreement on the philosophical justifications for such policies. For another example, the working party of the Nuffield Council on Bioethics was able to derive a 'consensus statement' on desirable further policies for animal experimentation despite the very deep philosophical disagreements held by the members who drew up the report.

A philosophical approach to public policy analysis, I believe, will be very likely to go wrong if it starts from the announcement of a set of principles or values claimed to be true. Where should it start then? Well, not all public policy areas need philosophical input. The ones that do are those that are beset by a problem. There is reason for taking an interest because of some sort of dispute or disagreement. Philosophers arrive on the scene rather like a (very slow moving) emergency service. There is a problem that needs resolution, if possible. Obviously, therefore, no progress can be made unless the problem is understood. If, for example, you want to make a contribution to the formulation of better regulations for animal experimentation or gambling or recreational drugs, then the first thing to do is to find out about the policy area. At least four types of investigation are likely to be needed, or at least helpful. First, and most obviously, you need to know about current practice, which might require attending to official statistics, books and papers describing activities, in all their varieties. Recall how important it was, in the chapters on safety and disability, to consider a range of empirical cases in the policy area, to avoid inappropriate generalization. Second, you will need to know about current regulations, and also what might be needed to make changes. I haven't discussed this in the main chapters of this book, but if you are really serious about proposing changes then you will have to learn about parliamentary procedure, the difference between primary legislation and other forms of state action, and the possibility of change given the many procedural difficulties you are likely to face. So, for example, committees I have worked with have rushed to complete a report in order not to miss a vital window of opportunity when the report had more chance of influencing debate. Third, it is often highly beneficial to understand the history of how current practice and regulation arose; not only to understand why we are where we are, but to observe how things once were different, and why changes were made in the past. And finally, most obviously, you need to understand what people currently disagree about. All of this together is hard work, or at least very time-consuming. And once more it can be enough to make one wonder whether all this work will have much of a pay-off. Often it won't, of course. Such are the frustrations of daring to stray across disciplinary boundaries.

A further frustration, we noted in connection with the regulation of drugs, is that in public policy the philosophers' weapon of choice is unavailable. It seems that there are no knock-down arguments in public policy, not even pointing out that a position is inconsistent. Of course, as we noted, if a position in public policy is baldly contradictory in the sense that it requires individuals both to do something and not do it, then there is a problem that needs urgent resolution. But showing that the government's treatment of, say, alcohol and ecstasy is inconsistent is an interesting curiosity, rather than the devastating objection that it would be in a philosophy seminar. Given that legislation is passed by different governments for different purposes at different times, one could hardly expect it to be consistent. Specialists in many areas can list inconsistencies, just as certain types of critics of religion delight in finding biblical contradictions. And in both cases the objections fail to have the power in the debate for which the critics hoped. While consistency is obviously a virtue it is not obvious that a consistent set of policies is always to be preferred to an inconsistent set. Most members of the British public seem happier with a policy that legalizes alcohol but not ecstasy, inconsistent though it seems, than they would be with a consistent policy that treats them both the same way. To the philosophical mind this is infuriating, but it is the everyday world of public policy. And, indeed, as I argued in the chapter on public safety, we can find that even within ourselves there are inconsistent, or at least conflicting, views. Many people, I conjectured, will be sympathetic both to the consequentialist idea that there is a limit to how much society should pay for safety improvements, and the absolutist view that it is wrong to put a value on life.

That example provides further reasons for the philosophically inclined to feel very uncomfortable. Current policies can indeed be represented as putting a price on life. Everyone, not only philosophers, will find this a difficult notion, and, as a first, and deep, instinct, will want to resist. Indeed, it is very easy to say the words 'it is immoral to put a price on life'. The answer, of course, is 'fine: tell us what else we should do'. In some cases philosophers have refused to take the next step, suggesting that it is legitimate to be a critic but without proposing an alternative. I sometimes have a good deal of sympathy for this reaction, but, once more, it is a way of resigning from the public policy debate. A policy is needed. Often we already have one, however imperfect. The urgent question is not whether there are objections to the existing policy, for there always are. Rather, is there an alternative that is an improvement on the current situation, and meets other criteria such as being widely acceptable and possible to implement given other constraints on the policy process? But as a first contribution to answering that

question, a broader issue needs to be addressed: what, even at the
level of pure theory, are the alternatives to current policy? Whether
one feels the need to take this question seriously is the test of
whether one is suited to philosophical engagement in public policy.
A refusal to get one's hands dirty is admirable, but unlikely to be
sustainable in public policy.

Furthermore, policy failure is always a threat. A policy introduced
for the best of intentions may or may not achieve its aims. One
reason for this can be that policies are advanced on the basis of
insufficiently examined empirical assumptions. We have seen a
couple of examples where assumptions about the consequences of
change have proven unfounded. A relatively minor case occurred
in relation to the discussion of gambling, where it was widely
assumed that widening opportunities for people to gamble would
enlarge the proportion of the population who became problem
gamblers. But at least in the current UK context this does not
appear to be so, although of course things could change. More
importantly we saw that one of the reasons for health-care reform
in the UK in the 1940s was to improve the health of those who did
not have access to health care. It seems obvious that the introduction
of a national health service would have this effect. But, according to
some analysts, it did not. And we are in danger of making the same
discovery in the US. In this case, however, I do not take the
empirical evidence as a reason for not introducing wider access to
health care, but rather for becoming more reflective about the reasons
why widening access is a desirable policy.

Another reason for policy failure is to make a false empirical
assumption of a different kind, an assumption about human motivation. Here, in fact, we noticed two opposing errors. In one type
of case the problem is that philosophers, and indeed members of
the public, can be too ready to think that the answer to a problem in
public policy is to pass a law. But, as we saw in the case of both drug
and gambling legislation, if we try to solve a problem by passing a
law, but the law is not generally obeyed, then we now have two

problems. In the UK we are learning this lesson again with legislation against fox hunting, which is turning out to be exceptionally difficult to enforce. To take the most extreme case I have seen, Primo Levi's autobiographical account of life in a concentration camp, If This Is A Man, contains various examples of the ways in which camp inmates broke rules in order to make their lives slightly more tolerable, knowing that they faced summary execution if found out (Levi 1958 [1947]). But if it is impossible generally to enforce rules in a concentration camp, where can they be enforced? The mistake here is to assume that people will treat laws as providing an absolute constraint on action, rather than changing the cost and risk profile of various forms of action. However, if the rewards of breaking the law are high enough, then the risks could be worth taking. The cost–benefit analysis can be in favour of breaking the law.

One mistake, then, is to forget that at least some human beings will approach the law in this cost–benefit manner at least some of the time. The opposite mistake is to overstate the degree to which human beings will do this; this mistake lies behind the assumption that increasing prison sentences will reduce crime. Our discussion of crime and punishment suggested that although this can be true for some people, on the whole length of sentences will have a very marginal effect on deterrence − a conjecture apparently supported by empirical studies, which also suggest that detection rates have a much greater effect (von Hirsch et al. 1999). The reason for this is that what counts as a cost and a benefit is a subtle matter and may be different for different people. But furthermore human motivation is highly complex in that there are differences between people, and over time. To the degree this is possible, policy makers will need to take human variation into account. Finally, on the topic of motivation, or at least of human response, it seems clear that there are important connections between different areas. The example in this book that best illustrates this rather banal point is the discussion of crime and punishment, where I suggested it will be difficult to understand our practices of punishment without first understanding why people find the prospect and experience of crime so problematic.

And we must not forget a further point about motivation, this time about the power of moral argument. In the discussion of experimentation on animals I pointed out that, at least in my own case, I often find that moral arguments have more power to make me feel guilty about my behaviour than to change that behaviour. Perhaps I am alone in this, but I suspect not. This suggests a dual lesson for philosophy and public policy: that moral argument, even when convincing, is not enough. We must also seek changes in the external conditions to allow people to continue to get what they want, but with a clean conscience. Structural change is needed to facilitate behavioural change. So, for example, although worried about climate change, and while prepared to make some financial sacrifices, few people will make a substantial change to their lifestyles unless there are acceptable alternatives. Many people would like to drive less, but they will not do so unless there are safe cycle routes or reliable and quick forms of public transport. Progress in this area, as in so many others, requires social and material change to accompany moral argument.

These methodological observations raise perhaps our central question. What is the role of philosophers in public policy discussions? I have argued against a naïve model in which philosophers formulate moral and political theories that are then applied to particular policy areas. I have also indicated a number of other difficulties that philosophers will encounter in trying to make a contribution to public policy debates. So what is left? Well, philosophers can do what philosophers do. Make distinctions. Work out what follows from what. Ask awkward questions. But still, it can fairly be asked, why would you need philosophers for that? Any intelligent person, surely, is just as well equipped? To a point this is correct, but as philosophers our life's work is to develop skills of analysis and argument, informed by a study of the history of the subject and the best contemporary work. We know about patterns of argument, with standard objections, and thoughtful replies. We are used to challenging and being challenged. We know how to depersonalize arguments and consider them on their merits rather than on the authority of the person that uttered them. There is work for us to do, but not necessarily the work we thought. Public policy needs philosophers more than it needs philosophy.

One important task for philosophers is illustrated in the chapter on animal experimentation. There I argued that the best way of understanding the position of people engaged in the debate is not as disagreeing on the classical philosophical question of what property makes a creature a member of the moral community. Rather there is an implicit acknowledgement that all sorts of features of animals are morally relevant, but disagreement about what weight they each should be given: do they provide an absolute constraint on action, or are they simply factors to be put in the balance against other factors? Whether or not animals have rights is not the best way to approach the issues. Perhaps an even better example comes from the work of Ronald Dworkin on abortion (Dworkin 1993). The debate on abortion is often posed as 'a woman's right to choose' pitted against 'the fetus's right to life'. These make good campaigning slogans, but, as Dworkin argues, they are not good statements of the positions people hold. For example, those who believe in a woman's right to choose, typically limit the right to the first two trimesters of pregnancy. But if a woman has a right to choose how can it be restricted? Why shouldn't a woman have a right to an abortion all the way up to the moment of birth? Clearly few people, if any, would accept such a practice, and this seems to go to show that the claimed right to choose is much more limited than appears on badges and T-shirts. Similarly many, although admittedly not all, opponents of abortion accept that abortion can be permissible in cases of rape or incest. But what has the fetus done to forfeit the right to life? How can the fetus's origin make such a difference? In fact, Dworkin argues, all sides in the debate give great concern to the interests both of the mother and of the fetus. Where they differ is how exactly to strike the balance. However, for campaigning purposes all sides present their position in an oversimplified, and strictly speaking, false way. But – and here is where there is work for the philosopher – the intellectual debate will suffer from frustrating unclarity if it proceeds along campaign-slogan lines. The philosopher is in a position – after hard work – to expose the core of the disagreement.

Once the disagreement is exposed, what next? The philosophical impulse is to try to work out which position in the debate is correct, by considering arguments, counterexamples and anything else that might usefully come to hand. But, as explained above, what matters in public policy debate is not convincing yourself that you have the best position, but carrying others with you. This is not so much a matter of pragmatic compromise, but of working out how people can get much of what they want without taking too much away from others. To illustrate using an example from road safety, as is well known, cars are extremely dangerous. Each year hundreds of thousands of people throughout the world die in car accidents. Yet stopping people from driving, although it would save many lives, would generally be considered a hugely disproportionate response. So what should we do? Well, what we in fact do is allow people to drive but not in the most dangerous ways. We put speed limits on driving, especially in highly populated areas. We have limits to how much people can drink before driving. We make cars pass safety tests. We try to build safe road systems. By such means we 'soften' the moral dilemma. We remove the most difficult cases, and thereby allow people to gain most of the advantages of driving while taking away at least some of the risks. Although we can always quibble about the details of such policies there is a chance of giving everyone much of what they want.

Of course the dilemma about driving is not one that has grabbed the attention of philosophers. Perhaps it is because the solution is rather obvious. But I would suggest that for some cases, though of course not all, it provides a model of how to make progress. We saw this, for example, in the chapter on gambling. In the UK it is permitted in restricted forms, so that the most potentially addictive forms of gambling are more difficult to access than they might have been. Another example, we saw, is that both defenders and critics of animal experimentation can accept, in a limited way, the doctrine of the three Rs – refinement, reduction and replacement. Both sides will be happy to reduce the number of animals used and to reduce the suffering of animals, especially where this does not compromise the science. But those who advocate experimenting on animals may well also be prepared to replace some of these experiments with procedures on tissue samples, even if the quality of information obtained is not as high. What is so encouraging about this type of example is that progress in public policy can come about through relatively small changes that amount to a large step forward for one group, but only a minimal concession for another. For example, it is now not possible to obtain a licence in the UK to test cosmetic products on animals as the aims are considered too trivial to justify the suffering. This was a triumph for animal welfare campaigners, but barely a loss at all to cosmetic companies. In some cases it may have been to their benefit for marketing purposes.

The limit to how far we might be able to go in policy areas, however, is illustrated again by the issue of disability. There, I noted, that although campaigners for disability rights argue for equality of opportunity, in practice their goals are not as comprehensive as this campaign slogan would suggest. Rather their goal is for disability no longer to be a special or further burden in 'life's race'. But this campaign pays no attention to the possible unfairness in the workplace that rewards high IQ or other talents. Rather, at least in some cases, campaigners want people with disabilities to be able to reap the full advantages of their abilities and skills. This is a worthy project – and it is mirrored in other campaigns for gender or racial justice – but it is not quite what it appears to be.

Philosophy can clearly help clarify these issues, but the argument of this book is that the benefit is mutual. For example, the discussion of animal experimentation shows that there is also a pay-off for philosophy in engaging in policy areas. I argued that by looking at our practices with regard to animals we can see that the debate about what makes a person or animal a member of the moral community is misguided. It seems that our attitudes are that it is not an 'all or nothing' thing, and how a person or animal should be treated depends, to a great extent, on its possession of morally relevant properties. Although derived from reflection on practices in a policy area, this is a conclusion of philosophical importance, and could, potentially, have an impact on purely philosophical debates. In my view, of course, it would considerably improve such debates. Even more telling, I believe, is the discussion of disability. Here looking at the concerns of disability activists and theorists one learns that much of the philosophical discussion of disability in relation to distributive justice is entirely irrelevant to the concerns of activists, and, if followed, would be a backward step. Making the appropriate adjustments to political philosophy so that it can engage with issues of disability pays dividends. Not only does it allow political philosophers to enter into the policy debates regarding disability, it also, in my view, enriches political philosophy to provide a better account of human well-being, and of the possibilities of political and public action. In this case, both sides benefit from the encounter.

I should also repeat a cautionary point I have made before. In trying to work out how moral and political philosophers can engage with, contribute to, and learn from policy debates, I am not at all suggesting that this is all philosophers in these areas should do. We continue to need a wide variety of approaches, methodologies and interests. This includes what has become known as 'ideal theory', where philosophers set out visions of how things should be, without worrying about the practicalities of implementation. As I have said, debate needs ideal theory. Without it, discussions would be limp and unimaginative. If a highly intelligent theorist has thought about an issue long and hard, and has come up with a systematic, elegant, imaginative or thorough proposal, then it needs to be taken seriously. It is unlikely that it will be completely wrong. On the other hand it is also unlikely that it will be completely right. Possibly the most common mistake in philosophy is to think one has the whole of the truth when one only has part.

Some may worry that the approach recommended here – essentially looking for small changes that will be seen as broadly beneficial – is too conservative. Large change, it will be said, is necessary from time to time and has happened. Think of, say, changes in the law in the direction of equality, regarding gender, race and sexual orientation. Massive progress has been made in a relatively short time, as a result of uncompromising advocacy of theories of justice. The status quo has been broken time and time again. How can that have happened, if I am right that there is an inevitable bias in favour of the status quo?

To consider this question it is worth looking at one of the most significant law reforms, from a moral point of view, in recent times: the change in legal status of homosexuality. In the UK, for example, forms of male homosexuality had been illegal since the sixteenth century, yet in 1967 the law changed so that homosexual acts, performed in private between consenting adults aged twenty-one or over, were no longer a criminal offence. The reform is usually thought to have been a result of the recommendations of the Wolfenden report, the *Report of the Committee on Homosexual Offences and Prostitution* (Home Office 1957), which made exactly this recommendation. How, then, was the Wolfenden report able to overturn the status quo in such a dramatic fashion?

It may help to make a distinction between two understandings of the status quo. One is the status quo of current laws and regulations. The other is the status quo of public opinion or values. Over time, as public views shift, there can be a tension between status quo laws and status quo values, and in this respect law can seem out of date and obstructive. At this point it may be possible to make a radical change in the laws, but underlying values cannot be ignored. As the Wolfenden report put the point: 'We clearly recognise that the laws of any society must be acceptable to the general moral sense of the community if they are to be respected and enforced. ... Certainly it is clear that if any legal enactment is markedly out of tune with public opinion it will quickly fall into disrepute' (Home Office 1957, 9, 10). And so what was public opinion on the desirability of decriminalization of homosexuality in the 1950s? Interestingly, the committee didn't seem to feel the need to explore this question in detail, commenting 'on the matters with which we are called upon to deal we have not succeeded in discovering an unequivocal "public opinion", and we have felt bound to try to reach conclusions for ourselves rather than to base them on what is often transient and seldom precisely ascertainable' (Home Office 1957, 10).

Yet this comment stands in contrast with a remark made in the same very short chapter, where the report's authors set out their view of the function of the law, or rather what its function is not: 'It is not, in our view, the function of the law to intervene in the private lives of citizens' (Home Office 1957, 10). Much later in the report, when discussing prostitution rather than homosexuality, the report quotes the earlier (1928) 'Street Offences Committee' in the following terms: 'We cannot do better than quote the words of the Street Offences Committee – "As a general proposition it will be universally accepted that the law is not concerned with private morals or with ethical standards. On the other hand, the law is plainly concerned with the outward conduct of citizens in so far as that conduct injuriously affects the rights of other citizens"'(Home Office 1957, 80).

It seems that the committee felt that it could not be shown that there was a clear, univocal public opinion on whether or not homosexual acts should remain illegal, although they did nothing to demonstrate this claim. At the same time, they set out a view of the purpose of the law that they thought was near-universally accepted, and argued that on this understanding the law needed to be changed. In this way, the report can be read as drawing on what they took to be an important public value, regarding the proper purpose of law, to argue that the law should retreat from criminalization of homosexual behaviour. Arguably, then, the authors were drawing on one strand of status quo values to challenge status quo regulation. It seems quite likely, however, that in 1957 a significant proportion of the general population had no desire to see the law changed. Yet there was enough tension here to put the possibility of radical change on the agenda. We should note, though, that there was a period of ten years between report and legal change, partly because of the lack of enthusiasm of successive governments to sponsor the bill. During this time pressure built up for change, highly influenced by the Wolfenden report, to a point where it became possible to say the laws and public values were no longer aligned. This created a climate in which a change of law could be publicly acceptable.

Broadly, then, if large change is to take place, the world needs to be ready for it. To illustrate further, it is said that the 'greenhouse effect' was first posited by a Swedish scientist Svante Arrhenius in the late nineteenth century. However it was not until the 1960s that his idea was taken up by other scientists and not until the end of the twentieth century that it became scientific orthodoxy (see for example Maslin 2008). Some draw the lesson that we may have been able to predict and mitigate global warming if only people had listened to Arrhenius. But in the year Arrhenius published his speculations no doubt there were many dozens or hundreds of new theories, potentially of great significance if true, that have subsequently turned out to be without merit. How could people have picked Arrhenius as providing the one theory of which we should all take note? To make any large-scale change we need many people, from different backgrounds and with different interests, arguing for similar conclusions, perhaps even for different reasons. The lone philosopher can contribute to this process, but few of us will ever be any more than one straw in the wind. But without such contributions there would be no change at all.

Note on the chapters

The history of the chapters, as far as I recall, is as follows. The Introduction and the final concluding chapter have been presented several times together, as a talk on political philosophy and public policy, including to the Association for Legal and Social Philosophy Conference in Edinburgh in 2009 (my thanks to Cecile Fabre for the invitation), but is previously unpublished.

Chapter 1 derives from work produced for the Nuffield Council on Bioethics and much of the central argument of the chapter can also be found in the resulting report of the working party (NCB 2005). It was written up as a separate paper for a conference on impartiality at the University of Reading, organized by Brian Feltham and funded by the Arts and Humanities Research Council.

Chapter 2 is based on work produced initially for the Gambling Review Body (DCMS 2001). I wrote a short piece on children and gambling for the *Guardian* newspaper in 2006 (Wolff 2006a), but the material in this chapter has not been published before or presented in its current form.

Chapter 3 is a rewritten version of a paper first appearing in the journal *Public Policy Research* called 'Harm and Hypocrisy: Have We Got It Wrong on Drugs?' (Wolff 2007b). It results from work with the Academy of Medical Science working party on drug futures, and the resulting report was published as *Brain Science, Addiction and Drugs* (Academy of Medical Sciences 2008).

Chapter 4 has not been published in this form before, but its origins can be traced to a report written for what is now called the

Rail Safety and Standards Board (Wolff 2002). This chapter also draws on two further published papers (Wolff 2006b, 2007a).

Chapter 5 has several sources. I was asked by the think tank Institute for Public Policy Research to join them in a project on crime, punishment and social justice. Their resulting report was published as Dixon *et al.* 2006. I was also a member of a group looking at the law of homicide, and especially the mandatory life sentence, although it did not produce a final report. Peter Cave invited me to give the first Bentham Lecture at University College London, in 2005, organized by the Humanist Philosophy Society, and the first half of the chapter was the basis of that lecture. Finally *Prospect* magazine asked me to write a piece on trends in imprisonment in the UK, and the chapter reproduces some of that article (Wolff 2008).

Chapter 6 derives, ultimately, from an invitation by Dan Brock and Dan Wikler to give a talk called 'Health Risks and the People Who Bear Them' at a conference, 'Population Level Bioethics: Mapping a New Agenda', at Harvard University Medical School in 2005. Subsequently the talk was substantially rewritten and presented as the first of my Boutwood Lectures at Corpus Christi College, Cambridge, in 2009. I am very grateful to the Master and Fellows for the invitation, and especially to Nigel Simmonds for arranging the lectures. I would also like to thank Ben Colburn, John Dunn, Serena Olsaretti and Diane Dawson for their exceptionally helpful comments. It also draws on some talks I recorded for BBC Radio 3 in 2008, at the invitation of Julia Johnson, to mark the sixtieth anniversary of the foundation of the British National Health Service. This chapter will also be published in Rosamund Rhodes, Margaret Battin and Anita Silvers (ed.) *Medicine and Social Justice*, 2nd edn (Oxford: Oxford University Press).

Chapter 7 dates back to work I started around 1998 and was first presented at that time at a seminar in London organized by Ronald Dworkin and a conference in Manchester organized by Hillel Steiner. I have presented the material many times since, and the resulting chapter draws on papers written over several years, but, coincidentally, all published in 2009 (Wolff 2009a, 2009b, 2009c).

Chapter 8 has two sources. One is a paper that has not been published before, and was originally written for a conference organized by Debra Satz at Stanford University in 2006 on Equality and the Market. The other is a paper written for a conference on equality in Copenhagen in 2004, organized by Kaspar Lippert-Rasmussen and Nils Holtug and published as Wolff 2007c.

Work on several chapters of this book was supported by the UK Arts and Humanities Research Council (AHRC), as part of the Ethics of Risk project at University College London. I am, of course, extremely grateful to the AHRC for their support of this, and other, work.

Further reading

INTRODUCTION

For related ideas on how disagreement is possible even between those with very different moral views see Sunstein (1995). And for a warning about how intervention in public life by philosophers and other intellectuals can go horribly wrong, see Lilla (2002).

CHAPTER 1: SCIENTIFIC EXPERIMENTS ON ANIMALS

The classic philosophical work on animal liberation is, of course, the book of that name by Peter Singer (Singer 1995). Richard Ryder's *Victims of Science* is well worth reading too (Ryder 1975). Peter Carruthers is a notorious critic of this position, suggesting that contemporary concern with animal rights is a sign of the moral decadence of the age (Carruthers 1992). A good survey of positions is DeGrazia (2002). Roger Scruton provides an elegant and interesting position of a rather conventional and conservative sort, albeit critical of certain current practices (Scruton 2000). Alison Hills has written an introductory book which tries to come to a philosophically reasoned defence of something closer to current practices, thereby rejecting the extreme positions of Singer and Carruthers (Hills 2005). The Nuffield Council report was published as NCB (Nuffield Council on Bioethics) (2005).

CHAPTER 2: GAMBLING

The *Gambling Review Body Report* – my first foray into collective public reasoning – is now hard to find, but I put some chapters on my website before they disappeared from the Department of Culture Media and Sport's own site. Currently they can be found here: http://www.homepages.ucl.ac.uk/~uctyjow/Gambling.

The classic account of problem gambling is Lesieur (1977), and a more recent treatment, by a long-standing professional in the field, is Bellringer (1999). A famous short novel, providing a florid account of the circle of hope and despair of the addicted gambler is Dostoevsky (2008 [1867]). For an excellent account of the life and thought of John Stuart Mill see Reeves (2007). Elster and Skog (1999) is a good collection of academic writings on addiction, and P. Adams (2008) and Doughney (2002) provide stark criticisms of the gambling regimes in New Zealand and Australia, respectively.

CHAPTER 3: DRUGS

Douglas Husak has been an important critic of drug laws, especially in the US, for many years. One excellent place to explore the philosophical debate in more detail is Husak and de Marneffe (2005). David Nutt's attempts to bring the British government to understand the relative harms of illegal drugs compared to tobacco and alcohol has its most scientific presentation in Nutt *et al.* (2007). Be warned, though, that this is essentially an opinion survey of scientists and professionals (a 'Delphic' study – so named after the mythical Delphic oracle) rather than an evidence-based study. However for an excellent, well-balanced account of the harms of one drug – cannabis – see W. Hall and Pacula (2003).

CHAPTER 4: SAFETY

For an account of the state of the railways in the UK in the immediate aftermath of privatization see Jack (2001) and Wolmar

(2001), and for detailed accounts of the train crashes described here, see S. Hall (2003). David Hare wrote a play based on the Hatfield crash. The play is called *The Permanent Way*: a pun that not everyone will have appreciated (D. Hare 2003). 'The permanent way' is the term railway engineers use to refer to the track. More generally on issues of risk and safety see J. Adams (1995) and Gigerenzer (2002). The Health and Safety Executive's account of their approach to safety (HSE 2001) is well worth examining.

CHAPTER 5: CRIME AND PUNISHMENT

While the topic of crime has not been one on which philosophers have spent much time, the philosophical literature on the justification of punishment is large and ever growing. A good selection of readings is Duff and Garland (1994), and Duff's own monograph is a very sophisticated account (Duff 2001). A rather speculative history of punishment is Foucault (1991 [1975]), which starts with a startlingly graphic depiction of the punishment of 'Damiens the regicide'. For a superb account of capital punishment in England see Gatrell (1994).

CHAPTER 6: HEALTH

Much of the discussion in this chapter is motivated by the issues set out in the Black report (Black et al. 1982). An excellent presentation of the social determinants of health is Marmot (2004). Richard Wilkinson is another pioneering figure in thinking about the social determinants of health; with Kate Pickett he has recently rather controversially extended his analysis to the relation between income inequality and other social ills (Wilkinson and Pickett 2009).

CHAPTER 7: DISABILITY

A superb account of how disability, if common, can be 'normalized' is Groce (1995), which explores a community living on

Martha's Vineyard in the US where many people had inherited a gene for deafness. The title of the book – *Everyone Here Spoke Sign Language* – tells the story. For a stimulating set of writings from disability activists see Shakespeare (1998), and for a sensitive philosophical discussion of the issues see Silvers *et al.* (1998). Important attempts to come to an understanding of issues of disability by major philosophers include MacIntyre (1999) and Nussbaum (2006).

CHAPTER 8: THE FREE MARKET

The classic discussion of the moral limits of the market is Marx's manuscript 'On Money' in his *Economic and Philosophical Manuscripts* (1975a [1844]). Michael Walzer reintroduced Marx's themes into contemporary debate (Walzer 1983), as did Margaret Radin (1996). Michael Sandel has added his own elegantly written contributions in his published Tanner Lectures (1998) and his so far unpublished Reith Lectures for the BBC, which may nevertheless be available in audio form on the BBC website (2009). Debra Satz (2010) is a recent major study of the issues.

CHAPTER 9: CONCLUSION

In writing this book I have become increasingly conscious of how influenced I have been by the writings of Bernard Williams – not just Williams 2005, which I mention in the chapter, but also Williams (2006 [1986]) – and Alasdair MacIntyre (1981, 1999), as well as Amartya Sen, especially (1999), but also Sen (2009), which sets out a general position similar in many ways to that of this chapter.

Bibliography

Academy of Medical Sciences (2008) *Brain Science, Addiction and Drugs* (London: Academy of Medical Sciences).

Acheson, D. (1998) *Independent Inquiry into Inequalities in Health* (London: The Stationery Office).

Adams, John (1995) *Risk* (London: UCL Press).

Adams, Peter J. (2008) *Gambling, Freedom and Democracy* (New York: Routledge).

Albrecht, Gary L. and Patrick J. Devlieger (1999) 'The Disability Paradox: High Quality of Life against All Odds', *Social Science and Medicine* 48: 977–88.

Allotey, Pascale, Daniel Reidpath, Aka Kouamé and Robert Cummins (2003) 'The DALY, Context and the Determinants of the Severity of Disease: An Exploratory Comparison of Paraplegia in Australia and Cameroon', *Social Science and Medicine* 57: 949–58.

Asch, Adrienne (2001) 'Critical Race Theory, Feminism and Disability: Reflections on Social Justice and Personal Identity', *Ohio State Law Journal* 62: 390–423.

Barry, Brian (2005) *Why Social Justice Matters* (Cambridge: Polity Press).

Beattie, J., S. Chilton, J. Covey, P. Dolan, L. Hopkins, M. Jones-Lee, G. Loomes, N. Pidgeon, A. Robinson and A. Spencer (1998) 'On the Contingent Valuation of Safety and the Safety of Contingent Valuation: Part 1 – *Caveat Investigator*', *Journal of Risk and Uncertainty*, 17: 5–25.

Bellringer, Paul (1999) *Understanding Problem Gamblers* (London: Free Association).

Bentham, Jeremy (1843 [1803]) *Panoptican versus New South Wales*, in *The Works of Jeremy Bentham*, 11 vols, ed. John Bowring (Edinburgh: William Tait).

——(1987 [1796]) *Nonsense upon Stilts*, ed. Jeremy Waldron (London: Methuen). (See 'Anarchical Fallacies' and 'Supply without Burden'.)

——(1996 [1781]) *An Introduction to the Principles of Morals and Legislation* (Oxford: Oxford University Press).

Berridge, V. (2010) 'The Black Report: Reinterpreting History', in H.J. Cook, S. Bhattacharya and A. Hardy (eds) *The History of the Social Determinants of Health* (Andhra Pradesh, India: Orient Blackswan).

Bickenback, Jerome (1993) *Physical Disability and Social Policy* (Toronto: University of Toronto Press).

Black, D., J.N. Morris, C. Smith and P. Townsend (1982) Inequalities in Health: The Black Report (London: Penguin).

Brock, Dan (1984) 'The Use of Drugs for Pleasure: Some Philosophical Issues', in H. Murray Thomas, Willard Gaylin and Ruth Macklin (eds) Feeling Good and Doing Better (Clifton, NJ: Humana Press), pp. 83–106.

Bruce, Anthony (1980) The Purchase System in the British Army 1660–1871 (London: Royal Historical Society).

Burke, Edmund (2009 [1790]) Reflections on the Revolution in France (Oxford: Oxford University Press).

Carruthers, Peter (1992) The Animals Issue (Cambridge: Cambridge University Press).

Daily Mail (2004) 'Gambling with Our Futures', Daily Mail, 15 October. http://www.dailymail.co.uk/news/article-322008/Gambling-futures.html#ixzz0Q3nm0gW0

Daniels, Norman (1985) Just Health Care (Cambridge: Cambridge University Press).

——(2007) Just Health (Cambridge: Cambridge University Press).

Davidson, Donald (1963) 'Actions, Reasons and Causes', Journal of Philosophy 60: 685–700.

Davies, A. (1991) 'The Police and the People: Gambling in Salford 1900–1939', Historical Journal 34: 87–115.

DCMS (Department of Culture Media and Sport, UK) (2001) Gambling Review Report (London: Stationery Office Books).

DeGrazia, David (2002) Animal Rights: A Very Short Introduction (Oxford: Oxford University Press).

Descartes, René (1985 [1637]) Discourse on Method, in The Philosophical Writings of Descartes, vol. 1, trans. J. Cottingham, R. Stoothoff and D. Murdoch (Cambridge: Cambridge University Press).

DfT (Department of Transport, UK) (2007) The Highway Code (London: HMSO Books).

DH (Department of Health, UK) (2005, amended 2006) United Kingdom Drug Situation 2005 Edition: UK Focal Point on Drugs (London: UK Focal Point on Drugs, DH).

Dixon, Mike, Howard Read, Ben Rogers and Lucy Stone (2006) CrimeShare: The Unequal Impact of Crime (London: Institute for Public Policy Research).

Dorling, D. (2004) 'Prime Suspect: Murder in Britain', in P. Hillyard, C. Pantazis, S. Tombs and D. Gordon (eds) Beyond Criminology: Taking Harm Seriously (London: Pluto Press).

Dostoevsky, F. (2008 [1867]) The Gambler, in 'Notes from the Underground' and 'The Gambler' (Oxford: Oxford University Press).

Doughney, James (2002) The Poker Machine State: Dilemmas in Ethics, Economics and Governance (Melbourne: Common Ground Publishing).

Duff, R.A. (2001) Punishment, Communication and Community (Oxford: Oxford University Press).

Duff, R.A. and D. Garland (ed.) (1994) A Reader on Punishment (Oxford: Oxford University Press).

Duffy, Simon (2010) "The Citizenship Theory of Social Justice: Exploring the Meaning of Personalisation for Social Workers", *Journal of Social Work Practice* 24, no. 3: 253–67.

Dunn, John (1990) 'Reconceiving the Content and Character of Modern Political Community', in *Interpreting Political Responsibility* (Cambridge: Polity Press).

Dworkin, Ronald (1981a) 'What Is Equality? Part 1: Equality of Welfare', *Philosophy and Public Affairs* 10: 185–246.

——(1981b) 'What Is Equality? Part 2: Equality of Resources', *Philosophy and Public Affairs* 10: 283–345.

——(1993) *Life's Dominion* (London: HarperCollins).

DWP (Department of Work and Pensions, UK) (2010) *Family Resources Survey 2008–9* (London: DWP). http://research.dwp.gov.uk/asd/frs

Elster, Jon and Ole-Jorgen Skog (ed.) (1999) *Getting Hooked* (Cambridge: Cambridge University Press).

Farrelly, Colin (2007) *Justice, Democracy, and Reasonable Agreement* (London: Palgrave).

Feinberg, Joel (1987) *Harm to Others* (New York: Oxford University Press).

Fergusson, David M., Richie Poulton, Paul F. Smith and Joseph M. Boden (2006) 'Cannabis and Psychosis', *British Medical Journal* 332: 172–75.

Foucault, Michel (1991 [1975]) *Discipline and Punish* (London: Penguin).

Freud, Sigmund (1963 [1930]) *Civilization and Its Discontents* (London: The Hogarth Press).

Gatrell, V.A.C. (1994) *The Hanging Tree: Execution and the English People 1770–1868* (Oxford: Oxford University Press).

Gigerenzer, Gerd (2002) *Reckoning with Risk* (London: Allen Lane).

Groce, Nora (1995) *Everyone Here Spoke Sign Language* (Cambridge, MA: Harvard University Press).

Haacker, Markus (2010) 'The Macroeconomics of HIV/AIDS', in M. Hannam and J. Wolff (eds) *Southern Africa: 2020 Vision* (London: e9 Publishing).

Hall, Stanley (2003) *Beyond Hidden Dangers* (London: Ian Allan Publishing).

Hall, Wayne (2006) 'Cannabis and Psychosis', *The Lancet* 367: 193–95.

Hall, Wayne and Rosalie Liccardo Pacula (2003) *Cannabis Use and Dependence* (Cambridge: Cambridge University Press).

Hare, David (2003) *The Permanent Way* (London: Faber & Faber).

Hare, R.M. (1952) *The Language of Morals* (Oxford: Oxford University Press).

Hart, H.L.A. (1997) *The Concept of Law*, 2nd edn (Oxford: Oxford University Press).

Hayek, F.A. [von Hayek, F.A.] (1937) 'Economics and Knowledge', *Economica* 4: 33–54.

Hickman, Matthew, Peter Vickerman, John Macleod, James Kirkbride and Peter B. Jones (2007) 'Cannabis and Schizophrenia: Model Projections of the Impact of the Rise in Cannabis Use on Historical and Future Trends in Schizophrenia in England and Wales', *Addiction* 102, no. 4: 597–606.

Hills, Alison (2005) *Do Animals Have Rights?* (Cambridge: Icon Books).

Holt, E.B. (ed.) (1912) *The New Realism: Cooperative Studies in Philosophy* (New York: Macmillan).

Home Office (1957) *Report of the Committee on Homosexual Offences and Prostitution* [the Wolfenden report] (London: Her Majesty's Stationery Office).

——(2007) *UK Drug Strategy*, National Archives (UK) website. http://webarchive. nationalarchives.gov.uk/20100419081707/drugs.homeoffice.gov.uk/drug-strategy/

——(2009) *Statistics of Scientific Procedures on Living Animals* (London: The Stationery Office). http://www.homeoffice.gov.uk/rds/pdfs09/spanimals08.pdf

——(2010) Drugs and the law, Drugs and Alcohol, Home Office website. http:// www.homeoffice.gov.uk/drugs/drug-law/.

Honderich, Ted (1971) *Punishment: The Supposed Justifications* (London: Pelican).

HSE (Health and Safety Executive) (2001) *Reducing Risk, Protecting People* (London: Her Majesty's Stationary Office).

Husak, Douglas (1989) 'Recreational Drugs and Paternalism', *Law and Philosophy* 8: 353–81.

——(1992) *Drugs and Rights* (New York: Cambridge University Press).

——(2002) *Legalise This! The Case for Decriminalizing Drugs* (London: Verso).

Husak, Douglas and Peter de Marneffe (2005) *The Legalization of Drugs* (Cambridge: Cambridge University Press).

ICPS (International Centre for Prison Studies) (2010) *World Prison Brief*, online resource (London: IC PS, King's College London). http://www.kcl.ac.uk/ depsta/law/research/icps/worldbrief/

Illich, I. (1977) *Limits to Medicine: Medical Nemesis – The Expropriation of Health* (London: Pelican).

Jack, Ian (2001) *The Crash That Stopped Britain* (London: Granta).

Jones-Lee, M.W., M. Hammerton and P.R. Philips (1985) 'The Value of Safety: Results of a National Sample Survey', *Economic Journal* 377: 49–72.

Juel, K., P. Bjerregaard and M. Madsen (2000) 'Mortality and Life Expectancy in Denmark and in Other European Countries: What Is Happening to Middle-aged Danes?' *European Journal of Public Health* 10: 93–100.

Kahneman, Daniel and Amos Tversky (1979) 'Prospect Theory: An Analysis of Decision under Risk', *Econometrica* 47: 263–91.

Kant, I. (1997) *Lectures on Ethics*, trans. and ed. P. Heath and J.B. Schneewind (Cambridge: Cambridge University Press).

Kaufman, Charles and Leonard A. Rosenblum (1967) 'Depression in Infant Monkeys Separated from Their Mothers', *Science* 155: 1030–31.

Keat, Russell (2000) *Cultural Goods and the Limits of the Market* (London: Palgrave Macmillan).

Kennedy, Randall (1997) *Race, Crime and the Law* (New York: Pantheon Books).

Kittay, Eva Feder (1999) *Love's Labour* (New York: Routledge).

Klinenberg, Eric (2003) *Heatwave: An Autopsy of Social Disaster in Chicago* (Chicago: University of Chicago Press).

Kynaston, David (2009) *Family Britain 1951–57* (London: Bloomsbury).

Lesieur, Henry (1977) *The Chase: Career of the Compulsive Gambler* (Garden City, NY: Anchor Press).

Levi, Primo (1958 [1947]) *If This Is a Man* (London: Abacus).

Levitt, Steven and Stephen Dubner (2005) *Freakonomics* (London: Allen Lane).

Lilla, Mark (2002) *The Reckless Mind* (New York: The New York Review of Books).

MacIntyre, Alasdair (1981) *After Virtue* (London: Duckworth).

——(1999) *Dependent Rational Animals* (London: Duckworth).

MacLeod, John and Matthew Hickman (2010) 'How Ideology Shapes the Evidence and the Policy: What Do We Know about Cannabis Use and What Should We Know?' *Addiction* 105, no. 8: 1325–30.

Marmot, M. (2004) *Status Syndrome* (London: Bloomsbury).

——(2006) 'Health in an Unequal World: Social Circumstances, Biology and Disease', *Clinical Medicine* 6: 559–72.

Marx, Karl (1969 [1863]) *Theories of Surplus Value*, vol. 1 (London: Lawrence & Wishart).

——(1975a [1844]) 'On Money', part of *1844 Manuscripts*, in *Karl Marx Early Writings* (London: Penguin).

——(1975b [1845]) 'Theses on Feuerbach', in *Karl Marx Early Writings* (London: Penguin).

Maslin, Mark (2008) *Global Warming: A Very Short Introduction* (Oxford: Oxford University Press).

Masters, Alexander (2005) *Stuart: A Life Backwards* (London: Harper).

McEwan, Ian (2005) *Saturday* (London: Jonathan Cape).

Milgram, Stanley (1974) *Obedience to Authority* (New York: Harper & Row).

Mill, John Stuart (1962a [1859]) On Liberty, in *'Utilitarianism' and Other Writings*, ed. M. Warnock (Glasgow: Collins).

——(1962b [1863]) Utilitarianism, in *'Utilitarianism' and Other Writings*, ed. M. Warnock (Glasgow: Collins).

——(1986) *Newspaper Writings*, ed. A.P. Robson and J.P. Robson (Toronto: University of Toronto Press).

Mishan, E.J. (1971) *Cost–Benefit Analysis* (London: George Allen & Unwin).

Moe, K. (1984) 'Should the Nazi Research Data Be Cited?', *Hastings Centre Report* 14: 5–7.

Mwenda, Lungowe (2005) 'Drug Offenders in England and Wales 2004', Home Office Statistical Bulletin 23, Home Office website. http://rds.homeoffice.gov.uk/rds/pdfs05/hosb2305.pdf

NCB (Nuffield Council on Bioethics) (2005) *The Ethics of Research Involving Animals* (London: Nuffield Council). http://www.nuffieldbioethics.org/go/ourwork/animalresearch/publication_178.html

NICE (National Institute for Health and Clinical Excellence) (2008) *Guide to the Methods of Technology Appraisal* (London: NICE).

NOMS (Ministry of Justice National Offender Management Service) (2010) 'Prison Population and Accommodation Briefing for 27th August 2010', Her

Majesty's Prison Service website. http://www.hmprisonservice.gov.uk/resour-cecentre/publicationsdocuments/index.asp?cat=85

Nozick, Robert (1974) *Anarchy, State, and Utopia* (Oxford: Blackwell).

Nussbaum, Martha (2000) *Women and Human Development* (Cambridge: Cambridge University Press).

——(2006) *Frontiers of Justice* (Cambridge, MA: Cambridge University Press).

Nutt, David (2006) 'A Tale of 2 Es', *Journal of Psychopharmacology* 20, no. 3: 315–17.

——(2009) 'Equasy: An Overlooked Addiction with Implications for the Current Debate on Drug Harms', *Journal of Psychopharmacology* 23: 3–5.

Nutt, David, Leslie A. King, William Saulsbury and Colin Blakemore (2007) 'Development of a Rational Scale to Assess the Harm of Drugs of Potential Misuse', *The Lancet* 369: 1047–53.

ONS (Office of National Statistics) (2009) *Road Casualties: Deaths on Britain's Roads at All Time Low* (London: ONS). http://www.statistics.gov.uk/cci/nugget.asp?id=1208

Radin, Margaret (1996) *Contested Commodities* (Cambridge, MA: Harvard University Press).

Rawls, John (1971) *A Theory of Justice* (Oxford: Oxford University Press).

——(1982) 'Social Unity and Primary Goods', in Amartya Sen and Bernard Williams (eds) *Utilitarianism and Beyond* (Cambridge: Cambridge University Press), pp. 159–85.

——(1989) *Political Liberalism* (New York: Columbia University Press).

——(1999a) *The Law of Peoples* (Cambridge, MA: Harvard University Press).

——(1999b) 'A Kantian Conception of Equality', in *Collected Papers* (Cambridge, MA: Harvard University Press), pp. 254–66.

RCG (Royal Commission on Gambling) (1978) *Royal Commission on Gambling (Rothschild Commission)* (London: Her Majesty's Stationary Office).

Reeves, Richard (2007) *John Stuart Mill: Victorian Firebrand* (London: Atlantic Books).

Ricaurte, G.A., J. Yuan, G. Hatzidimitriou, B.J. Cord, and U.D. McCann (2002) 'Severe Dopaminergic Neurotoxicity in Primates after Common Recreational Dose Regimen of MDMA ("Ecstasy")', *Science* 297, no. 5590: 2260–63.

——(2003) 'Retraction', letter to the editor to retract Ricaurte *et al.* 2002, *Science* 301, no. 5639: 1479.

Rousseau, Jean-Jacques (1973a [1754]) *Discourse on Inequality*, in *The Social Contract and Discourses*, ed. G.D.H. Cole, J.H. Brumfitt and John C. Hall (London: Everyman).

——(1973b [1762]) *The Social Contract*, in *The Social Contract and Discourses*, ed. G.D.H. Cole, J.H. Brumfitt and John C. Hall (London: Everyman).

RSSB (Rail Safety and Standards Board) (2008) *ASPR Overview 2008* (London: RSSB). http://www.rssb.co.uk/sitecollectiondocuments/pdf/reports/ASPR%202008%20Overview.pdf

Russell, W.M.S. and R.L. Burch (1959) *The Principles of Humane Experimental Technique* (London: Methuen).

Ryder, Richard (1975) *Victims of Science* (London: Davis-Poynter).

Sandel, Michael (1998) *What Money Can't Buy: The Moral Limits to Markets*, The Tanner Lectures in Human Values (Salt Lake City, UT: Tanner Humanities Center,

University of Utah). http://www.tannerlectures.utah.edu/lectures/documents/sandel00.pdf

——'A New Citizenship', Reith Lectures, BBC Radio 4, 9–30 June. http://www.bbc.co.uk/programmes/b00kt7sh

Satz, Debra (2010) *Why Some Things Should Not Be for Sale* (New York: Oxford University Press).

Sayre-McCord, Geoffrey (ed.) (1988) *Essays on Moral Realism* (Ithaca, NY: Cornell University Press).

Schelling, Thomas (1984 [1968]) 'The Life You Save May Be Your Own', rpt. in Thomas Schelling (ed.) *Choice and Consequence* (Cambridge, MA: Harvard University Press); originally published in S. Chase (ed.) *Problems in Public Expenditure Analysis* (Washington, DC: The Brookings Institution, 1968).

Scruton, Roger (2000) *Animal Rights and Wrongs*, 3rd edn (London: Metro).

Sen, Amartya (1980) 'Equality of What?', in S. McMurrin (ed.) *Tanner Lectures on Human Values* (Cambridge: Cambridge University Press), pp. 195–220.

——(1999) *Development as Freedom* (Oxford: Oxford University Press).

——(2009) *The Idea of Justice* (London: Allen Lane).

Shakespeare, Tom (ed.) (1998) *The Disability Reader* (London: Cassell).

——(2006) *Disability Rights and Wrongs* (London: Routledge).

Shaw, G.B. (1946) *The Doctor's Dilemma* (London: Penguin). (First produced 1906, published 1911.)

Sher, George (2003) 'On the Decriminalization of Drugs', *Criminal Justice Ethics* 22: 12–15.

Silvers, Anita, David Wasserman and Mary B. Mahowald (1998) *Disability, Difference, Discrimination* (Lanham, MD: Rowman & Littlefield).

Singer, Peter (1989) 'All Animals Are Equal', in T. Regan and P. Singer (eds) *Animal Rights and Human Obligations*, 2nd edn (Englewood Cliffs, NJ: Prentice-Hall), pp. 148–62.

——(1995) *Animal Liberation*, 4th edn (London: Pimlico).

Smith, Adam (2003 [1777]) *The Wealth of Nations*, bks I–III (London: Penguin).

Sproston, Kerry, Bob Erens and Jim Orford (2000) *Gambling Behaviour in Britain: Results from The British Gambling Prevalence Survey* (London: National Centre for Survey Research). http://www.gamblingcommission.gov.uk/research_consultations/research/bgps/bgps_2000.aspx

STC (House of Commons Science and Technology Committee) (2006) *Drug Classification: Making a Hash of It?* (London: The Stationary Office).

Stuckler, D., S. Basu and M. McKee (2010) 'Budget Crises, Health, and Social Welfare Programmes', *British Medical Journal* 340: c3311.

Sunstein, Cass R. (1995) 'Incompletely Theorized Agreements', *Harvard Law Review* 108: 1733–72.

——(2002) *Risk and Reason* (Cambridge: Cambridge University Press).

Szasz, Thomas (1992) *Our Right to Drugs* (New York: Praeger).

Terzi, L. (2004) 'The Social Model of Disability: A Philosophical Critique', *Journal of Applied Philosophy* 2: 141–57.

Thaler, R.H. and C. Sunstein (2008) *Nudge* (New Haven, CT: Yale University Press).

Titmuss, Richard (1970) *The Gift Relationship: From Human Blood to Social Policy* (London: Allen & Unwin).

Tremain, Shelley (1996) 'Dworkin on Disablement and Resources', *Canadian Journal of Law and Jurisprudence* 9: 343–59.

United Nations (1948) *Universal Declaration of Human Rights*, United Nations website. http://www.un.org/en/documents/udhr/ (accessed 27 June 2010).

von Hirsch, Andrew, Anthony E. Bottoms, Elizabeth Burney and P.-O. Wikstrom (1999) *Criminal Deterrence and Sentence Severity: An Analysis of Recent Research* (Oxford: Hart Publishing).

Waal, Helge (1999) 'To Legalize or Not to Legalize: Is That the Question?', in Jon Elster and Ole-Jorgen Skog (eds) *Getting Hooked* (Cambridge: Cambridge University Press).

Walzer, M. (1983) *Spheres of Justice* (New York: Basic Books).

Wardle, Heather, Kerry Sproston, Jim Orford, Bob Erens, Mark Griffiths, Rebecca Constantine and Sarah Pigott (2007) *British Gambling Prevalence Survey 2007* (London: National Centre for Survey Research). http://www.gamblingcommission. gov.uk/research_consultations/research/bgps/bgps_2007.aspx

Webster, C. (2002). *The National Health Service: A Political History*, 2nd edn (Oxford: Oxford University Press).

WHO (World Health Organization) (2000) *World Health Report 2000* (Geneva: WHO).

——(2006) *Basic Documents* (Geneva: WHO). http://apps.who.int/gb/bd/PDF/bd47/EN/constitution-en.pdf (accessed 27 June 2010).

——(2008) *The Top Ten Causes of Death*, Fact Sheet 310 (Geneva: WHO). http://www.who.int/mediacentre/factsheets/fs310/en/index.html (accessed 27 June 2010).

——(2009) *World Health Statistics* (Geneva: WHO).

Wilkinson, R. and K. Pickett (2009) *The Spirit Level* (London: Allen Lane).

Wikler, Daniel (1979) 'Paternalism and the Mildly Retarded', *Philosophy and Public Affairs* 8: 377–92.

Wilkinson, R. (2001) *Mind the Gap* (New Haven, CT: Yale University Press).

Williams, Bernard (2005) *In the Beginning Was the Deed* (Princeton, NJ: Princeton University Press).

——(2006 [1986]) *Ethics and the Limits of Philosophy* (London: Routledge).

Wittgenstein, Ludwig (2009 [1953]) *Philosophical Investigations* (Oxford: Blackwell).

Wolff, Jonathan (2002) *Railway Safety and the Ethics of the Tolerability of Risk* (London: Rail Safety and Standards Board). http://www.rssb.co.uk/SiteCollectionDocuments/pdf/policy_risk.pdf

——(2006a) 'High Stakes', *Guardian*, 5 December. http://www.guardian.co.uk/education/2006/dec/05/schools.news

——(2006b) 'Risk, Fear, Blame, Shame and the Regulation of Public Safety', *Economics and Philosophy* 22: 409–27.

Wolff, Jonathan (2007a) 'What Is the Value of Preventing a Fatality?', in Tim Lewens (ed.) *Risk: Philosophical Perspectives* (London: Routledge).

——(2007b) 'Harm and Hypocrisy: Have We Got It Wrong on Drugs?', *Public Policy Research* 14: 126–35.

——(2007c) 'Market Failure, Common Interests, and the Titanic Puzzle', in K. Lippert-Rasmussen and N. Holtug (eds) *Egalitarianism: New Essays on the Nature and Value of Equality* (Oxford: Oxford University Press.)

——(2008) 'Crime and Punishment', *Prospect* 144, 28 March.

——(2009a) 'Disability among Equals', in Kimberlee Brownlee and Adam Cureton (eds) *Disability and Disadvantage* (Oxford: Oxford University Press), pp. 112–37.

——(2009b) 'Disability, Status Enhancement, Personal Enhancement and Resource Allocation', *Economics and Philosophy* 25: 49–68.

——(2009c) 'Cognitive Disability in a Society of Equals', *Metaphilosophy* 40: 402–15.

Wolff, Jonathan and Avner de-Shalit (2007) *Disadvantage* (Oxford: Oxford University Press).

Wollstonecraft, Mary (2008 [1792]) *'A Vindication of the Rights of Women'* and *'A Vindication of the Rights of Men'* (Oxford: Oxford University Press).

Wolmar, Christian (2001) *Broken Rails* (London: Aurum).

Wootton, D. (2006) *Bad Medicine: Doctors Doing Harm since Hypocrites* (Oxford: Oxford University Press).

Index